Sport Public Relations and Communication

Sport Public Relations and Communication

Maria Hopwood
Paul Kitchin
James Skinner

AMSTERDAM • BOSTON • HEIDELBERG • LONDON • NEW YORK • OXFORD
PARIS • SAN DIEGO • SAN FRANCISCO • SINGAPORE • SYDNEY • TOKYO
Butterworth-Heinemann is an imprint of Elsevier

ELSEVIER

Butterworth-Heinemann is an Imprint of Elsevier
The Boulevard, Langford Lane, Kidlington, Oxford, OX5 1GB
30 Corporate Drive, Suite 400, Burlington, MA 01803, USA

First edition 2010

Notice
No responsibility is assumed by the publisher for any injury and/or damage to persons or
property as a matter of products liability, negligence or otherwise, or from any use or operation of
any methods, products, instructions or ideas contained in the material herein. Because of
rapid advances in the medical sciences, in particular, independent verification of diagnoses and
drug dosages should be made

British Library Cataloguing in Publication Data
A catalogue record for this book is available from the British Library

Library of Congress Cataloging-in-Publication Data
A catalog record for this book is available from the Library of Congress

ISBN: 978-1-85617-615-6

For information on all Butterworth-Heinemann publications
visit our web site at books.elsevier.com

Printed and bound in Great Britain

10 11 12 10 9 8 7 6 5 4 3 2 1

Working together to grow
libraries in developing countries

www.elsevier.com | www.bookaid.org | www.sabre.org

ELSEVIER   BOOK AID
International   Sabre Foundation

Contents

v

Author Profiles

Laurence Chalip is Professor and Co-ordinator of the Sport Management Program at the University of Texas at Austin. His research focuses on policy and marketing. He has published three books, four research monographs and over 70 articles and book chapters. He is a Research Fellow of the North American Society for Sport Management and has served as Editor of *Sport Management Review* and *Journal of Sport Management*. He consults to sport organisations throughout the world. He has won two service awards from the Sport Management Association of Australia and New Zealand, the Earle F. Zeigler Award from the North American Society for Sport Management and was named to the International Chair of Olympism by the International Olympic Committee and the Centre for Olympic Studies.

Dr Allan Edwards was formerly the Head of Sport and Business Management at Hartpury College, University of the West of England and a faculty member at the University of Ulster. Now being a member of faculty at Griffith University Dr Edwards research brings sociological theory to the study of sport business. Dr Edwards has extensive sport industry experience and have conducted a number of consultancies for national and international sport organisations.

B. Christine Green is Associate Professor of Sport Management and Co-ordinator of undergraduate programs in the Department of Kinesiology and Health Education at the University of Texas at Austin. She earned her Masters and PhD degrees in Sport Management from the University of Maryland. She has authored or co-authored a book and 50 articles or book chapters. She is a Research Fellow of the North American Society for Sport Management, the former Editor of *Sport Management Review* and an Associate Editor of *Journal of Sport and Tourism*. She works extensively with the sport industry, including design and management of volunteer support for the British Olympic Holding Camp during the Sydney Olympics and service on the Board of Directors for Australian University Sport – North. She has earned an Academic Innovation Award from the RGK Center for Philanthropy and Community Service for her work on designing volunteer systems.

Maria Hopwood is Senior Lecturer in Public Relations at Leeds Business School, Leeds Metropolitan University. Her research interest is into sport public relations which means that her work bridges the disciplines of both public relations and sport management. Maria joined Leeds Metropolitan in May 2009 following 3 years' teaching at Bond University on Queensland's Gold Coast prior to which she had completed 20 years at the University of Teesside in North East England. Maria has gained extensive experience working in a consultancy capacity with professional sport organisations in both Australia and the UK such as Durham County Cricket Club, Middlesbrough Football Club, Queensland Roar Football Club and Gold Coast United Football Club. She is a member of the editorial boards for the journals *PR Review* and the *International Journal of Sport Communication*.

Paul Kitchin is Lecturer in Sport Management at the University of Ulster where he teaches strategy, marketing and sport policy. Paul is currently Deputy Editor of the *International Journal of Sport Marketing and Sponsorship* and an editorial board member of the *International Journal of Sport Management and Marketing*. Paul has experience working with UK third-sector sporting organisations in the provision of research, planning and consultancy services. A graduate of University of Tasmania and Deakin University he is currently completing his PhD at Loughborough University investigating sporting participation and self-identity in young people with disabilities.

Jacquie L'Etang is author of *Public Relations in Britain: A History of Professional Practice* (2004), *Public Relations: Issues, Practice and Critique* (2008) and *Sport Public Relations: Contexts and Issues* (forthcoming); and co-author and co-editor of *Critical Perspectives on Public Relations* (1996) and *Public Relations: Critical Issues and Contemporary Practice* (2006). She is also author of around 50 journal articles and book chapters on a range of topics including propaganda, public diplomacy, rhetoric, corporate social responsibility, tourism public relations. Her research interests are currently focused on the role of public relations in culture and is pursuing the theme of public relations anthropology. She is Director of the MSc in Strategic Public Relations and Communication Management and also of the MLitt in Public Relations Theory, Research and Education at the University of Stirling and supervises many PhDs.

Rob Lewis is Old South Walian by birth and heritage, despite a Cambridge degree in English Literature and an MBA from Warwick Business School, Rob followed a career in marketing and strategic management in the corporate world before switching to the study of sport from a marketing, public policy and social perspective through an MA at London Metropolitan University. His main interest has lain in the intersection of new technology and marketing and in how sport organisations adapt their management to take advantage of new potential. Married with three children and three terriers, he spends his time juggling teaching and consultancy opportunities while squeezing in as much watching of Fulham and London Welsh as he can in between the Guardian crossword and managing domestic cuisine.

Katherine Rowe is a graduate of the Bachelor of Applied Science (Exercise and Sport) and the Bachelor of Commerce (Honours) at Deakin University. Katherine's research has focused on marketing as it relates to children's sport, with particular interests in how sport marketing theory and practice may be used to increase participation in physical activity. Katherine has taught in sport management, sport science and health and has been a Research Assistant in the Sport Management Program at the School of Management and Marketing at Deakin University.

Professor David Shilbury is the Foundation Chair in Sport Management and a former Head of the School of Management and Marketing at Deakin University. He has a PhD from Monash University and a Master of Science (Sport Management) from the University of Massachusetts. He is a former editor of *Sport Management Review*, a member of the editorial board for the *Journal of Sport Management* and is the lead author of the text *Strategic Sport Marketing*. His research interests include sport governance, sport development and strategic marketing. He is a research fellow of the North American Society for Sport Management.

James Skinner is an Associate Professor in Sport Management at Griffith University, Nathan Campus. His research has appeared in leading sport management journals such as the *Journal of Sport Management, European Sport Management Quarterly, Sport Management Review* and the *International Journal of Sport Management*. He has published two books on Sport Management Research and is a member of the editorial review board for the International Journal of Sport Communication. James has conducted consultancies for international and national sporting organisations, the Australian Sport Commission and state and local government departments of sport and recreation.

Professor Kristine Toohey is currently Head of the Department of Tourism, Leisure, Hotel and Sport Management and Professor of Sport Management in the Griffith Business School, Griffith University. She has acted as a consultant to various organisations such as the Olympic Co-ordination Authority, the Australian Sport Commission, the Australian Jockey Club, Womensport Australia, Netball Australia and the International Olympic Committee. In her professional career she has won a number of awards including the UTS 'Excellence in Teaching Award' and in 1999 was Visiting Professor at the International Olympic Academy in Olympia,

Greece. Kristine has published widely as the author and co-author of a number of journal articles and books, most dealing with Olympic and sporting themes. Her books include *The Olympic Games: A Social Science Perspective* (Toohey and Veal) and *The Contribution of the Higher Education Sector to the Sydney 2000 Olympic Games* (Cashman and Toohey).

Dr Wayne Usher's research examines twenty-first century paedagogical approaches that engage the teacher/interventionists and the student/audience in the co-construction of meaning, value and knowledge associated with school/community health education and sport coaching. He gives specific attention to modern communication technologies and how they are creating a paradigm shift surrounding traditional barriers of power and information dissemination. Other areas of research include the Internet, WWW and Social Media applications. Current research includes examining the promotion of online health information and the impacts of health websites on the relationship between the general practitioner and e-health consumer.

CHAPTER 1

Bringing Public Relations and Communication Studies to Sport

Maria Hopwood
Leeds Metropolitan University

Paul Kitchin
University of Ulster

James Skinner
Griffith University

In March 2009, the Sri Lankan cricket team toured Pakistan for a series of matches. On route to a match at the Gaddafi stadium in Lahore the team and their International Cricket Council (ICC) test match umpires were attacked by terrorists. The two buses carrying each group were targeted and eight playing staff of the Sri Lankan team were injured. Sadly a driver and six local police officers were killed in the attack, as well as nine policemen were seriously injured. Later that day match referee Chris Broad, one of the umpires in the second vehicle, addressed the media to respond to the growing pressure for details of the attack. Referee Broad was scathing in his criticism of the security arrangements provided to the umpires and the visiting team. As a key stakeholder of the ICC, Broad's comments added to the pressure on the event hosts (the Pakistan Cricket Board) and also on his organisation through his action. It is remarkable that a senior employee of an organisation, who could realistically be expected to be in a state of shock, was able to address the media without his statements being approved by the ICC public relations and communication officers. His comments started a public verbal confrontation with the Chairman of Pakistan Cricket, Ejaz Butt who did little to ease the situation. The situation exposed operational procedures concerning the safety and security of players and officials. However, it also exposed a serious flaw in the public relations and communication strategies of not only the ICC, but also some of its key stakeholders – the national cricket organisations that play in its tournaments.

Formula 1 racing has always been a cavalier sport where technology and passion meet in the desire to win. Unfortunately, in the recent past the sport has suffered from some cavalier management techniques. In 2007 the McLaren team was fined $100 million for spying on the rivals, Ferrari. At the start of the 2009 season the same team was involved in an incident where race stewards were lied to about the use of less-than-legal tactics. However, an incident at the 2008 Singapore Grand Prix was described by sport writer Simon Barnes as 'the worst single piece of cheating in the history of sport' (Barnes, 2009, *online*). In brief, Renault driver Nelson Piquet Jr was part of a conspiracy with team principal Flavio Briatore and his number two Pat Symonds to crash his car on the Singapore circuit allowing his unknowing teammate to win the race (FIA, 2009). The crash brought out the yellow (caution) flags and allowed the teammate to effectively get his pit-stop strategy correct and therefore win. The public relations (PR) dilemma of this incident does not just affect the team involved in the incident but the entire sport, its fans, sponsors and partners and the governing authority of the sport itself (Fédération Internationale de l'Automobile – FIA). The sport is a network of organisations that creates one of the world's most watched sporting events. Despite the furore over the race-fixing a number of stakeholders took action to minimise the PR dilemma of the incident. First, Renault's major sponsor Dutch bank ING and partner Spanish insurer Mutua Madrilena withdrew their sponsorship immediately after FIA established wrong-doing to disassociate themselves from the team. However, this may have been premature as the corporation Renault ensured that the F1 team Renault responded immediately to the investigation by sacking Briatore and Symonds and ensuring that all staff cooperated with the government body's enquiry (Piquet had been released by the organisation in July). Also the governing body FIA released its findings to the press to ensurethe justification for its decision, ultimately to keep the team in the competition on a suspended sentence, which would allay fears of a whitewash or cover up and maintain the sport's integrity. This decision was in no small part due to the management of relationships within the sport that can be enhanced by sound public relations and communication principles. Both the sport and the Renault team are tarred by this event, however, steps have been taken to repair these reputations.

It is clear from the above examples that there is a need for further development of public relations and communication strategies, knowledge and understanding of the management of sport. As seen in the above situations, even successful international sporting organisations have a need for well-honed practices. The coordinated implementation of sport public relations through sport communication methods can minimise the negative impacts on the organisation's publics occurring.

There is no doubt that sport has transformed over the last 30 years. At the elite end of the sport continuum it has become a complex commercial enterprise, while at the 'participation' end it has become quite sophisticated in marketing its activities to local communities. As a consequence, sport marketing is now a recognised and rapidly developing sector with universities offering sport marketing degrees. However, the one area where sport marketing is underdeveloped is in public relations and communication strategies. For the most part, sport management students have been forced to go to the generic management literature to further their understanding. In many respects this has not been a bad thing, but it often means that some of the 'nuances' and special features of sport are not given sufficient focus. This book customises its discussion of public relations and communications so that it is directly relevant to the sport management student. It provides a concise guide as to how public relations and communication strategies and principles can be applied to sport management and marketing issues and problems. In short, it demonstrates how the principles of public relations and communications can be successfully applied in practice within a sport context (Stewart, 2002).

The book is structured to address the wide and varied activities in sport organisations that public relations and communications can develop in order to achieve wider business objectives. Underpinning all of these themes is an acknowledgement that sport organisations rely on a network of partners and publics that constitutes stakeholders. Each chapter is structured around a common approach consisting of learning outcomes, a presentation of the chapter's key terms, an overview of the chapter and the main body. The main body consists of a discussion of the theory of public relations and communications within non-sport business and sport business situations. Each chapter contains a case or a number of cases to highlight how various organisations and their stakeholders are utilising the Sport Public Relations and Communications (SPRC) function to achieve their objectives. Following the main body is a series of discussion questions that can allow the reader to extend their understanding and critically reflect on the chapter's main points. The reader is also directed towards suggested readings and supporting websites that assist in developing further the chapter content.

PUBLIC RELATIONS AND COMMUNICATION IN SPORT

This chapter serves to provide the theoretical basis for this publication. Maria Hopwood provides an overview of PR theory and practice that is encapsulated initially as organisations *doing the right things at the right time*. By establishing the basis of PR activity as a crucial management activity Hopwood provides a crucial distinction as to how the public perceptions of PR have been tainted by its past associations with propaganda and its current connotation with spin. Following a series of definitions on PR that covers the academic and practitioner environments, the author presents a critique of how well-managed PR can be used to convert negative situations into positive ones. The second part of the chapter examines the background to the two key areas of the textbook. Sport Public Relations and Sport Communications is all about relationships, which is a theme that runs throughout the book. However, Hopwood here defines it as a separate form of sport communication as the former is the activities by which relationships are managed and the latter is the modes of media that are chosen. This distinction is highlighted through a case study on the England and Wales Cricket Board's development of Twenty20 cricket in 2003 and its subsequent success.

SPORT RELATIONSHIP MANAGEMENT

David Shilbury and Katherine Rowe address the importance of managing the relationship with the sport organisation's stakeholders and publics. Their chapter begins with an overview of why a strategic approach to relationship management is essential. They stress that difficulties arise when organisations view their publics as static and assume that they will respond predictably to certain events and situations. Sport organisations should manage their publics through a strategic approach to relationship management that can minimise these eventualities. The chapter then focuses on Ledingham's (2003) work on organisation–public relationships and the importance of management consideration of strategic publics. The work required by organisations to develop relationships with these strategic publics may be time- and resource-consuming; however, these efforts can offer the sport organisations benefits over the long term. The case study highlights such a situation where the Canterbury Bulldogs RLF Club used SPRC to sustain its relationship with its key strategic publics; its fans. The case addresses how this was done through a five-step process that saw the club increase its attendances in light of its situation. The chapter concludes with an overview of the importance of relationship management in the context of sport outlining some of the key authors in the area and providing a platform for further study and investigation.

SPORT MARKETING PUBLIC RELATIONS

Chapter 4 serves to introduce the concept of sport marketing public relations (SMPR) and its place within the management and marketing of sporting organisations. Hopwood serves up the SMPR Rugby Ball model which represents the environment and context for the collection of marketing communication-related activities and presents where SMPR is positioned within the organisation. This is highlighted in the case of Durham County Cricket Club which forms one of two chapter cases. Following this is the application of Harris' (1993) key areas where traditional marketing public relations (MPR) (sans Sport) is applied to the sport industry. Hopwood then concludes with an examination of one of the key issues within this text. That of how does sport public relations and communications differ from the practices of sport marketing.

SPORT SOCIAL RESPONSIBILITY

Despite the increasing commercialisation and professionalisation of sporting practices organisations need to consider their impact on their wider international, national and local communities. James Skinner discusses the importance of adhering to principles of corporate social responsibility (CSR) for organisations in wishing to examine their community impact. The author extends Carroll's (1979) model of CSR to the sporting industry to provide an overview of sport social responsibility and the resultant SPRC benefits that arise from such an approach. Through a discussion of economic, legal, ethical and discretionary responsibilities, Skinner addresses how sporting organisations across the globe are positioning their work for CSR goals. This is highlighted in two cases, the first on the National Football League (NFL) and their use of the Super Bowl to produce public relations benefits for the game as a whole and the second case demonstrates how English football has repositioned itself through its national governing association, the Football Association (FA), to engage with CSR activities.

COMMUNITY RELATIONS AND ENGAGEMENT

Throughout the local, national and international there are many examples of how sport organisations do good work in local and international communities. Paul Kitchin and Rob Lewis address the importance of using SPRC to highlight these community relations and engagement situations. The development of community programmes of sport organisations or the sport-related community programmes of non-sport organisations has led to increasing media clutter for good news stories. Many organisations are yet to use this work to reach its potential benefits through the strategic application of SPRC in order to break this clutter. The first case focuses on the challenges that exist for a small not-for-profit sport organisation implementing SPRC on minimal resources. The case highlights how an organisation of this size works with partners and agencies to provide sport activities that compliment the work of partners and hence provide SPRC opportunities throughout these partnerships. Capitalising on community involvement organisations can look to develop cause-related marketing (cause-RM) initiatives that use sport and physical activities to achieve a number of organisational goals. Many of these initiatives have been developed due to the rise of socially conscious consumers (Webster, 1975), more recently known as the ethical consumers. The second case study in this chapter focuses on two such programmes. Both programmes aimed to get young people active to increase long-term participation, however, the specifications of the programme highlighted how the SPRC benefits can vary. The chapter concludes with a discussion of the management implications for cause-RM and other community programme partnerships.

SPORT VOLUNTEERISM

B. Christine Green and Lawrence Chalip examine how the SPRC function can be used to assist in the recruitment and retention of volunteers and how these volunteers can be used to achieve a range of benefits for the sport organisation. The authors' focus on how volunteer involvement can be beneficial not only for making volunteers feel more valued but also for heightening organisational profile and reputation. Additionally, by providing the local community with speakers to present a range of issues important to the sport organisation links can be developed with the local stakeholders. The first case focuses on how Special Olympics International uses it volunteers to fulfil key SPRC roles and increases awareness and understanding of the movement in the community. The second case focuses on the Purple Armband Games (also used in Chapter 11), which was established by supporter groups to highlight the plight of those caught up in violent and abusive situations. This volunteer programme was used by sport organisation to further develop links with stakeholders and create a proactive stance on these serious issues. The chapter concludes with a discussion on the benefits of using volunteers within the SPRC function itself. Although challenging, this can assist the organisation in achieving its objectives without requiring significant financial resources.

CRISIS COMMUNICATIONS AND SPORT PUBLIC RELATIONS

The importance of the SPRC function is instrumental when the sport organisation suffers a crisis situation. Allan Edwards and Wayne Usher focus on the need for crisis management practices. This is developed through considering the naturalist and positivist perspectives of crisis management. This chapter develops into a discussion of crisis communication strategies in light of the case of the Brisbane Broncos RLFC. Edwards and Usher then draw attention to approaches used by sporting organisations in a number of contexts and focus on the Gonzalez-Herrero and Pratt (1996) model of crisis communications. Finally the chapter focuses on the professional sport leagues in the USA and the inability of two of their leagues to implement more proactive public relations in light of the incidents. Recommendations for practice are presented.

THE PUBLIC RELATIONS ROLE OF FANS AND SUPPORTERS' GROUPS

In this chapter we will be looking specifically at the role that fans and supporters play in sport public relations and communications. Referring to specific supporter groups such as the Barmy Army, Maria Hopwood highlights their intense public relations value to sport organisations and contends that those organisations need to use their fans and supporters' groups strategically for public relations purposes. Fans and supporters are the highly visible representation of sport public relations and communications as they are the living and breathing representation – the heart and soul – of sport. Fans and supporters are the lifeblood of any sport organisation. Without their support, the sport organisation would arguably cease to exist and function. For the astute sport organisation, fans and supporters are a key public relations tool. They only say good things about the sport organisation and they support it through thick and thin. Even more importantly, they are likely to pass on their passion for the sport organisation to their children and others. For this reason and others, fans and supporters' groups are extremely important brand ambassadors for any sport organisation and, consequentially, are an extremely powerful sport public relations and communication resource. Hopwood has included a case study based on the time she and her family spent with the Barmy Army at the 2004 test match series between England and the West Indies at Antigua when Brian Lara made his historic 400 not out.

CROSS-CULTURAL SPORT PUBLIC RELATIONS AND COMMUNICATION

Developing communication strategies that are designed to cross borders and cultures is a challenge for those involved in managing the SPRC function. Jacquie L'Etang discusses these challenges facing public relations in complex and increasingly international contexts. L'Etang takes a critical perspective to discuss the role and function of public relations in these environments. The importance of cultural analysis is considered in light of its implications for communication. This is applied through a brief analysis of mayoral justifications of four cities bidding for the 2012 Olympic Games. In this regard the reader is encouraged to compare and contrast bidding communications rhetoric. L'Etang then carries out a detailed discussion of factors that add complexity to the SPRC function with regard to cultures, borders and the forces of globalisation before presenting a critical review of its potential impact on sport business.

NEW COMMUNICATIONS MEDIA FOR SPORT

The rapid rise of telecommunication systems such as satellite television to the development of social networking sites has progressed beyond all early predictions. In this chapter Lewis and Kitchin address the evolution and role of new media and communications in developing SPRC strategies. The authors begin by presenting an overview of the PR uses of the Internet from

1996 to 2005. At this time sporting organisations were deemed to be reactionary towards SPRC opportunities but additionally faced with increased challenges presented by heightened stakeholder interest in these organisations. The first case addresses the Purple Armband Games (also discussed in Chapter 6) and how the movement was supported by a website that coordinated the group's advocacy work. The chapter then considers the paradigm shift of Web 2.0 and its implications for SPRC. A number of Web 2.0 tools are developed in light of their potential benefit to SPRC. The second case examines MyColts.net, a social networking site developed for the Indianapolis Colts NFL team. This chapter discusses social media and why it is important to sporting organisations looking to break through the communications clutter. The authors present a series of guidelines for developing a social media strategy for sporting organisations.

PUBLIC RELATIONS FOR PLAYERS

In Chapter 12, Skinner draws predominately on the work of Summers and Morgan (2008) to explore the role of public relations in professional sport. In doing this, particular emphasis on how public relations and communication strategies can be used when dealing with potentially damaging situations for players, the sport organisation and the sport itself are discussed. A failure by sport public relations professionals to deal with a player's crisis can lead to unsavoury or bad press about players and has the potential to call into question a player's reputation and lead to poor public perception of the sport organisation and/or sport. This negative press has the potential to impact on future participation problems and a reduction in a range of revenue streams including sponsorships and player endorsements (Bruce and Tini, 2008). This chapter suggests that given the 'market value' of a player's image and the reputation of the sport hinges on public perception, which is the domain of the sport public relations professional, it is vital for this professional to nurture and defend a player's image and a sport's reputation. It is argued that at its best public relations should be proactive in its efforts to create a positive player image and reputation; however, it is often forced to react to negative situations by using strategies to repair a tarnished player image or reputation in order to defuse a public perception crisis. The chapter concludes by highlighting that it is essential that sport public relations professionals need to focus on protecting and enhancing a positive player image and reputation through building and maintaining mutually beneficial relationships with key publics, in particular their fans (Hopwood, 2007).

INTERNATIONAL SPORT PUBLIC RELATIONS

In the final chapter, Skinner is joined by Kristine Toohey in examining the rise of international sport public relations. The authors first examine the rise in international public relations as a consequence of increasing international trade, communications and politics. Focusing on international SPRC the chapter examines previous use of the Olympic Games to provide non-sporting agendas to be broadcast across the globe. The first case examines the Olympic Torch Relay and the public relations difficulties the International Olympic Committee (IOC) and the Beijing 2008 organisers faced as it travelled from Greece to the Bird's Nest stadium in Beijing. Skinner and Toohey go on to focus on the role that International Non-Governmental Organisation (INGO – of which the IOC is one) can play in the development of society through sport. The public relations issues that these INGOs face in this work are discussed. Once again focusing on the IOC, and in this case on the Salt Lake City Bribery scandal, the authors highlight how the appointment of a well-known PR consultancy assisted in resolving stakeholder management issues.

RECOMMENDED WEBSITES

For coverage of the terrorist attack on the Sri Lankan cricket team readers can be directed to the BBC and Cricinfo websites at <http://news.bbc.co.uk/1/hi/world/south_asia/7920677.stm> and <http://www.cricinfo.com/infocus/content/story/infocus.html?subject=38>, respectively.

For coverage of the Singapore Grand Prix race-fixing scandal see the following: <http://en.wikipedia.org/wiki/Renault_Formula_One_crash_controversy>.

For journals relating to Sport Public Relations and Communication see:

International Journal of Sport Communication – <http://hk.humankinetics.com/ijsc/journalAbout.cfm>.

Journal of Sport Media – <http://muse.jhu.edu/journals/journal_of_sport_media/>.

Additionally a special edition from Public Relations Review – <https://enduser.elsevier.com/campaigntypes/specissue/index.cfm?campaign=public_relations_sport>.

International Journal of Sport Marketing and Sponsorship – <http://www.im-reports.com/SM/IJSM/?type=current>.

For a general blog site on the area of Sport PR – <http://sportprblog.com/blog/>.

REFERENCES

Barnes, S., 2009. The worst act of cheating in the history of sport. Times Online. Retrieved on 17 September 2009 from: <http://www.timesonline.co.uk/tol/sport/formula_1/article6837713.ece>.

Bruce, T., Tini, T., 2008. Unique crisis response strategies in sport public relations: Rugby League and the case for diversion. Public Relations Review 34, 108–115.

Carroll, A.B., 1979. A three dimensional model of corporate performance. Academy of Management Review 4 (4), 497–505.

Fédération Internationale de l'Automobile, 2009. Press release: World Motor Sport Council. FIA Online. Retrieved on 22 September 2009 from: <http://www.fia.com/en-GB/mediacentre/pressreleases/wmsc/2009/Pages/wmsc_210909.aspx>.

Gonzalez-Herrero, A., Pratt, C.B., 1996. An integrated model for crisis communication management. Journal of Public Relations Research 8 (2), 79–105.

Harris, T.L., 1993. How MPR adds value to integrated marketing communications. Public Relations Quarterly 38 (2), 13–19.

Hopwood, M.K., 2007. The sport integrated communications mix: sport public relations. In: Beech, J., Chadwick, S. (Eds.), The Marketing of Sport. Prentice Hall, Harlow, England, pp. 292–317.

Ledingham, J.A., 2003. Explicating relationship management as a general theory of public relations. Journal of Public Relations Research 15 (2), 188–198.

Stewart, B., 2002. Foreword. In: Edwards, A., Gilbert, K., Skinner, J. Extending the Boundaries: Theoretical Frameworks for Research in Sport Management. Melbourne, Victoria, Common Ground Publications, p. XI.

Summers, J., Morgan, M.J., 2008. More than just the media: considering the role of public relations in the creation of sporting celebrity and the management of fan expectations. Public Relations Review 34, 176–182.

Webster Jr., F.E., 1975. Characteristics of the socially conscious consumer. Journal of Consumer Research 2, 188–196.

CHAPTER 2

Public Relations and Communication in Sport

Maria Hopwood
Leeds Metropolitan University

Learning Outcomes

Upon completion of this chapter the reader should be able to:

- Understand basic public relations theory and be able to apply it within the context of sport
- Understand the nature of public relations and identify the distinguishing characteristics of public relations
- Understand the concept of contemporary sport communication
- Address issues pertaining to the effective use of public relations in sport

---

CHAPTER OVERVIEW

Public relations is increasingly becoming a dominant force in contemporary marketing communications, yet it is also probably the least understood and appreciated communications technique for all sorts of reasons. Widely associated with such words as 'spin', 'deception', 'subterfuge' and 'lying', public relations' immense significance, value and potential in sport communication and business have yet to be fully realised. Again, the reasons behind this are various but the basic one is that it tends to be the case that people who work in sport business are familiar with the concept of 'marketing', but have limited understanding of the theory and processes of communication and, as a result, public relations.

To compete in the contemporary sport business environment, the understanding of and ability to implement a range of communication strategies is essential. The global interest in and consumption of sport continue to grow and with that increasing demands and need for knowledge are placed on those who supply that demand. Anyone who is involved with the operations of sport entities at any level needs to know about communication and relationship management – both of which form the core of successful public relations. Public relations is a communications discipline, founded on communication theory and guided by those principles. Sport communication is a modern variant of communication and is thus also founded on the same theories and guided by the same principles. Therefore, sport public relations and communication are inextricably linked and this chapter will explore that potentially formidable partnership.

WHAT IS PUBLIC RELATIONS?

This is a frequently asked question and one which generates any number of different responses. According to Ledingham and Bruning (2000, p. xi), public relations 'is a field which is more often characterised by what it does rather than what it is'. They say that the overall aim and function of public relations must be to create goodwill and good feelings about the organisation and anything it produces. This includes sport organisations. This can be achieved partly through the establishment of a sound corporate (or organisational) reputation and partly by getting people to think positively about what the organisation is doing. Encouraging the way people think and feel about an organisation can be a lengthy and time-consuming process but where knowledge of public relations exists within the organisation and when public relations is a recognised and well-managed element of the overall communications function, it is known that public relations can lead to very real and measurable benefits. For a sport organisation, public relations can, if implemented strategically and professionally, become its most cost effective and productive communications mechanism. Sport public relations is all about making sure that the sport organisation does the right things at the right times and ensuring that everyone who needs to know what it is doing does so when necessary. In other words, sport public relations is concerned with establishing, managing and maintaining a whole range of mutually influential and beneficial relationships.

Despite the relatively recent critical interest and examination that public relations has attracted, as both a practice and concept it has its roots that go back to the ancient Greeks and beyond. Public relations is many things, a persuasive communications technique being one of them. Persuasion, of course, takes many forms and one of the most notorious of these is propaganda. Hitler's Minister for Propaganda, Joseph Goebbels, acknowledged the published writings of Edward Bernays (widely referred to as 'the founding father of public relations') as the inspiration for his speeches which is one reason why public relations continues to bear the stigma of unpleasant association.

Another reason for the frequently negative opinion of public relations is its association with 'spin' and other dubious techniques which have been widely implemented by companies and individuals who patently have no understanding or appreciation of the essence or immense potential and value of excellent professional public relations and have given the practice a bad name and reputation which it is striving hard to overcome.

PUBLIC RELATIONS DEFINED

There are hundreds of written definitions of public relations which try to encapsulate the essence of the discipline. The majority of them focus on the technical or operational aspects of public relations – i.e. what it *does* rather than what it *is*. However, it is worth analysing some of the more widely used ones in both academia and professional practice in order to appreciate the unique characteristics and intentions of public relations.

In the 1970s, American public relations academic and professional, Rex F. Harlow famously collected almost 500 definitions which he attempted to distil into one, rather lengthy and wordy, definition:

> *Public relations is the distinctive management function which helps establish and maintain mutual lines of communication, understanding, acceptance and co-operation between an organisation and its publics; involves the management of problems or issues; helps management to keep informed on and responsive to public opinion; defines and emphasises the responsibility of management to serve the public interest; helps management keep abreast of and effectively utilise change, serving as an early warning system to help anticipate trends; and uses research and sound and ethical communication as its principal tools.*
>
> (Harlow, 1976 cited in Broom, 2009, p. 24)

Though not exactly concise, Harlow's definition has informed numerous definitions which have emerged since this one originally appeared in 1976 in the highly respected academic journal *Public Relations Review*. On close reading, it provides a very good summary of what professional public relations is all about. It focuses on the *management* aspect of the discipline and illustrates just how all encompassing public relations really is. This definition provides an excellent starting point for considering public relations within the context of sport. Try inserting the word sport at various points throughout this definition and you will get the idea.

Another widely used definition is the one created by renowned US public relations authors Cutlip, Center and Broom in the early editions of their internationally famous textbook *Effective Public Relations*. This text is now in its 10th edition and is a highly recommended source for information on the original American growth and history of public relations. Their definition states that:

> *Public relations is the management function that establishes and maintains mutually beneficial relationships between an organisation and the publics on whom its success or failure depends.*
> (Broom, 2009, p. 21)

What stands out in this definition is the phrase '*management function*'. This clearly emphasises that really effective public relations has to be much more than writing news releases and organising press conferences, it is all about *managing* communication, *managing* reputation and *managing* relationships.

Moving on from the academic and textbook definitions, the Chartered Institute of Public Relations, which is the professional body for public relations practitioners in the UK, cites this definition on its website:

> *Public relations is about reputation – the result of what you do, what you say and what others say about you. Public relations is the discipline which looks after reputation, with the aim of earning understanding and support and influencing opinion and behaviour. It is the planned and sustained effort to establish and maintain goodwill and mutual understanding between an organisation and its publics.*
> (CIPR, 2009, *online*)

This provides another useful starting point for developing an understanding of public relations because it focuses specifically on reputation. For a sport entity nowadays – whether it is a premier league football club or a young swimmer approaching businesses for potential sponsorship – reputation is paramount. Reputation and image combine to create an *impression* which can be good, bad or indifferent but which is vital to the success of the sport entity. Positive responses, such as goodwill, support – financial or otherwise – and participation, are all generated by reputation, i.e. how people think and feel about the sport entity. Reputation is an immensely powerful intangible quality which cannot be bought and which is not entirely dependent on success or financial worth. Reputation is priceless, it takes a great deal of time and effort to create and can be destroyed in seconds if it is not protected and nurtured. Public relations, when it is properly understood and implemented, *is the guardian of reputation*. Reputation management is what contemporary public relations is all about. Successful reputation management is founded on the following prerequisites:

- Mutual understanding
- Goodwill
- Support
- Mutually beneficial relationships

Finally, in an attempt to define public relations in its simplest form and to show that it can be effectively used at both the organisational and individual level, here is my definition: *'Public relations is everything you say, everything you do and everything anyone says or thinks about you.'*

As will be demonstrated in later chapters, public relations is continuing to evolve but the following list will help in summarising, briefly, what public relations is:

- The management of relationships
- The management of reputation
- The management of goodwill and mutual understanding
- The eyes and ears of the organisation
- The instigator of two-way communication between the organisation and its publics
- It helps the organisation (or individual) achieve its full potential

In an attempt to describe public relations in clear, basic, functional terms, L'Etang (2008, p. 18) offers the following explanation which provides an excellent summary of public relations for the purposes of this text:

Public relations involves the communication and exchange of ideas either in response to, or to facilitate change. It entails argument and case-making … Organisations need specialists to perform that function and to interface between the organisation and those groups

with which it has or would like to have relationships. Public relations
entails the analysis of organisational actions which may impact on
relationships of reputation.

SOME ADVANTAGES AND DISADVANTAGES OF PUBLIC RELATIONS

Just in case there are any remaining doubts concerning the benefits to sport
organisations of learning about and implementing public relations, I will
conclude with a brief summary of the major advantages and disadvantages
that public relations can offer. When applied professionally, public relations
can offer the following distinct advantages over other major marketing
communications tools:

Credibility: Unlike advertising messages, public relations messages are
often generated by a source which is not the sport organisation. This is
referred to as 'third-party endorsement' and is a very powerful way of
gaining credibility for a message and thus the sport organisation. Having
somebody else say good things about your organisation and your product is
priceless, especially if that person is respected and/or recognised by your
publics.

Cost: As mentioned previously, public relations is considerably more cost
effective than other communications tools.

Cutting through the clutter: Public relations efforts frequently lead to
publicity and are usually considered eminently newsworthy, particularly by
the local news media. As a result, public relations messages are often in
a class of their own and considered distinct from the proliferation of
advertising and sales promotion messages which can often overwhelm and
confuse potential consumers.

Ability to reach specific groups: Understanding publics and their behaviour
as discussed earlier in this chapter allows for the implementation of
specifically targeted communications and relationship building strategies.

Image building: The tireless development of effective public relations
strategies can lead directly to the creation of a strong image and identity for
the sport organisation. As has been mentioned above, this can result in very
real benefits to the organisation, both financial and non-financial.

Public relations' main disadvantage is the lack of understanding that
surrounds the discipline in some quarters and the uncontrollability of
publicity. The more people involved in the business of sport learn about

public relations, the better it will undoubtedly be for all sport generally as according to Halbwirth and Toohey (2005):

> *Sport like any business is operating in a complex global market. Sport management needs to be adaptive to change, effectively manage risk, integrate technology advances and build stakeholder intimacy.*

THE PUBLICS OF PUBLIC RELATIONS

There is a much more detailed discussion around the concept of publics in Chapter 3, but it will be useful here to explain why we use the word 'publics' within the context of sport public relations and communication.

Publics is a relatively uncommon word and is only really used within the context of public relations as a way of describing all those groups and individuals with whom an organisation wants to develop long-term, mutually beneficial relationships. For example, as a supporter of Gold Coast United Football Club, I am an individual public but I am also part of the much bigger supporter group public. As a season ticket holder, I am a member of that public. As a supporter of football generally, I am a member of that global public, and so it goes on. It soon becomes clear, therefore, that all sport entities – whether they are clubs, individual athletes or sport governing bodies – have very many publics, all of whom have different needs and expectations.

In the example given above, I have referred to myself as what is known as an 'external public'. External publics, which also include sponsors, the media, funding bodies and investors amongst others, are clearly vital to the success of the sport organisation. However, all sport organisations also have to use public relations to communicate with another kind of public known as the 'internal public'. Internal publics are anyone who works for the sport organisation, for example, shareholders, ground staff, administrators, volunteers, players, caterers and coaching staff to name but a very few. Internal publics have a different relationship with the organisation to external publics and so they are perhaps the most important public because if they feel they are working for a good organisation, if they are happy and feel valued and are communicated with well then they become a powerful public relations tool in their own right because they will speak positively about the organisation using the important technique of 'word of mouth' communication. Everyone, including sponsors and prospective players, for example, wants to be associated with a good company which is doing good things.

In the competitive business world, organisations are becoming acutely aware of the necessity to 'analyse' their publics, which means they utilise professional public relations strategies and tactics to 'get to know' their many publics. Sport organisations, on the other hand, are notoriously bad at doing this and for taking their publics for granted. There seems to be two main reasons for this:

1. Many sport organisations do not practice public relations because they do not understand what it is.
2. There is the wide assumption in sport organisations that people will continue to support and engage with them whatever happens.

Sport itself is now operating in an extremely competitive business environment and it is obvious that the old practices are no longer relevant and that a new focus on excellent public relations and communication is required in order to continue to be successful.

SOME USEFUL MODELS OF PUBLIC RELATIONS

As with all abstract concepts, it can be helpful to illustrate the public relations function in a model form. Though there are not many specific public relations models available in the literature, here are some of the most useful.

The public relations transfer process

In 1988, the late Frank Jefkins who was one of the UK's pioneers in public relations professionalism and education, devised a model which he called *The Public Relations Transfer Process* and which clearly and straightforwardly illustrates the intended function of public relations. This is shown in Fig. 2.1.

The Public Relations Transfer Process shows us that professionally handled public relations has the power to convert a negative situation into

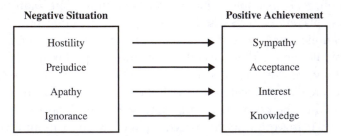

*When the negative situation is converted into positive achievement – through knowledge – the result is the primary objective of public relations, **understanding.***

FIGURE 2.1 *The Public Relations Transfer Process* (Source: Jefkins, 1994).

a positive one and this is achieved through creating relationships and dialogue between the organisation and its publics. It requires a complete knowledge of all the public groups and it requires truth, openness, honesty and clarity in all organisation–publics communications. Time after time, emotions such as those listed in the Negative Situation box are converted, through the implementation of specific and well thought through public relations techniques, to those emotions and responses listed in the Positive Situation box. This is a particularly useful model to apply to sport public relations because of its strong emotional dimension.

Dozier et al.'s new model of symmetry

In 1995, renowned American public relations theorists and academics, David Dozier, Larissa Grunig and James E. Grunig created their *'New Model of Symmetry as Two-Way Practices'* in an attempt to demonstrate that when an organisation creates and develops trusting and reliable relationships with its publics through excellent communications and public relations practices, it is entirely possible for both the organisation and the publics to gain something positive from the relationship and communication exchanges that take place surrounding it. This, of course, should be the ultimate goal for any sport organisation or entity in today's sport business-oriented environment.

In the model, as shown in Fig. 2.2, the most desirable outcome in communication terms is 3, the Two-Way Model of communication which results in a balanced (symmetric) relationship between the organisation and its publics. In 1 and 2, either the organisation or the public dominates the communication which makes it imbalanced (asymmetrical) and suggests lack of relationship building and understanding. Truly symmetric communication is a challenge and, many would argue, an idealistic and improbable ambition. However, the incorporation of the 'Win–Win Zone' in the new model suggests that even if the balance of communication power is sometimes skewed – either in favour of the organisation or the publics – the strength of the *relationship* between the two parties will ensure that goodwill and mutual understanding exist and that compromise can occur with both parties being satisfied with the outcome. For example, if your favourite rugby club suddenly raised its membership prices for the forthcoming season without any explanation, reasoning or advanced warning then you would quite naturally feel aggrieved and quite possibly think twice about renewing your membership. If, on the other hand, the rugby club thoroughly engaged in consultation with all its members and came to an agreement that a proportion of the fee increase would be invested in local grassroots initiatives such as junior rugby leagues then,

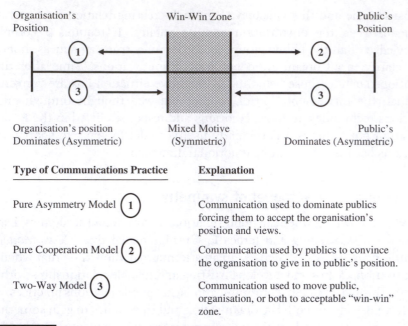

FIGURE 2.2 *New Model of Symmetry as Two-Way Practices. Adapted from Gruning in Heath (2001, p. 26).*

though you might still feel aggrieved at the price hike, you would probably be more likely to renew your membership at the increased rate because you would feel that you had been consulted on the reasons and, because you used to play in the junior leagues yourself, you appreciate how difficult it is to raise much needed funds and will therefore feel a certain satisfaction at being able to 'give back' in some small part – an example of a 'Win–Win' public relations solution.

The purpose of including the Jefkins and Dozier models is to illustrate how theorists have tried to conceptualise the sometimes rather abstract explanations and definitions of public relations into something more concrete and tangible. As with the definitions of public relations given earlier in the chapter, the insertion of the word 'sport' into these models at appropriate junctures makes their value and relevance to sport public relations immediately apparent.

SPORT PUBLIC RELATIONS

Because of its unique nature, sport demands its own public relations specialism. The phrase 'sport public relations' has only really emerged within the last 5 years in acknowledgement of the fact that sport marketing no longer fully encapsulates the distinct qualities of sport public relations. In recent years it has become evident that sport public relations and sport marketing have completely different objectives. Whereas sport marketing's primary objective is to ensure the sport entity is profitable, sport public relations' main priority is the establishment and maintenance of long-term relationships. This priority does, of course, support the marketing objective but there is much more to it than merely making a profit.

The objectives of sport public relations are as follows (Hopwood, 2005):

- To establish and maintain mutually beneficial long-term relationships
- To raise awareness
- To inform
- To educate
- To build trust
- To make friends
- To give people a reason to support
- To create fan acceptance

Sport public relations is all about relationships – relationship management and relationship building (Ledingham and Bruning, 2000, Shilbury and Rowe, next chapter). Relationships are intangible meaning that you cannot really measure or evaluate them in hard figures but public relations, and by extension sport public relations, is very much concerned with intangibles which, according to The Centre for Business Performance at Cranfield School of Management in the UK, are crucial to the ongoing success of any business, including sport business:

> *Intangible assets (such as long term relationships) are the sources of value and the levers for sustainable business performance in today's competitive economic context. They are the sources of competitive advantages and above normal financial returns.*

Distinct definitions have also begun to emerge for sport public relations in an attempt to encapsulate the importance of public relations in sport:

> *Sport public relations encompasses all the processes through which sport organisations can create and develop long-term mutually beneficial relationships with a range of publics.*
>
> (Hopwood, 2005, p. 175)

In their book '*Sport Public Relations: Managing Organizational Communication*', American authors Stoldt et al. (2006, p. 19) define sport public relations as follows:

> *Sport public relations is a managerial communication-based function designed to identify a sport organisation's key publics, evaluate its relationships with those publics, and foster desirable relationships between the sport organisation and those publics.*

Both of these definitions focus on a number of key aspects which are of critical importance to the sport entity. Firstly, the emphasis is very much on the managerial aspect of sport public relations. The Stoldt et al. definition explicitly states that public relations is a management level function which is just as critical to the success and effectiveness of the sport organisation as other managerial activities such as human resource management and marketing (Stoldt et al., 2006). Public relations actually overlaps with all the other management functions in the organisation precisely because it is a communications based activity and deals with internal as well as external publics. For that very reason, public relations cannot be effective unless it is fully integrated into the organisation's management function (Dozier et al., 1995).

Secondly, sport public relations is communication directed. Though not all sport public relations is composed of communication-based activities, communication is the cornerstone of the practice. Effective communication is the lifeblood of healthy and long-lasting relationships and sport public relations is totally relationship directed. As Lagae (2005, p. 76) states:

> *PR through sport also fits into an interactive communication strategy, making use of the various media to obtain understanding, attention and support for the values and aims of an organisation among clearly specified groups.*

WHAT IS SPORT COMMUNICATION?

In the above paragraph it states that not all sport public relations is composed of communication-based activities which recognise the fact that a significant element of sport public relations is emotional and intangible. It will be useful at this point, therefore, to focus more directly on sport communication in order to create a distinction between the two elements.

In their book entitled *Strategic Sport Communication*, Pedersen et al. (2007, p. 76) define sport communication as follows:

> *Sport communication is a process by which people in sport, in a sport setting, or through a sport endeavour share symbols as they create meaning through interaction.*

In their explanation of this definition Pedersen et al. (2007) conclude that *any* example of communication which occurs in and through sport will fit this definition which makes it a very broad definition indeed and, by implication, would also encompass sport public relations as well as, arguably, all the components of sport marketing, sport marketing communication, sport management and sport business. Sport communication, therefore, is an immensely generic term which really needs to be given its own identity. For this reason, it is suggested that the term sport communication be used to refer to the *techniques* and *media* which are used in the sport communication process. For example, newspaper articles could be considered as examples of sport communication when they are giving a direct report of a sporting event and its result and outcome. In the UK, these are the types of articles you find on the back pages of many newspapers, the kind of articles that people read in order to get the facts about what happened during the event, reports on websites are another such example. Articles such as these are principally sending an asymmetric communication message though feedback can be created when people share or discuss the article. The point here though is that this type of sport communication article is different from an article which is written from a sport public relations' perspective. In suggesting that sport communication refers to the techniques and media or 'technical aspects' of sport it becomes clear that the persuasive and relational elements of sport public relations are missing. Sky Television's broadcast of the 2009 Ashes series is an example of sport communication as is Channel 9's Monday Night Football in Australia. Two mates discussing the football in the pub after the match is an example of sport communication as is a coach conducting a pre-match team briefing.

The symbols mentioned in the Pedersen et al. (2007) definition refer to the components which are used in the communication of the sport message, for example, words, signs, images, sounds, logos, songs, chants, the stadium or venue and so on. All of these have been developed in order to create shared communication amongst all the many publics involved in any given sport. Think of your favourite sport team and the chances are you will visualise the club logo or perhaps their home venue or even the colour of their kit – these are all symbols and they are hugely important in both sport communication and sport public relations. In sport communication terms they will identify the team, in sport public relations terms they will create and inspire a powerful emotional and relational attachment. Again, think about your favourite sport team – how do you feel when you are out and about and you see a complete stranger wearing the team shirt? The chances are that you will feel an immediate emotional response and an inexplicable warmth towards the person wearing the shirt because you are fellow supporters, you might even strike up a conversation. Would the same emotions occur if that same stranger were wearing the team shirt of your team's fiercest rivals? Probably not.

Symbols in sport communication are extremely powerful which is why they are often closely guarded and protected by their owners. They are used by sport organisations, for example, to create and reinforce organisational culture and identity which is a core element of sport public relations, when they are used to transmit messages, that is, sport communication.

Pedersen et al.'s definition also focusses on meaning created through interaction and this is where sport communication begins to merge more closely with sport public relations. Interaction and shared experience are key elements of the relational aspect of sport public relations. Attending and participating in a sporting event creates a shared meaning which is generally only experienced by those directly involved but which can then become a powerful example of sport public relations. Through word of mouth communication, i.e. by talking about the experience, others who were not at the event could potentially develop an interest in the sport and go along to the next event as they want to be a part of that interaction. Fans interacting at a sporting event can create meaning and atmosphere which communicate a whole range of messages about the sport. The unfortunate interaction between West Ham and Millwall football fans in August 2009 created a specific meaning about a certain dimension of football. On the other hand, the interaction of the Barmy Army at England's cricket matches has created a new meaning for a sport which traditionally has had a relatively low supporter base.

Sport communication, is therefore, a distinct element in its own right and it provides the techniques and media through which sport public relations occurs. Because public relations is founded on communications, the two are inseparable and as we have seen, the same applies within the context of sport.

CASE STUDY 2.1: Sport Public Relations and Communication in Action: Twenty20 Cricket

There can be few sport that have undergone the same kind of transformation as cricket. In a few short years, the image of the game has changed from that of dull, boring and only watched by middle-aged men to exciting, entertaining, colourful and fun. The reason for this complete turnaround is Twenty20 cricket, the bright, brash version of the sport which has taken the world by storm and which is having a significant influence on the whole structure of the game, not only in England but wherever in the world cricket is being played.

Twenty20 cricket is an example of excellent sport public relations. It was created by the England and Wales Cricket Board (ECB) which, in the late 1990s, realised that support for the game was declining and attendances at cricket matches throughout the UK were falling year on year. In order to address this serious problem, the ECB conducted a national survey in 2001 and came up with a number of key findings about how people felt about the sport:

- Nineteen million people had an interest in cricket and thought about it in a positive way.
- Seventeen million of those had never attended a live game.
- It was boring.
- It took too long.
- It was incomprehensible.
- It was played at the wrong time while people were at work.
- It was watched mainly by middle-aged and retired men.

As a result of the survey, the ECB recognised a number of key issues which had to be addressed if cricket was to remain relevant to the British public:

- Cricket competes in the very busy entertainment industry.
- Today's younger – and less committed – cricket audiences want a result and excitement from their entertainment.

- Regular audiences recognise the need for change … but want to keep the sport's core values.
- The total cricket offering must compete and justify the significant leisure time and money invested.
- Cricket is capable of being played in many different formats. It is essential to recognise the publics who want these different formats and structure the game with them in mind.
- Once publics have experienced cricket for the first time, they come back for more. Getting them to come for the first time is key.
- Barriers to publics paying to watch the sport needed to be removed through product diversification.

It was clear from the research that people appreciated the values and character of the sport. There are, after all, a number of phrases used in common parlance such as 'it's not cricket', 'sticky wicket', 'hit for six', 'bowl over' which illustrate the extent to which the sport has infiltrated the national psyche but it was also clear that cricket in its present form was perceived as being outdated and out of reach to a younger, entertainment oriented public. Taking the findings very seriously, the ECB decided that a new version of the cricket product had to be created which would appeal to a different target public who is a younger consumer, who considers the longer form of the game 'tolerable' but who has never attended a live match. The Twenty20 Cup was the outcome, which according to John Carr, former ECB director of cricket operations:

> … was one of my hobby-horses. We wanted to make the most of the appeal of county cricket, bring in a new audience and not lose the interest of the game's long-term supporters.
>
> (Berry, 2009, p. 58)

The short format of the game was born during the English county cricket season of 2003 to a typically English mixed reception of dire forebodings and great excitement and anticipation. The 2003 Twenty20 Cup was launched with

Continued

relatively little fanfare yet played out with the glitz, glamour and hype usually only reserved for football (the round ball version of the game). That first euphoric season concluded with unimaginable success and a previously unseen support for cricket together with a typically English response of 'well, we always knew it was a brilliant idea, didn't we?!' For a sport which is often saddled with adjectives such as 'outdated' and 'out of touch' overnight, cricket became the spectator sport of choice attracting and appealing to a range of unfamiliar audiences – namely children, families and females. Having fun at the cricket and playing to sell out crowds on balmy English summer evenings was a match made in heaven for a sport which had come to be seen generally as boring, irrelevant and having limited appeal. Since then the publics' (and the players') appetite for the short form of the game has gathered momentum to the extent that Twenty20 has become arguably the dominant force in the world game of cricket and, as reported in the 2009 edition of the Wisden Almanack, in the English 2008 cricket season 'for two and a half weeks in June it was impossible to avoid Twenty20 – more watched than ever before.' (Berry (2009), p. 816)

The continuing success of Twenty20 cricket clearly shows that in order to remain relevant and reach new audiences, the sport product can be differentiated, diversified and extended in similar ways to other consumer products. Twenty20 cricket is a result of what Peters and Waterman (1982, p. 156) describe as 'staying close to the customer'. Most stakeholder publics were clearly identified and communicated with during the research stages demonstrating that Grunig's two-way symmetrical communication strategy can and does work. The capacity crowds are evidence of the demand for this new form of cricket. When the tournament began in 2003, a third of the paying customers had never attended a live cricket match before. Not only that, Twenty20 cricket has, for the first time in county cricket, created a culture of advance ticket sales. The fact that large numbers of supporters have watched more than one game of this type provides clear evidence that publics will display long-term loyalty and repeat purchase behaviour to a company, brand or service if a relationally based grounding is applied in the form of effective sport public relations practice.

During the 2009 Test Series between South Africa and Australia, revered cricket commentator, Richie Benaud said during an interview 'with test cricket, parents take their kids – with Twenty20 the kids take their parents.' This comment really encapsulates the success of the role of sport public relations in Twenty20 cricket. The audiences at all Twenty20 matches around the world are entirely different to those who attend other forms of cricket matches. Twenty20 cricket is a complete entertainment package that appeals to everyone. The ECB describes it as 'family friendly, fun and fast' – the match lasts three hours, there is plenty of action and each county provides plenty of peripheral entertainment to add to the fun such as face painting, bouncy castles, cheerleaders, hot tubs, speed dating to name but a few. On the international stage, Twenty20 cricket has become even more glitzy and the crowds love it, so much so that in the 2010 season, the cricket schedules around the world will be incorporating even more of it at the expense of some of the longer formats of the game. Adam Gilchrist, the retired Australian wicket-keeper batsman in delivering the 2009 Cowdrey Lecture sums up the raison d'etre for Twenty20 cricket perfectly:

> By playing a cricket match over a 3 hour time frame 20/20 cricket brings the game into the 21st century in terms of its ability to adapt to the busy, time poor world in which we all live … Most importantly, it has introduced a number of new demographics to cricket that weren't there before.
>
> (Cricinfo.com, 2009)

The example of Twenty20 cricket is a clear endorsement of the value of sport public relations and communication because, as Adam Gilchrist observes 'it has changed cricket forever'.

SUMMARY

This chapter has illustrated the immense importance of public relations and communication to sport and there can be no doubt that this importance will only continue to grow as all sport become more aware of the need for establishing and maintaining long-term relationships with those upon whom it relies for its existence. It is apparent that sport organisations tend to perpetuate the view that marketing is the main business operation but as Hopwood (2007, p. 315) observes: 'It is clear ... that public relations goes beyond marketing and promotion. Public relations, if conducted properly, can provide the roots from which marketing can grow'. The special nature of the sport product in all its forms means that traditional marketing, promotional and general business principles have to be adapted to meet the needs of sport and all its publics, therefore the more transactional focussed approaches and attitudes found in those areas have to be rethought and given a relational focus. Important basic public relations theories and models have been included in order to illustrate that public relations is founded upon distinct theoretical concepts which can be applied to the sport context in order to create specialist sport public relations. This theoretical base also affirms the assertion that sport public relations is much more than sport media relations and publicity. The case study on Twenty20 cricket is illustrative of the efficacy and efficiency of sport public relations.

Sport communication has been considered as a separate but inclusive element of sport public relations based on the notion that sport communication is more to do with the *technical aspects* or the tools and media of sport public relations such as newspaper articles, websites and sport event television broadcasts. Symbols and interaction were also discussed in relation to the Pedersen et al. (2007) definition of sport communication.

Public relations and communication in sport are the foundations of success for any sporting enterprise as sport itself can be regarded as both public relations and communication. In his editorial in the April 2009 edition of the *International Journal of Sport Marketing and Sponsorship*, Professor Michel Desbordes states:

> *These are interesting times for the sport industry and its partners, as the economic downturn and the reducing availability of credit usher in a sea change in the commercial confidence in sport...authenticity and substance have become the hallmarks of the relationship approach that will hopefully dominate future practices.*
>
> (p. 197)

It seems that the time for better education in and greater knowledge of sport public relations has arrived.

KEY TERMS

Public Relations   Public relations is the discipline which looks after reputation, with the aim of earning understanding and support and influencing opinion and behaviour. It is the planned and sustained effort to establish and maintain goodwill and mutual understanding between an organisation and its publics.

Sport Public Relations   Encompasses all the processes through which sport organisations can create and develop long-term mutually beneficial relationships with a range of publics.

Sport Communication   The process by which people in sport, in a sport setting, or through a sport endeavour share symbols as they create meaning through interaction.

Relationship Management   The process of fostering good relations with customers to build long-term loyalty, goodwill and mutual understanding and support.

Publics   John Dewey, philosopher and educator defined a public as an active social unit with a common interest. Public relations professionals identify strategic publics to whom they target specific messages because they know that the public will care about the message and respond to it in some way.

Intangible Assets   Are defined as identifiable non-monetary assets that cannot be seen, touched or physically measured, which are created through time and/or effort and that are identifiable as a separate asset, e.g. relationships, emotional attachment to a sport organisation, reputation.

DISCUSSION QUESTIONS

1. The function of the Public Relations Transfer Process Model is to demonstrate how negative attitudes can be changed to positive ones through the use of public relations. Identify any recent examples of sporting events, incidents, entities or organisation where this model could be applied.

2. For any sport organisation with which you are familiar, critically analyse its use of sport public relations and communication putting yourself in the position of a public.

3. A new girl's football team has been admitted to your local junior Sunday league and they have asked you to advise them on how they can raise awareness and build relationships in the local community. Develop a strategy on how they can use public relations and communication to achieve their objectives.

4. How do you see the role of public relations in sport developing in the future?

GUIDED READING

Hopwood, M.K., 2007. Sport public relations. In: Beech, J., Chadwick, S. (Eds.), The Marketing of Sport. Prentice Hall, Harlow (Chapter 14).

Hopwood, M.K., 2005. Applying the public relations function to the business of sport. International Journal of Sport Marketing and Sponsorship 6 (3), 174–188.

In June 2008, a Special Issue on Sport Public Relations of the journal Public Relations Review (Volume 34 Issue 2) was published, edited by myself and Dr Jacquie L'Etang. It is available online through university libraries and contains a varied and interesting range of articles by authors from around the world.

RECOMMENDED WEBSITES

The Chartered Institute of Public Relations (CIPR) – <http://www.cipr.co.uk>.
   The Global Alliance for Public Relations and Communication Management – <http://www.globalalliancepr.org/>.
   Cricket20 the home of Twenty20 Cricket – <http://www.cricket20.com/>.

REFERENCES

Berry, S. (Ed.), 2009. Wisden Cricketer's Almanack, 146th ed. A & C Black Publishers Ltd, London.

Broom, G.M., 2009. Cutlip and Center's Effective Public Relations, 10th ed. Prentice Hall, Upper Saddle River, NJ.

Cricinfo, 2009. Adam Gilchrist's Cowdrey Lecture 2009. Cricinfo.com Retrieved on 25 June 2009 from: <http://www.cricinfo.com/ci/content/current/story/410365.html>.

Dozier, D.M., Grunig, L.A., Grunig, J.E., 1995. Manager's Guide to Excellence in Public Relations and Communications Management. Lawrence Erlbaum Associates, Mahwah, NJ.

ECB, 2009. Twenty-20 cup. ECB Online. Retrieved on 21 September 2009 from: <http://www.ecb.co.uk/news/domestic/twenty20-cup>.

Halbwirth, S., Toohey, K., 2005. Leveraging knowledge: sport and success. In: The 12th International Association for Sport Information Proceedings, Beijing, pp. 278–285.

Heath, R.L., 2001. Handbook of Public Relations. Sage Publications Inc., Thousand Oaks, CA.

Hopwood, M.K., 2005. Applying the public relations function to the business of sport. International Journal of Sport Marketing and Sponsorship 6 (3), 174–188.

Hopwood, M.K., 2007. Sport public relations. In: Beech, J., Chadwick, S. (Eds.), The Marketing of Sport. Pearson Education Limited, Harlow.

Jefkins, F., 1994. Public Relations Techniques, second ed. Butterworth Heinemann, Oxford.

L'Etang, J., 2008. Public Relations: Concepts, Practice and Critique. SAGE Publications Ltd, London.

Lagae, W., 2005. Sport Sponsorship and Marketing Communications: A European Perspective. Financial Times. Prentice Hall, Harlow.

Ledingham, J.A., Bruning, S.D., 2000. Public Relations as Relationship Management: A Relational Approach to the Study and Practice of Public Relations. Lawrence Erlbaum Associates, Mahwah, NJ.

Pedersen, P.M., Miloch, K.S., Laucella, P.C., 2007. Strategic Sport Communication. Human Kinetics, Champaign, Illinois.

Peters, T., Waterman Jr., R.H., 1982. In Search of Excellence: Lessons from America's Best Known Companies. Harper & Row, New York.

Stoldt, G.C., Dittmore, S.W., Branvold, S.E., 2006. Sport Public Relations: Managing Organisational Communication. Human Kinetics, Champaign, Illinois.

CHAPTER 3

Sport Relationship Management

David Shilbury
Deakin University

Katherine Rowe
Deakin University

Learning Outcomes

Upon completion of this chapter you should be able to:

- Explain the differences between four models of communication
- Recognise the significance of the two-way symmetrical model of communication in establishing and maintaining relationships
- Understand the importance of public relations as a management function designed to build and maintain long-term relationships
- Identify processes that assist in the management of organisation–public relations
- Appreciate the value of relationships in the context of sport

---

CHAPTER OVERVIEW

Public relations is conceptualised and used by organisations very differently depending on their objectives and available resources. A traditional view of public relations is that the practice is simply a communications activity used to improve company image and *reputation* (Ledingham and Bruning, 1998). From this perspective, a football club wanting to boost public opinion might consider hosting a charity event, sponsoring an aid-related effort or otherwise linking itself to a community-minded organisation. This traditional view, however, has gradually started to be overtaken by a more strategic way of conceptualising public relations.

Grunig (1993) suggests that public relations practitioners, who preoccupy themselves with corporate image alone and use the media simply to build symbolic relationships rather than behavioural relationships with publics, offer little value to the organisations they serve. He suggests that for public relations to be of benefit to an organisation, the goal of communications activities must be about 'building long-term behavioural relationships with strategic publics' (p. 136). This focus on relationship building as an objective of public relations is becoming more widely accepted across the industry, resulting in public relations now more commonly being considered to be a management function that uses communications strategically to build relationships with publics (Ledingham and Bruning, 1998). This chapter will discuss the concept of *relationship management* in the context of sport but first we look at the concept of *relationship management* as a general theory of public relations.

PUBLIC RELATIONS IN MANAGING RELATIONSHIPS

Cutlip et al. (2006, p. 5) define public relations as a 'management function that establishes and maintains mutually beneficial relationships between an organisation and the publics on whom its success or failure depends'. This definition encapsulates the importance of making public relations activities strategic and focused on developing relationships with key publics rather than simply building symbolic relationships that do little more than superficially boost or improve company image. When deciding who they should establish relationships with, organisations must first understand who their 'publics' are.

Organisations have a series of *stakeholders*, who are individuals or groups of people who can affect or be affected by the actions, goals, decisions and policies of that organisation (Hunt and Grunig, 1994). In the case of a National Basketball Association (NBA) club, stakeholders might include season ticket holders, fans, sponsors, TV networks, community groups and employees, for example. These stakeholders are made up of a range of different types of publics, dependent upon the level of influence and involvement each group has regarding a particular problem or issue related to that organisation (Cutlip et al., 2006). Further expanding on the NBA club example, one specific public in the stakeholder group labelled as 'fans' might be a group of mothers who disagree with the off-court behaviour of players and decide to collectively take action against the club they had once supported. Another public in this situation could be a group of young male fans whose opinion of the club is not influenced by this behaviour. These two very distinct and different publics will require different public relations strategies, despite the fact that they exist as part of the same stakeholder group.

An organisation will generally divide its stakeholders into publics based on individual responses to a particular issue or problem that arises, and the level of influence they have on the organisation and vice versa. Grunig and Hunt's (1984) seminal work identified four distinct types of publics, referred to as: non-publics, latent publics, aware publics and active publics, which are widely accepted and used in public relations texts (Dozier and Ehling, 1992; Hunt and Grunig, 1994; Dozier et al., 1995; Cutlip et al., 2006), and specifically in the domain of sport public relations (Stoldt et al., 2006).

Non-publics are groups of people who have little impact on an organisation and the organisation has little impact on them. In order for a public to exist, a problem or issue must be present which causes people to become similarly affected by the organisation's behaviour or act collaboratively to influence the organisation's behaviour. In the case of a non-public, this condition is not satisfied. *Latent publics* are connected to or affected by an organisation in regards to a certain issue, but are unaware that the link exists. This group has the potential to become active if they become aware of the connection. *Aware publics* realise that they are affected by or involved in an issue but have not communicated with other people or taken collaborative action. *Active publics* form when people in aware publics begin to communicate and plan to take coordinated action about the situation or issue.

For an active public to exist, they must meet three conditions. A group of people must face a similar problem, recognise that the problem exists and organise to do something about the problem (Grunig and Hunt, 1984). In a sporting context, an active public could be a group of athletes who take coordinated action to expose drug cheats in their sport. A public is more likely to be active if its constituents have a high level of involvement (feel that the organisation's actions affect them) and problem recognition (recognise that the actions of the organisation are a problem) with a low level of constraint recognition (feeling constrained from taking action about the organisation's behaviour) (Hunt and Grunig, 1994). As the level of involvement and problem recognition increase and constraint recognition decreases, a latent public can become an aware or active public.

Organisations using public relations for strategic, relationship management purposes need to identify their *strategic/key publics* (publics that affect the organisation's ability to achieve their goals) in order to develop communication strategies that target these groups. Unfortunately, not all public relations activities are as strategic and coordinated as they ideally could be and many provide little support in terms of relationship development with strategic publics. In order to understand how public relations can be most effectively used to build relationships, we must first understand the different ways organisations communicate with their publics.

Grunig and Hunt (1984) have identified four models of public relations that are generally practiced by organisations which are commonly referred to in texts (Dozier et al., 1995; Hon, 2007; Witmer, 2006) and used in academic research (Grunig et al., 1995). These models vary significantly in their level of effectiveness and ethical merit, which make them relevant to investigate in determining the role of public relations in relationship management.

Press agentry model: A common model employed in the area of sport. This model is a *one-way* model of communication where the organisation develops communications strategies giving little to no consideration of the opinions of publics. It is also an *asymmetrical* model in that the organisation seeks a change in the behaviour of its publics rather than its own. Securing mass media publicity which reflects positively on the organisation is often the goal in this model and organisations with little regard given to the importance of reporting all of the facts. This simplistic approach to public relations provides little support in terms of relationship building and management. The role of the Sport Information Directors (SIDs) in the US collegiate system is a good example of this model. Essentially, SIDs produce timely press releases and score reporting, game/athlete stories, game programs, media guides and promotional pieces and operate in-game scoring statistical programs. This task is largely about disseminating information about the performance of the various athletic teams within a university or college.

Public information model: This model is similar to press agentry in that communications are not based on research or strategic planning. Public relations practitioners objectively report information to publics about the organisations they represent, with the intent of disseminating information rather than persuading these publics towards a particular viewpoint or type of behaviour. In this model, organisations generally present the full story to publics rather than reporting on the parts that make the organisation look good. SIDs can also fulfil this role, which is similar to press agentry. In this case, the public information model may be used to provide details in relation to a prominent athlete or athletes who may have broken team rules, been apprehended by police or been the centre of attention in relation to drug testing results. In all cases, the SID would clarify the details relating to the matter at hand and communicate them in the most appropriate format, either via press release or press conference.

Two-way asymmetrical model: In *two-way* models of public relations, organisations first determine the attitudes of publics and then develop messages designed to alter these attitudes and ultimately behaviours in a way that suits the organisation. By designing communications based on public attitudes, this model generally produces greater success in achieving the desired outcome from publics than *one-way* models. However, this model is *asymmetrical* in that it seeks change from its publics rather than making changes itself. This model can be most effectively used when the public stand to gain from a change in their behaviour, such as a public health campaign, encouraging the population to get active in order to reduce their risk of life-style diseases. Changes to ticketing systems or new stadia can require the use of this model. In Melbourne, Australia, the introduction of a new state-of-the-art football stadium with a roof that closes required the use of a two-way asymmetrical model. Most Australian rules' patrons had been used to purchasing tickets on game day on a walk-up basis. With the introduction of a smaller boutique stadium, patrons had to be advised and cajoled into thinking about ticket purchases well in advance of game day. In the first few years of the new stadium's life, entry to the stadium was encumbered by the need to purchase specific seats and evaluate all the various seating options and prices, if the purchase was left to game day. Entry to the stadium was consequently time-consuming and frustrating, until it became obvious that a communications strategy was required to outline ticket-purchasing options.

Two-way symmetrical model: This model is based on negotiation and compromise by both parties where the organisation assesses opinions of their strategic publics and communicates with them on an area of conflict in order to develop a mutual resolution. In the context of sport, perhaps a club decides that it wants to change its uniform and members object to the decision. A compromise could be reached by allowing member input regarding the new uniform design or keeping the old uniform for home games. Communicating with this key publics (disapproving members) and reaching a suitable compromise assist in reducing the damage inflicted on this important relationship.

Ledingham (2003, p. 181) proposes that from a relationship management perspective, 'public relations balances the interests of organisations and publics through management of *organisation–public relationships*'. By using communication as a way of managing conflict and reaching a compromise on issues, relationships are more likely to be an outcome of the two-way symmetrical model of communication than the other models. By seeking to understand, rather than simply persuade its publics, organisations are more strategically positioned to establish and maintain relationships with these key groups of people (Thomlison, 2000).

Having defined terms such as stakeholder and public in the context of public relations practice, and outlined the different communication styles that organisations use, this chapter will now delve a little deeper to focus on how sport organisations can strategically employ public relations techniques to manage relationships with these important groups.

ORGANISATION–PUBLIC RELATIONSHIPS

Sport organisations have relationships with a range of different publics. So what exactly is a relationship in the context of public relations? An organisation–public relationship can been defined as 'the state which exists between an organisation and its key publics, in which the actions of either can impact the economical, social, cultural, or political well being of the other' (Ledingham and Bruning, 1998, p. 62). In order to maintain quality relationships with key/strategic publics, organisations must design a range of communications strategies that cater for the stance of each public on a specific issue, as individuals who make up each of the publics will differ as will their response to the problem or issue at hand. Each of these publics has the ability to affect the organisation differently, just as the organisation itself can affect each of them in different ways. For this reason, we must investigate the notion of organisation–public relationships and understand how public relations practitioners representing sport organisations can foster quality, long-term relationships with strategic publics of the organisations.

It is important to first consider this concept of strategic publics, which was briefly discussed earlier in the chapter. How can an organisation determine who it should be communicating with in order to develop and maintain long-term, valuable relationships? Grunig and Repper (1992) explain that stakeholders, publics and issues evolve outside of the control of the organisation in most cases. The role of the public relations practitioner is to scan the environment and determine who these groups are, the extent of their influence on the organisation and their stance on particular issues.

Many stakeholders are passive and it is only once they become *aware* and/or *active* that they are considered as *public* by a particular organisation. Grunig and Repper (1992) posit that the first step in strategic public relations is to determine all those individuals or groups who have a stake in the organisation. This can be achieved by scanning the environment using methods such as opinion polls, studying the mass media, consulting political or community leaders, using internal records and information management, along with a host of other scanning options. Environmental scanning should produce a list of stakeholders who may then be ranked or assigned weights, depending on the degree of influence they have on the organisation or the extent to which the organisation believes that it must moderate its impact on them. Resources should be allocated based on this ranking system, with those ranked/weighted highest receiving the most attention. Communicating with stakeholders 'is especially important as it helps to develop stable, long-term relationships... and to manage conflict when it occurs' (Grunig and Repper, 1992, p. 127). Stoldt et al. (2006) concur with this notion of managing stakeholder relationships in order to increase the probability of receiving a positive response from stakeholders in the future if issues arise or the organisation requires their support.

In addition to managing relationships with stakeholders it is most important that sport organisations pay particular attention to relationships with strategic publics. Publics are not selected, rather they evolve as situations or issues arise. As these publics emerge they will each take a different degree of interest in the issue or problem based upon variables such as their degree of problem recognition, involvement and the constraint recognition they display. These variables determine whether publics are non-publics, latent publics, aware publics and active publics. Grunig's situational theory explains that publics can take a different stance on different issues which means that organisations may need to manage relationships differently depending on the situation and issue at hand (Grunig and Hunt, 1984). Logically, active publics, who have the greatest impact on an organisation or are themselves greatly impacted on by an organisation, should be the first considered in developing communication strategies.

When David Beckham announced his plan to leave Spanish side, Real Madrid at the completion of season 2007, non-publics and/or passive publics regarding this issue might have included a group of LA Galaxy 'supporters' who were aligned with the team to which Beckham would subsequently move, but rarely attended games and did not hold memberships. These fans were unaware of this issue as they did not follow the press and were not aware that Beckham was moving to their club (limited problem recognition and involvement). Upon Beckham's arrival at the LA-based side, these fans may have become aware or active regarding the issue of Beckham's move, realising the connection they had to this issue (aware) and taking action to purchase a membership in season 2008 due to renewed interest (active). It can be seen that these aware and active publics would then require different styles and levels of communication than was originally required when classified as latent or non-publics regarding this issue.

Cutlip et al. (2006, p. 323) examine the process of strategically defining publics, stating that 'the key to defining publics strategically is to identify how people are involved and affected in the situation for which the program intervention is being developed, which requires greater information-gathering efforts than simply labelling groups of people who appear to have something in common'. The authors add, it is important to understand 'what they know, how they feel, and what they do, combined with who and where they are' (p. 323) in order to set useful program objectives for each target public. This further reinforces Grunig and Hunt's (1984) contention that two-way communication through identification of publics and their stance on issues is most effective when organisations seek to build relationships with their key publics.

In the case of the 2007 outbreak of equine influenza in several Australian states, the potential for devastation of the Australian racing industry was immense, resulting in a need for public relations efforts in order to contain the issue, ensuring speculation and hysteria were minimised. How would an organisation such as Racing New South Wales (Racing NSW), an Australian racing governing body, have determined its stakeholders and subsequent publics regarding the issue, in order to communicate with them appropriately? Immediate action taken by this organisation would have the potential to exacerbate or diffuse the subsequent damage to relationships with key stakeholders.

Firstly, the organisation must map its stakeholders. State governments, state racing associations, venue managers, employees, event sponsors, media representatives, horse owners, bookmakers and racegoers are examples of stakeholders. The organisation must then identify the response of key stakeholders to the issue or 'crisis'. A group of regular race meet sponsors might threaten to pull their support for future race events as a result of the issue. Racing NSW would need to communicate with this group in order to ensure that positive relationships were maintained. Relationships with these publics in a situation such as this would be far easier to manage if the organisation had made efforts to establish mutually beneficial relationships with these groups as stakeholders before the issue emerged. The following case study describes a situation where an Australian rugby league club was able draw upon well-established relationships with a key stakeholder group in order to reduce the impact of the crisis on the organisation's success.

CASE STUDY 3.1: Canterbury Bulldogs Rugby League Football Club (RLFC)

The Canterbury Bulldogs are strong competitors in Australia's National Rugby League (NRL) who have suffered from numerous off-field incidents in recent years. In August 2002, the club was exposed for breaching the league's salary cap by close to AUD$1 million. An investigation carried out by Bruce and Tini (2008) analysed articles published in both the Australian and New Zealand media. The authors discovered that the club employed several crisis communication strategies in their attempts to manage the situation including denial, provocation and corrective action amongst others, each of which had little impact, some in fact making matters worse. The only strategy which appeared to have a positive impact in restoring the Bulldogs' standing amongst the rugby community was based on the club's understanding of the power well-established relationships with fans could have if managed effectively, in rescuing the club from a potentially disastrous situation.

The Bulldogs' attempted to gain leverage from its relationships with fans by shifting the blame for the breaches wholly onto club management. Fans did not feel an alliance with Bulldogs' management; it was with the players and coaches the strongest bonds existed. The club attempted to paint a picture of players, coaches and most importantly fans as victims in the situation, using the CEO and the board of the club as scapegoats, blamed for deliberately breaching the salary cap. The public responded well. Bruce and Tini (2008, p. 113) suggest that 'by protecting the players and coach, with whom fans have the strongest emotional connection, and sacrificing the management team, the organisation ensured that the relationship with at least one key stakeholder group would continue'.

Several media outlets criticised this portrayal of players as 'victims' in the situation given that they were being paid far better than players from the other clubs. Despite such criticism, Bulldogs' fans would not budge. Their support for players and their club remained strong with increased spectatorship being seen in the year following the crisis. This was perhaps a sign of fans' support for the players and the suffering they had endured as a result of an NRL-imposed ban from participating in the finals series 2002, the cause of which in the minds of fans lay solely with the decision of management to breach the salary cap.

In this case, strong relationships with stakeholders saved the club from a potentially disastrous situation. Sport organisations in many cases have the advantage of experiencing the benefits of strong emotional connection from supporters and other stakeholders. In this case, these relationships made blaming management (for the situation the club found itself in) the obvious decision, separating the players and the team from the scandal. Without this strong bond, fans may have attributed the salary cap breaches to unrealistic player demands and greed, potentially leading to a very different outcome for the Canterbury Bulldogs.

How then did the Canterbury Bulldogs set about the task of managing organisation–public relationships? Ledingham (2000) in his five-step approach to managing organisation–public relationships illustrates the decision-making processes that might have been evident at the Bulldogs. In order for this approach to be successfully implemented, organisations must understand that organisation–public relationships go through a series of phases as they develop and then degenerate. Figure 3.1 outlines these phases. Being able to identify the state of the relationship assists practitioners in developing appropriate communications strategies.

Managing Organisation–Public Relationships at the Canterbury Bulldogs

(1) *Identify your key publics*:
Main stakeholder group and strategic public here were identified as fans/supporters and members.
(2) *Determine the state of the relationship*:
Use Fig. 3.1 to determine the state of important relationships inviting input from all key personnel within the organisation and other external parties where necessary. In this case, supporters and members felt an alliance with the club, attending matches and supporting their team publicly. This would indicate that

Continued

this relationship had reached the 'Fidelity Phase'. Their relationship did not extend to those associated with managing the club.

(3) *Find out how your publics view the relationship*: Through feedback from fans and supporters, the strongest alliances were with players, coaches and those associated with the team's on-field performance, as this aspect of the sport organisation was what bound them most tightly with their supporters.

(4) *Develop strategies to manage relationships*: In the salary cap scandal of 2002, the club sought to maintain the 'strong' relationships they had established with fans by using the CEO and the board of the club as scapegoats, portraying them as being solely responsible for breaching the salary cap, while players and coaches were said to be victims of poor management.

(5) *Communicate your behaviours to key publics*: In order to ensure fans felt the club was taking action against those responsible for this salary cap breach, an act of poor management, Football Manager Garry Hughes was sacked, with the resignation of CEO, Steve Mortimer, also welcomed by the club, indicating to fans that the club would not stand for such deceitful behaviour within its upper levels of management. These actions communicated to members and supporters that the club was taking action to prevent such scandals in the future in order to spare fans, coaches and players from further distress and embarrassment at the hands-on management actions.

By applying this theory to the study, it is clear that the Canterbury Bulldogs applied a well-planned, strategic approach to managing its valuable relationship with supporters and members, displayed by this overview of actions taken by club's public relations representatives. Ledingham's (2000) staged approach to managing relationships clarifies how organisations should behave if they are to develop and maintain long-term relationships with key publics. When following this process, organisations must ensure that the communications objectives they develop do not seek to solely influence the attitudes and behaviours of publics. It must also include actions the organisation itself can take in order to be perceived in a positive light by publics. For example, rather than establishing an advertising campaign to convince members that they should donate money to their basketball club, the organisation could issue a report which outlines budget cuts management themselves have made to reduce costs. Such cuts might, for example, include limiting the amount of club-funded corporate travel and downsizing offices to reduce leasing costs. By communicating these acts of organisational compromise, publics are made aware of management's own sacrifices for the good of the club and in return, it is hoped that key publics will follow suit. *Stewardship* is another approach to maintaining organisation–public relationships and is an important final step in the standard management process of conducting research, setting objectives, developing and implementing the program and evaluating its success (Kelly, 2001).

STEWARDSHIP

Stewardship provides a method of nurturing relationships between organisations and their publics. Stoldt et al. (2006, p. 29) refer to the value stewardship offers sport organisations in "nurturing relationships with the business community as potential sponsors, suppliers and consumers". It focuses on two-way, symmetrical communication concepts in interacting with publics as illustrated in Fig. 3.2. Kelly (2001, p. 284) contends that 'as stewards… public relations practitioners are attentive to every aspect of the

The coming TOGETHER of a relationship	The coming APART of a relationship

Phase 1: Introductory Phase
- Getting to know you phase.
- General factual information is exchanged between the organisation and its key public.

Phase 1: Contrasting Phase
- Either party begins to focus on the differences between the organisation and its publics, more often than similarities and agreement.
- Cause of such differences must be identified and addressed quickly if the relationship is to be saved.

Phase 2: Exploration Phase
- Roles and expectations are explored and each party assess whether developing a relationship will offer worthwhile benefits.
- Many relationships will not progress from here.

Phase 2: The Spiralling Phase
- Frequency and quality of communication between parties declines and can often be dishonest or not completely open.
- Both the organisation and publics are less willing to invest time money and effort into sustaining the relationship.

Phase 3: Escalating Phase
- Both parties gain confidence that they understand each other's position and needs.
- The relationship progresses once those needs are constant.

Phase 3: The Idling Phase
- Relationship is in 'neutral' with less effort being put into resolving differences as parties feel that is 'just isn't worth it'. Relationship is not beyond repair but lacks energy and commitment.

Phase 4: Assimilating Phase
- Public members generally support the position taken by the organisation on many political, economic and social issues.
- Organisation and public see their values as being intertwined and publics perceive organisation's behaviour to be open and forthright.

Phase 4: The Evading Phase
- Both parties avoid communication resulting in calls to the organisation going unanswered and the views of publics not being sought by the organisation.

Phase 5: Fidelity Phase
- Public displays a public expression of loyalty to the organisation.
- Organisation behaves in a manner which supports the interests of the public and therefore, the public is predisposed to support future organisational pursuits.
- This period will last for as long as mutual trust, openness and commitment exist.

Phase 5: Discontinue Phase
- The organisation and its key public decide to write each other off.
- Any communication that occurs is often stilted and uncomfortable and each blocks access from the other while also pursuing relationships with other key publics or organisations.

FIGURE 3.1 *Phases of an Organisational Public Relationship*

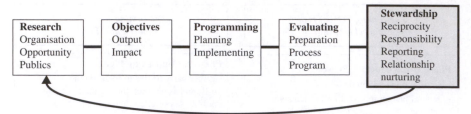

Source: Adapted from Kelly, (2001, p. 281).

FIGURE 3.2 *Stewardship*

organisation's behaviour that might affect relations with supportive publics'. Their role is to ensure organisational objectives and behaviours consider the position, needs and wants of its key publics, rather than simply being about making front page newspaper. They must nurture those publics who support the organisation in order to secure their long-term commitment and loyalty. The four elements of stewardship assist in reinforcing organisation–public relationships and in supporting the notion of relationship management. They also build on the five-step approach to relationship management proposed by Ledingham (2000), as they can be integrated into strategies developed by organisations. The four elements of stewardship are outlined in the following discussion.

Organisations should endeavour to integrate the concept of *reciprocity* into their communications activities in order to demonstrate their gratitude for support offered by publics on previous occasions. Reciprocity in the sporting domain could take the form of a football club handing out free merchandise to supporters who attend a match in which their team has no chance of winning. The Mumbai Cricket Association in India, for example, might provide test match tickets to a group of volunteers who have organised junior cricket leagues across Mumbai. Saying thank you, whether by giving gifts or offering public commendations, shows these individuals that the organisation is grateful for their support and recognises their efforts. These acts of reciprocity reinforce the positive attitudes and behaviours of these publics and assist with the establishment of long-term relationships.

Responsibility is the second element of stewardship. In essence, organisations must act in a manner considered socially responsible by strategic publics. Codes of conduct were introduced into Australian rugby league clubs in an attempt to assist with this concept of practicing socially responsible behaviour. The goal is to reduce the negative behaviour demonstrated by those representing rugby clubs (players) which should in turn reduce the opportunity for harm to be inflicted upon organisation–public relationships due to publics losing faith in clubs' level of social responsibility. Organisations must also honour their word where publics are concerned. If Netball England offered to provide coaching clinics to schools that had placed a large focus on netball in their physical education curriculum, later to renege on this agreement without sufficient reason or apology, it could potentially alienate this particular public and damage the relationship the action was initially seeking to enhance.

Organisations must keep publics informed of any developments that occur regarding a problem or issue for which a certain public has previously offered its support. This is the *reporting* element of stewardship. If fundraising was conducted for a local tennis club with the goal of purchasing new lights for their courts and the installation of those lights was delayed by 18 months due to council restrictions, those publics who supported the cause must be kept informed to ensure that the support they had shown for the club is not undermined. Miscommunication in this situation could potentially damage this relationship, resulting in a less-supportive public next time the organisation requires support.

Finally, *relationship nurturing* encompasses those elements already discussed in addition to asking public relations practitioners to 'accept the importance of supportive publics and keep them at the forefront of the organisation's consciousnesses' (Kelly, 2001, p. 286). The volunteers who make the Australian Open (Tennis) possible, the parents who take their children to support their favourite soccer team in the middle of winter, sponsors who provide funds for equipment and uniforms must all be considered in management decisions, should be thanked and kept informed by the organisations they serve in order to nurture these organisation–public relationships and encourage long-term support and loyalty.

The issue of building relationships with volunteers is especially relevant in the context of sport as many competitions and events would not be able to operate if not for the support of dedicated volunteers. In securing long-term support from volunteers, it is critical that those offering their time have a positive experience in their role. As has already been discussed, recognising and thanking these individuals is critical in ensuring that the volunteers are satisfied with their experience. Farrell et al. (1998) surveyed volunteers at a sporting event in order to identify what makes a satisfying experience as a volunteer. They discovered that recognition received was a major predictor of volunteer satisfaction, confirming importance of reciprocity as an element of relationship building.

Volunteer satisfaction was also assessed by Costa et al. (2006) who identified other factors that influenced volunteers' evaluation of their experiences. They found that volunteers believed it was important to be given the opportunity to make a noticeable contribution to the event by sharing their opinions and experiences. Feeling a sense of belonging with fellow volunteers was another factor that increased their satisfaction as volunteers. The authors suggest that many volunteers are 'often attracted not to the job, but to the subculture of the sport or event' (p. 177). It is important that management looking to recruit and build relationships with volunteers considers each of these aspects regarding the volunteer experience and incorporates them into strategic planning activities.

This discussion of organisation–public relationships has highlighted the value of managing relationships with both stakeholders and publics effectively in order to gain their trust and support in future dealings, thus making it simpler for the organisation to achieve its objectives and function as part of the community. Strategies for maintaining such relationships have also been proposed and discussed with the importance of understanding an organisation's key publics and the state of those relationships before setting objectives, developing strategies and finally communicating with those publics. Additional concepts of stewardship explained how further attention to thanking, considering and being open with publics further assists with nurturing these fragile relationships. The final section of this chapter will address relationship management issues that are particularly relevant in the sporting context.

RELATIONSHIP MANAGEMENT IN THE CONTEXT OF SPORT

The focus of this chapter to this point has largely been relationship management as a theory of public relations, including strategies that can assist in the development and maintenance of organisation–public relationships. Whilst the strategic public relation and relationship management literature continues to grow, specific resources relating to sport relationship management are in short supply. L'Etang (2006, p. 245) highlights this deficiency:

> …to date, sport literature does not seem to appreciate that public relations defines and analyses key stakeholders and newly emerging publics and interest groups with a view to understanding not only their perceptions of, and relationships with, the organisation but also with each other.

Hopwood (2005) and Bruce and Tini (2008) also found in their research into public relations practices in sport organisations that public relations really is not 'formally implemented to the extent that it should be' with organisations often being 'content to rely on history, tradition and, perhaps mythology, to assuage potentially damaging image and reputation issues' (Hopwood, 2005, p. 202). This section of the chapter focuses on relationship management issues of particular relevance to sport organisations, drawing on sport-specific resources.

Stoldt et al. (2006), for example, place an emphasis on issue and reputation management when considering strategic management approaches to public relations in sport. Regarding issue management, the authors explain the importance of not only identifying key publics, but also understanding those issues and concerns likely to result in a connection forming between the organisation and those publics. In order to achieve excellence in issue management, managers must be able to successfully follow a three-staged approach (Wartick and Heugens, 2003). This approach involves *environmental scanning*, *issue interpretation and development of appropriate issue responses*. These three separate but inter-related stages ensure that organisations are prepared to deal with emerging issues that could potentially jeopardise relationships with key stakeholders. 'Stakeholders will make a judgement regarding an issue based on whether its interests match those of the organisation (i.e., whether the organisation's behaviour is desirable or undesirable) and whether the issue is judged to be morally right or wrong' (Parent, 2008, p. 139). It is the role of management to communicate with stakeholders in a manner appropriate to the particular stakeholder's stance.

Parent (2008) identified a series of issue categories and specific issues that were faced by the organising committee of the 1999 Pan American Games held in Winnipeg, Canada (see Table 3.1). This study also found that specific issues emerged at different phases of the event organisation process and are shown in Table 3.2, perhaps indicating that sporting event planners may be able to predict the types of issues likely to emerge at different phases when organising major-sport-event events. By constantly scanning the environment for the presence of such issues and identifying the response of stakeholders, organisations are able to formulate appropriate issue response strategies.

Issues are the key factors that cause individuals within stakeholder groups to develop into publics. In domains outside of major event organisation, sport organisations can deal with issues ranging from drug scandals and player violence to financial issues, salary cap breaches and changes to league rules. Issues will not always be met with hostility, however, it is important for sport organisations to be aware of issues likely to emerge, and devise strategies to reduce their impact on key organisation–public relationships. Being prepared and systematic about this process appears to be the most effective way to offset the impact issues have on such relationships.

In addition to issue management, Stoldt et al. (2006) also consider the importance of managing *reputations* through communication. Organisations

Table 3.1	Issue Categories Faced by an Organising Committee
Issue Category	**Specific Issue**
Politics	Power and politics, lobbying, government support, intercity competition, egos and protocol
Visibility	Reputation, image and public/corporate support
Financial	Cost control, budget management, sponsorship, ticket sales, marketing and licensing
Organising	Planning, decision-making, structure, management activities, team composition, deadlines and effectiveness
Relationships	Negotiation, discussion with stakeholders, managing expectations, building and maintaining relationships, accountability and authority
Operations	Venues and facilities, technology, ceremonies and cultural events, defections, medical, security, contingencies, food, travel, games, transportation, accommodation, accreditations, logistics, commissions and decommissioning
Sport	Delegation size, qualification standards, sanctions, fields of play, officials, readiness, delivery, event quality, resources and equipment, test events, practices and water
Infrastructure	Traffic, street, existing facilities, city/public transportation, tourism, weather and municipal services (e.g., garbage collection)
Human resources	Staff or volunteer management and roles, leadership, motivation and teamwork
Media	Media coverage and broadcast rights
Interdependence	Coordination, communication, divisional and hierarchical linkages and information management
Participation	Involvement, recognition, experience, fun, excitement and ticket availability
Legacy	New facilities, know-how, final report and knowledge transfer, resource management, trade opportunities, pride, benefits and networking

Source: Reprinted, with permission, from M.M. Parent, 2008, 'Evolution and issue patterns for major-sport-event organizing committees and their stakeholders.' Journal of Sport Management 22(2), 151.

need to identify what their key publics value about the organisation and attempt to maximise the emphasis they place on such attributes when communicating with them. The authors explain that efforts to improve the organisation's reputation can also go a long way towards producing tangible benefits such as increases in memberships, sponsorships and supporter bases. They suggest that assessing 'stakeholder awareness, attitudes and perceptions about the organisation will be useful in judging reputation strengths and weaknesses' (p. 39), all dimensions also important in assessing the quality and state of relationships. In many ways, reputation management can be considered a component of relationship management processes and it is suggested that 'as sport organisations nurture relationships with all of their relevant publics, they must also make strategic choices about their reputation' (Stoldt et al., 2006, p. 39). Moreover, Hopwood (2005, p. 184) explains that 'creating the correct image… is necessary as this [develops] the reputation that helps turn strangers into long-term friends and associates'.

Table 3.2	Issue Categories Faced at Different Event Organisation Phases	
Mode	**Phase**	**Issue Categories Faced**
Planning	Bid	Politics, relationships, financial, organising, infrastructure and visibility
	Business plan	Politics, organising, interdependence, financial and relationships
	Operational plan	Politics, organising, financial, interdependence, human resources, operations and infrastructure
	Work packages	Politics, interdependence, financial, operations, infrastructure and relationships
Implementation	Venue plans	Politics, interdependence, operations, infrastructure, human resources, sport and participation
	Games time	Sport, operations, interdependence, human resources, participation, infrastructure, media and politics
Wrap-up	Final report and post-games	Legacy, operations and human resources

Source: Reprinted, with permission, from M.M. Parent, 2008, 'Evolution and issue patterns for major-sport-event organizing committees and their stakeholders.' Journal of Sport Management 22(2), 152.

Reputation is said to reflect 'the ability of the organisation to meet the expectations of its publics and the strength of the relationship various stakeholders have with the organisation' (Stoldt et al., 2006, p. 35). The repeated act of meeting and exceeding the expectations of organisations builds confidence and trust between both parties, which in turn can result in the establishment of a behavioural relationship with key publics. If an organisation acts in a manner which undermines this trust and faith of these publics, however, the relationship can be jeopardised, with the bond once existing between the organisation and its publics beginning to break down, as Fig. 3.1 has demonstrated.

Not only are the activities and behaviours of the organisation able to jeopardise relationship with key publics, those individuals who represent the organisation are also able to either enhance or damage the relationships with publics. Organisations generally have individuals or groups of individuals who represent them and interact with members of stakeholder groups and publics. Employees are one such group in a typical organisation. Sport organisations face a more complex task of also being concerned with the behaviour of athletes and to an extent participants and supporters as they can often be perceived as being elements of the organisation's behaviour and as such have the ability to influence the reputation of the organisation and relationships with key publics. Football (soccer) is perhaps the best example of an association between a sport and the behaviour of its fans, with various football clubs and associations often having to manage the 'fallout' from spectator hooliganism.

L'Etang (2006, p. 392) suggests that often 'sport celebrities are commodified and become part of the currency of the sport business and, more widely, in promotional culture' which can both benefit and pose as a threat to sport organisations. The behaviours of athletes and sport celebrities are often difficult to regulate as the organisation is extremely reliant on their support in order to be successful. Furthermore, their behaviours cannot simply be monitored in a typical 'workplace' environment where management is able to monitor their behaviours at close quarters. The most significant player indiscretions often occur off the field in non-sport time, where media scrutiny is high, making controlling of such behaviours a difficult task – a discussion taken up in more detail in Chapter 12. Although it could be argued that the high media presence is a controlling variable, with players mindful of the exposure generated by an indiscretion. Nonetheless, some professional athletes still find ways to become embroiled in headline-capturing incidents.

Stakeholders in the world of sport extend far beyond supporters and members. Organisations must also consider the impact management decisions and the actions taken by those who represent them can have on the relationships with sponsors and investors. One example of a situation where player behaviour resulted in severe damage to a sport sponsor relationship was in Australian Rules football when the Richmond Football Club's partnership with the Traffic Accident Commission (TAC), a body charged with promoting road safety in the Australian community, was terminated after 16 years in partnership. The cause for this relationship breakdown in 2005 was repeated drink driving and speeding offences involving players from the club. On this occasion, the players' disregard for the objectives of the club sponsor, the TAC, resulted in the organisation cutting ties with the football club and withdrawing support as it felt that being associated with the football club was detrimental to their overall objectives.

Sport organisations have a wide range of stakeholders, each having a very different interest in the organisation. It is critical that these organisations constantly identify issues that could potentially damage their reputation and relationships with key stakeholders. The high degree of media scrutiny that exists within sport means that sport organisations must be strategic in their approach to managing relationships, monitoring the behaviours of those representing them and implementing issue management, reputation management and relationship management strategies in order to prevent damage to the valuable organisation–public relationships.

SUMMARY

This chapter has highlighted the importance of managing relationships with key stakeholders and strategic publics. It is essential that sport organisations identify stakeholders, their reaction to issues and subsequently devise communication strategies which are appropriate to the degree of influence they have over the organisation and the particular group's stance on the issue at hand. Public relations activities which seek only to improve organisational image and reputation have been shown to have little impact on improving organisation–public relationships, thus indicating that such practices serve limited purpose in the realm of relationship management.

Sport organisations must be careful to understand and value their relationships with stakeholders and key publics. Relationships constantly change and are influenced by issues that arise as a result of environmental changes, the decisions of management and the behaviour of organisations and their representatives. Managers need to be proactive in their efforts to nurture relationships, implementing strategies discussed in this chapter. By employing strategic approaches to public relations including conducting research, setting objectives and goals, developing strategies and practicing two-way symmetrical communications, sport organisations place themselves in the best position to prevent damage to relationships with stakeholders and key publics by anticipating issues and implementing appropriate communications strategies.

KEY TERMS

Relationship Management   The act of balancing the interests of an organisation and a specific public, resulting in mutual benefit for both parties.

Two-way Symmetrical Communication   An approach to public relations based on negotiation and compromise whereby organisations assess opinions of their strategic publics and communicate with them on areas of conflict in order to develop a mutual resolution.

Organisation–Public Relationship   The state which exists between an organisation and its key publics, in which the actions of either can impact the economical, social, cultural or political well-being of the other (Ledingham and Bruning, 1998, p. 62).

Strategic/Key Public   Groups of individuals, known as publics affecting the organisation's ability to achieve their goals, or is affected by the organisation's behaviours to a large extent. These groups are generally targeted in public relations activities.

Stewardship The process of fostering relationships with important stakeholders and publics by applying the concepts of reciprocity, responsibility, reporting and relationship nurturing.

Issue The product of problems, opportunities, uncertainties and controversies (Dale, 2002). Issues emerge as a result of environmental changes, organisational behaviours and management decisions and are the key factors that cause individuals within stakeholder groups to develop into publics based upon their respective responses.

Reputation Composed of those images and opinions publics have about the organisation that relate to the organisation's perceived prestige when compared with other organisations. Reputation often reflects the ability of the organisation to meet public expectations.

DISCUSSION QUESTIONS

1. Provide an example of an issue or situation which might require two-way symmetrical communications by a sport organisation to ensure that relationships are not compromised. Discuss.

2. Develop a stakeholder map for your favourite sporting club. Discuss issues that could potentially arise between this club and one of the stakeholders you have identified and how the organisation might set about managing such issues to prevent damage to the relationship.

3. What factors are important to consider when sport organisations want to establish and manage relationships with volunteers that result in their long-term support?

4. How could stewardship be used by a sport organisation to manage relationships with an important sponsor?

GUIDED READINGS

Sport Public Relations (2006) by Stoldt, Dittmore and Branvold provides a valuable explanation of how public relations can be used as a strategic management tool in a sporting context, also explaining the process of reputation management in depth.

Public Relations: Critical debates and contemporary practice (2006) by Jacquie L'Etang and Magda Pieczka frame relationship building and management in sport in L'Etang's chapter on Public relations in sport health and tourism.

Sport Public Relations (2007) by Maria Hopwood, in The Marketing of Sport by John Beech and Simon Chadwick (Eds) discusses important public relations issues and management approaches specifically relevant in the domain of sport.

RECOMMENDED WEBSITES

International Association for Sport Information – <http://sportinfo.ning.com/>.
  Sport Customer Relationship Management – <http://www.sportscrm.com/>.

REFERENCES

Bruce, T., Tini, T., 2008. Unique crisis response strategies in sport public relations: Rugby League and the case for diversion. Public Relations Review 34, 108–115.

Costa, C.A., Chalip, L., Green, C.B., 2006. Reconsidering the role of training in event volunteers' satisfaction. Sport Management Review 9, 165–182.

Cutlip, S.M., Center, A.H., Broom, G.M., 2006. Effective Public Relations, ninth ed. Prentice Hall, Upper Saddle River, NJ.

Dale, M.W., 2002. Issue driven strategy formation. Strategic Change 11, 131–142.

Dozier, D.M., Ehling, W.P., 1992. Evaluation of public relations programs: what literature tells us about their effects. In: Grunig, J.E. (Ed.), Excellence in Public Relations and Communication Management. Lawrence Erlbaum Associates, Inc., Hillsdale, NJ, pp. 159–184.

Dozier, D.M., Grunig, L.A., Grunig, J.E., 1995. Manager's guide to excellence in public relations and communication management. Lawrence Erlbaum Associates, Mahwah, NJ.

Farrell, J.M., Johnston, M.E., Twynam, G.D., 1998. Volunteer motivation, satisfaction, and management at an elite sporting competition. Journal of Sport Management 12 (4), 288–300.

Grunig, J.E., 1993. Image and substance: from symbolic to behavioural relationships. Public Relations Review 19 (2), 121–139.

Grunig, J.E., Grunig, L.A., Sriamesh, K., Huang, Y., Lyra, A., 1995. Models of public relations in an international setting. Journal of Public Relations Research 7 (3), 163–186.

Grunig, J.E., Hunt, T., 1984. Managing public relations. Holt, Rinehart & Winston, Inc., Orlando, Florida.

Grunig, J.E., Repper, F.C., 1998. Strategic management, publics and issues. In: Grunig, J. (Ed.), Excellence in Public Relations and Communications Management. Lawrence Erlbaum Associates, Inc., Hillsdale, NJ, pp. 117–158.

Hon, L., 2007. How public relations knowledge has entered public relations practice. In: Toth, E. (Ed.), The Future of Excellence in Public Relations Communication Management: Challenges for the Next Generation. Lawrence Erlbaum Associates, Mahwah, NJ, pp. 3–23.

Hopwood, M.K., 2005. Applying the public relations function to the business of sport. International Journal of Sport Marketing and Sponsorship 6 (3), 174–188.

Hunt, T., Grunig, J.E., 1994. Public Relations Techniques. Holt, Rinehart and Winston, Inc., Orlando, Florida.

Kelly, K.S., 2001. Stewardship: the fifth step in the public relations process. In: Heath, R. (Ed.), Handbook of Public Relations. Sage Publications, Inc., Thousand Oaks, California, pp. 279–290.

L'Etang, J., 2006. Public relations in sport, health and tourism. In: L'Etang, J., Pieczka, M. (Eds.), Public Relations: Critical Debates and Contemporary Practices. Lawrence Erlbaum Associates, Mahwah, NJ, pp. 241–262.

Ledingham, J.A., 2000. Guidelines to building and maintaining strong organisation–public relationships. Public Relations Quarterly 45 (3), 44–46.

Ledingham, J.A., 2003. Explicating relationship management as a general theory of public relations. Journal of Public Relations Research 15 (2), 188–198.

Ledingham, J.A., Bruning, S.D., 1998. Relationship management and public relations: dimensions of an organisation–public relationship. Public Relations Review 24, 55–65.

Ledingham, J.A., Bruning, S.D., 1998. Relationship management in public relations: dimensions of an organisation–public relationship. Public Relations Review 24 (1), 55–65.

Parent, M.M., 2008. Evolution and issue patterns for major-sport-event organizing committees and their stakeholders. Journal of Sport Management 22, 135–164.

Stoldt, G.C., Dittmore, S.W., Branvold, S.E., 2006. Sport Public Relations: Managing Organisational Communication. Human Kinetics, Champaign, Illinois.

Thomlison, T.D., 2000. An interpersonal primer with implications for public relations. In: Ledingham, J.A., Bruning, S.D. (Eds.), Public Relations as Relationship Management: A Relational Approach to the Study and Practice of Public Relations. Lawrence Erlbaum Associates, Mahwah, NJ, pp. 177–203.

Wartick, S.L., Heugens, P.M.A.R., 2003. Future directions for issue management. Corporate Reputation Review 6 (1), 7–18.

Witmer, D.F., 2006. Overcoming systems and cultural boundaries: public relations from a structuration perspective. In: Botan, C., Hazleton, V. (Eds.), Public Relations Theory II. Lawrence Erlbaum Associates, Mahwah, NJ, pp. 361–374.

CHAPTER 4

Sport Marketing Public Relations

Maria Hopwood

Leeds Metropolitan University

When people you trust and admire talk about a product, you are more likely to buy it so you, too, can become part of the conversation.

Giannini, Jr, 2009, p. 3

Learning Outcomes

Upon completion of this chapter the reader should be able to:

- Understand the concept of Sport Marketing Public Relations (SMPR)
- Define and identify the concepts of Marketing Public Relations (MPR) within the sport context
- Differentiate between SMPR and Sport Marketing
- Appreciate the position of SMPR within Sport Communications and be able to identify the practice within the operations of sport organisations
- Address issues relating to the practice and management of SMPR in the context of sport

---

CHAPTER OVERVIEW

This chapter introduces the reader to the newly emerging concept of *Sport Marketing Public Relations (SMPR)*. SMPR is unlikely to be familiar to most readers as it is a hybrid concept of *sport marketing* and *sport public relations* which has not been widely used in the literature but which is an idea that the author has been developing through her continuing research into the way that sport organisations implement sport communications. Sport organisations continually say that they engage in sport marketing activities, when in reality the vast majority of activities they undertake and techniques they employ are SMPR. For all sorts of good reasons, the author argues that in today's competitive and challenging sport business environment sport organisations should strongly consider altering their orientation to one of SMPR rather than simply marketing.

This chapter will put the case of the adoption within sport communication of SMPR by discussing from where the idea has originated and upon which theories and concepts it is founded within the disciplines of both marketing and public relations. It will highlight the distinct differences between Sport Marketing and SMPR and clearly position SMPR within contemporary sport business and communications. The case study which concludes the chapter will present the reader with an opportunity to identify SMPR in operation within the highly successful operations of a recent innovation within cricket – the Indian Premier League.

WHAT IS SMPR AND WHERE DOES IT COME FROM?

Sport Marketing Public Relations is a new concept which is in the process of ongoing development in an attempt to address the unique requirements of sport public relations and communication. One of the overriding principles of this book has been to emphasise that although we can understand and accept that contemporary sport operates within a competitive business environment, sport in all its forms and permutations cannot be marketed or promoted in the same way as any other consumer commodity. As Ferrand and McCarthy (2009, p. 7) so concisely point out: 'The relational approach suits the situation and goals of sport organisations better than a transactional approach'.

In a 2009 interview with SportBusiness International magazine, FC Barcelona President Joan Laporta said:

> *In times of crisis there are few activities which give people a reason to live … but one of them is football.*
> (*SportBusiness International*, June 2009, Issue 146, p. 28)

The context in which he made this statement was in a discussion on the importance of football's *social* role.

At the World's Sport Forum in March 2000, Louise Frechette, UN Deputy Secretary General said:

The power of sport is far more than symbolic. You are the engines of economic growth. You are a force for gender equality. You can bring youth and others in from the margins, strengthening the social fabric. You can promote communication and help heal divisions between people, communities and entire nations. You can set an example of fair play.

(L'Etang, 2006)

Following the England Cricket team's sensational regaining of the Ashes from Australia in August 2009, the Mayor of London, Boris Johnson said:

I hope this amazing feat will inspire kids who may have never played cricket to pick up a bat or a ball in the hope of becoming the next Freddie Flintoff, Monty Panesar or Jonathan Trott.

(*The Times*, 24 August 2009, p. 4)

Adding that the victory was made even more impressive by:

... the way the team has dealt with adversity, injury and the huge expectations of a nation hungry for cricketing success.

(*The Times*, 24 August 2009, p. 4)

It is immediately obvious from this small selection of quotations that contemporary sport is much more than purely making money and this is one of the reasons why SMPR has such an important role to play in today's sport business.

Another important reason is the strong, potentially lifelong relationships that people develop with their chosen sport. Whether as supporters, participants or administrators, individuals expend huge amounts of time, emotional capital, money and sometimes sacrifice other relationships in the pursuit of their sporting love. As Joan Laporta argues during times of crisis, adversity or economic downturn the sporting mega-events such as the football World Cup and the Olympic Games can unite nations and create a 'feel good factor' that is rarely achieved outside sport. It is for such reasons, and many others, that sport needs to be approached with an SMPR rather than with sport marketing mindset.

SMPR is an innovative concept which utilises the best practices from sport marketing, sport integrated marketing communications and sport public relations and is illustrated in the 'Rugby Ball' diagram of Fig. 4.1.

The SMPR Rugby Ball has been designed to show the position of SMPR within the sport organisation. The model acknowledges that the practices of sport marketing, sport integrated marketing communications and sport public relations can be conducted as separated functional

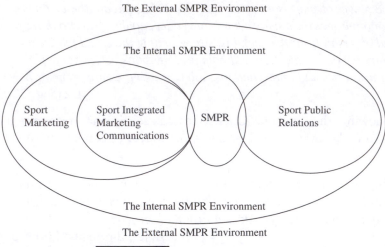

The External SMPR Environment

The Internal SMPR Environment

Sport Marketing

Sport Integrated Marketing Communications

SMPR

Sport Public Relations

The Internal SMPR Environment

The External SMPR Environment

FIGURE 4.1 *The SMPR Rugby Ball.*

disciplines in their own right and to productive effect depending on the promotions or communications issue. However, when all the practices are brought together synergistically then the outcome is Sport Marketing Public Relations (SMPR). SMPR represents the potentially powerful collaboration of *all* sport communication practices and creates the opportunity for true relationship communication in the form of relationship creation and management, promotional communication and transactional communication – a remarkably powerful collaboration which exactly meets the unique needs of the sport organisation or entity. The outside edge of the rugby ball symbolises the boundary between the sport organisation and its publics. The internal SMPR environment includes *all* internal publics to the organisation and is the place where the sport communication functions and operations originate, hence their inclusion inside the rugby ball. The external SMPR environment includes *all* the external publics with which the sport organisation or entity wants to engage for purposes of long term, mutually beneficial relationship building in all its many forms.

SMPR is the parts of 'sport public relations that are most focussed towards marketing-relevant activities' (Hopwood, 2007, p. 306). The whole range of sport communication tools and techniques can be used to achieve SMPR objectives. However, the key to successful SMPR is being able to successfully encourage publics and other intermediaries (including the media) to communicate the SMPR message on the sport organisation's behalf. New communications media and technology are continually creating new and improved opportunities for SMPR and sport organisations are increasingly realising the value of maintaining an interesting, exciting and regularly updated website for SMPR purposes (also as discussed in chapter 11). The following case study illustrates how a sport organisation can successfully use its website to achieve specific SMPR objectives.

CASE STUDY 4.1: Durham County Cricket Club At <http://www.durhamccc.co.uk/home>

Durham County Cricket Club is one of the 18 First Class Counties playing in the English County Cricket Championships. The youngest of the First Class Counties, having achieved that status in 1991, Durham's home is at Chester-le-Street which is in North East England making them the northernmost county of all the First Class clubs. They are very much rooted in the North East community and the majority of the players at all levels from the school boys and girls to the England representative players were born and grew up in the area. The club therefore has a unique character and it is this which underpins their whole public relations philosophy. In common with many sport organisations, Durham County Cricket Club has adopted an active SMPR approach by using its website as a communication tool with which to communicate with both internal and external publics (http://www.durhamccc.co.uk/). As well as providing information about the club and its progress in the various tournaments played throughout the summer, it gives information about the players – which is intended to attract both potential sponsors and fans; it contains links to all the partner websites – an excellent promotional mechanism for both parties and it incorporates Durham TV which provides the existing loyal supporters with an opportunity to relive the magical and emotional highs and lows of the season and allows potential supporters a glimpse of what they have missed yet could experience if they join the club. Crucially, it is also a virtual ticket office which provides the opportunity to purchase membership, season tickets and match tickets and the virtual club shop allows supporters worldwide the opportunity to purchase club merchandise. As the Riverside at Chester-le-Street is a designated Test Match ground, there is a dedicated section for international cricket and a facility to buy tickets for international matches. For the internal publics, such SMPR mechanisms provide an opportunity for them to feel pride in their club and to be able to encourage friends and family, who might be scattered far and wide around the globe, to engage with the club remotely. For expatriate Durham supporters, who still consider themselves to be very much a part of the internal public, it is a mechanism for keeping in touch with the club and its fortunes from afar, again focussing on the strong emotional dimension to SMPR.

It is clear from this case study that a successful SMPR strategy is limited only by the ability of the sport organisation to understand its publics. Durham County Cricket Club's website is a successful example of how a sport organisation has embraced technology for SMPR purposes. This website is not, by far, the most glamorous or visually stimulating of sport websites when compared with some of the premier league football or international sport organisations' websites, but it is successful precisely because it meets the needs of the club's specific publics and communicates with them in a way to which they can relate. A strategic SMPR focus will allow sport organisations the opportunity to offer publics what Kevin Roberts, CEO of Saatchi & Saatchi calls

Table 4.1 The Scope and Techniques of Sport Marketing Public Relations

The Scope of SMPR	The Techniques of SMPR
■ Raise awareness	■ Media relations
■ Inform	■ Publicity
■ Interest	■ Publications
■ Excite	■ Corporate communication
■ Educate	■ Public affairs and community relations
■ Generate understanding	■ Lobbying
■ Build trust	■ Sponsorship/donations
■ Encourage loyalty	■ Events management
■ Generate relationship management outcomes	■ Crisis management
	■ Research and analysis

'Priceless Value' and to create for the sport organisation 'Loyalty Beyond Reason':

> *There are massive opportunities through sport to build Loyalty Beyond Reason and to do so by using new media in a way which is not simply more effective but actually cuts costs. We have moved from an attention economy to a participation economy and successful (sport) brands will create those opportunities to participate ... We have to involve fans in new ways ...and by offering specialist content that builds on relationships and takes them into entirely new areas.*
>
> (Roberts, 2009, p. 30)

Table 4.1, though not exhaustive, illustrates both the scope and the techniques of SMPR.

SOME ANTECEDENTS OF SMPR

Having explained the concept of SMPR and given an example of how a sport organisation can actively engage in SMPR communication, we will now turn our attention to SMPR's antecedents.

In an article written in 1978 entitled *Marketing and Public Relations: Should They Be Partners or Rivals?* the highly regarded Professors of Marketing Kotler and Mindak (1978, p. 13) wrote:

One can sense the growing confusion as to the future roles of marketing and public relations in the modern organisation:

■ *Marketing people* are increasingly interested in incorporating publicity as a tool within the marketing mix, although this tool has normally been controlled by public relations.

■ *Public relations* people are growing increasingly concerned with their company's marketing practices, questioning whether they "square" with the company's social responsibility. They seek more influence over marketing and more of a counselling and policy-making role.

This seminal article raised the question whether or not marketing and public relations should be kept as separate disciplines in business organisation or whether they should be merged for the greater good of the organisation as the boundaries between the two disciplines were becoming so blurred. The authors were prescient in their observation that 'the neat and tidy divisions separating marketing and public relations are breaking down.' (Kolter & Mindak, 1978, p. 19). The research upon which this article was founded illustrated that as far back as the 1970s growing similarities between the two disciplines were emerging for example both talk in terms of publics and markets, both recognise the need for market segmentation, both acknowledge the importance of market attitudes, perceptions and images in formulating programmes and both acknowledge a management process consisting of analysis, planning, implementation and control. The resulting outcome of the research was a 'Joint Methodology of Marketing and Public Relations' which I propose as the basis for my thoughts on sport marketing public relations:

1. Auditing the present position of the sport organisation/entity and its products in the minds of target market and publics.
2. Defining the desired position for the sport organisation/entity and its products.
3. Developing a well-balanced portfolio of products and services which will ensure long term mutually beneficial relationships and meet the needs of *all* the target publics both within and outside the sport organisation.
4. Developing sport marketing public relations objectives, policies and strategies.
5. Formulating specific tactics and a timetable.
6. Implementing actions and evaluating results with all publics.

During the 1980s and 1990s, the International Association of Business Communicators (IABC) in the USA commissioned a research project known as the IABC Excellence Project which was led by James and Larissa Grunig from the University of Maryland. This lengthy project concluded that although public relations and marketing worked better when kept as separate disciplines because of their theoretical differences, 'discussion and research are needed to resolve these differences and *to integrate the theories into a broader communication theory*' (my italics) (Grunig and Grunig 1998, p. 141). The Grunigs' 'broader communication theory' developed into the concept of Integrated Marketing Communication (IMC) which I have expanded into Sport Integrated Marketing Communication (SIMC) in another text (Hopwood, 2007, p. 306) and into which concept SMPR fits very well because it is an integrated discipline in its own right.

In 1993, notable American public relations professional and former Vice Chairman of Golin/Harris Communications, Thomas L. Harris, published an article in which he talked about what he proposed as the 'New Hybrid' and stated:

> *I take the view that marketing and public relations can, should and must be compatible. I make a clear distinction between those public relations functions which support marketing which I call MPR and the other public relations activities that define the corporation's relationships with its non-customer publics which I label CPR.*
>
> (Harris, 1993, p. 15)

Harris (1993) takes the view that in a message saturated society, marketing public relations can help regain a share of voice meaning that people are looking for more than just a clever advertising campaign or short-term promotions push, they are looking for a meaningful relationship which exactly resonates with what sport organisations need to strive towards. Marketing public relations can also, according to Harris, win a greater share of heart and mind and it can deliver a better and more effective voice than marketing alone in specific instances. I believe that sport is one such specific instance.

Sport publics are already tied into their chosen sport or sport so advertising and promotion have limited or no effect – fans will go and support their team regardless of whether or not there is a buy one get one free promotion running. Harris identified seven key areas in which MPR can add value to marketing and marketing communications, all of which can be adapted to fit the sport context:

1. *Builds marketplace excitement before media advertising breaks*

Each year between one end of the northern hemisphere football season and the beginning of the other, newspapers, websites and magazines continue to carry stories about clubs, players, transfers and so on in order to keep fans interested until the television and other media advertising starts to break during late July early August.

2. *Makes advertising news where there is no product news*

Sport apparel companies frequently find themselves in the news because of controversy surrounding their practices. In 2003 sportwear brands Adidas and Umbro came under fire because of the use of kangaroo leather in their sport shoes.

3. *Introduces a product when there is little or no advertising*

When a new player joins a football club, for example, the message is communicated via the club website, mass media reports and television coverage.

4. *Provides a value added customer service*

The use of fans forums on websites, face to face contact, players engaging in community relations' activities, coaching clinics, stadium tours are all examples of SMPR tactics which really bring the sport organisation close to the publics.

5. *Builds brand to customer bonds*

Within the sport context this is probably the most important and lucrative benefit that SMPR can bring to the organisation. Many commentators believe that the organisation–fan relationship should be paramount in the sport communication dynamic. Karren Brady, former Managing Director of English football club Birmingham City encapsulated this by saying:

You have to understand (when running) a football club, you don't own the club, the supporters do. The passion they feel for the football club (is something) people can't understand.

(Jacobs, 2008)

6. *Influences the influentials*

In times of economic downturn, many sport organisations discover that engaging a sponsor becomes more challenging especially for those sport in the lower echelons of the sport hierarchy. Effectively employing SMPR to engage with potential sponsors and others with influence is key as Kevin Roberts of Saatchi & Saatchi observes:

Sport is made for these times… People have become disenfranchised and disassociated from many aspects of life and they are finding solace in sport. It is tribal and gives them somewhere they really belong and can feel part of life.

(Roberts, 2009, p. 29)

7. *Defends products at risk and gives consumers permission to buy*

Many sport organisations have been saved from bankruptcy because a financial backer has stepped in as a result of being convinced by the value of the organisation beyond that of the purely monetary. Relationships, personality, culture, character and values are reasons frequently cited in rescue bids. Players behaving badly are a frequent cause of crisis situations for sport organisations but strong relationships with publics together with open and honest communication through the media regularly save the reputation of many sport organisations and individuals.

According to Giannini (2009, p. 6) 'MPR's task is ultimately one of communication between an organisation and its stakeholders. This communication is accomplished through channels – typically interpersonal or media'. He also takes the view that there are a series of seven related goals which savvy organisations hope to achieve through skilful communication with those stakeholders. Once again, by inserting the word sport at strategic points we can apply this thinking to sport organisations and entities:

- Building the identity of the sport organisation or sport product.
- Increasing the visibility of an established sport organisation or sport product.
- Establishing a sport organisation or sport individual as an expert in a given field.
- Educating stakeholders on issues critical to the sport organisation.
- Shaping public opinion about a sport organisation, sport related idea or sport individual.
- Maintaining the image of a sport organisation or sport product – over time or during a crisis.
- Stimulating the trial or repeat usage of a sport product.

Having considered some of the antecedents of SMPR we can see that, within the marketing and public relations literature, interest in the MPR concept is ongoing. From a sport public relations and communication perspective, it is essential to be aware of and to keep abreast of developments and thinking in this area because MPR is the cornerstone of SMPR.

THE DIFFERENCE BETWEEN SPORT MARKETING AND SMPR

Following an examination of some of the antecedents of SMPR it will be helpful at this point to give a brief explanation of the key difference between sport marketing and SMPR. In 2004, Pickton and Broderick described MPR as '...a healthy offspring of two parents: marketing and PR'. This is a straightforward, concise and very useful interpretation of the MPR concept and one which can be applied just as well to SMPR which can be described as the healthy offspring of the two parents: sport marketing and sport public relations. Clearly, SMPR extends beyond the boundaries of sport marketing, combining certain elements of that function with sport public relations. Most definitions of sport marketing focus on the *commercial* aspects of sport. Consider this definition from a widely used US sport marketing text:

> *Sport marketing consists of all the activities designed to meet the needs and wants of sport consumers through exchange processes. Sport marketing has developed two major thrusts: the marketing of sport products and services directly to consumers of sport, and the marketing of other consumer and industrial products or services through the use of sport promotions.*
>
> (Mullin et al., 2007, p. 11)

The marketing *of* sport and marketing *through* sport as highlighted in Mullin et al. definition are what most of us are exposed to and have become familiar with over time. It is very much an American sport marketing model which is grounded in the highly commercialised American sport culture. It is also the model which has been widely adopted by sport organisations in the UK, Europe and elsewhere in the world but what is immediately obvious is the glaring omission of any mention of relationships or any publics beyond those of consumers. This is where SMPR differs fundamentally from sport marketing. SMPR is grounded in relationships and communication; sport marketing is grounded in monetary transactions and promotions.

CASE STUDY 4.2: It's Sub-Continental Cricket But Not As We Know It

The sport of cricket – steeped in history and tradition and the widely accepted metaphor for fair play and gentlemanly conduct – according to many involved with the sport changed forever on Friday 18 April 2008. That day saw the opening ceremony and first round matches of the inaugural DLF Indian Premier League (IPL) Twenty20 cricket competition, the fast paced short form of the game which is completely changing the way in which cricket around the world is played, watched, commentated upon, sponsored and engaged with generally.

Twenty20 cricket burst onto the sporting stage during the 2003 English cricket season. Concerned by consistently

Continued

declining audience figures and participation levels in cricket, the England and Wales Cricket Board (ECB) engaged in extensive marketing and public relations research and discovered that the general image of cricket was that it was irrelevant, boring, took too long, anachronistic, outdated and only watched by older people. Seriously disturbed by the findings, the ECB decided that the time had come to diversify the cricket product in order to create relationships with a range of new publics and so Twenty20 was created. With previously unheard of sell-out crowds being reported at all the county grounds and a markedly different audience demographic of young women, families and children obviously enjoying summer evenings at the cricket, Twenty20 has become a cricketing success story and an excellent example of sport public relations.

It was clearly only a matter of time before the game's obvious appeals started to attract interest from elsewhere. Five years later, on Friday 18 April 2008, Twenty20 cricket became a part of a new world order in sport when Bollywood and big business – the eight team franchises were bought by an unusual combination of both Indian and international business entities and Bollywood stars – combined with Indian Cricket's governing body, the BCCI, in the launch of the inaugural DLF Indian Premier League (the IPL).

Audience and financial figures for the first year of operations saw the team franchise owners recouping 80% of their original investment to the BCCI from the central television and sponsorship revenue generated by the tournament and 101 million global television viewers enjoying the mediated version of the 6-week long spectacle. The IPL 2009 is likely to provide an even bigger bonanza for investors, participants and audiences alike.

2008 and the birth of the IPL is an example of how excellent public relations and sound product diversification can inject new life into an old sport. The case study illustrates that sport public relations has more profound cultural implications than that of mere promotions and publicity and suggests that the resounding success of the IPL provides an excellent example of the role of public relations in building national identity. It further argues that public engagement and relationship management form the heart of contemporary sport management. The IPL provides a fascinating example of product diversification and public relations engagement. It has significantly added to the success of Twenty20 cricket in terms of attracting new publics to become cricket fans and the full effect of its influence is yet to emerge. Cricket will never be the same again.

SUMMARY

This chapter provides the reader with some thoughts and ideas concerning the emerging concept of Sport Marketing Public Relations (SMPR). Based on the theoretical principles of Marketing Public Relations (MPR) originally developed by Kotler and Mindak (1978) and later by Harris (1993) and Giannini (2009) we can see that as a concept, SMPR makes complete sense to contemporary sport business. The Rugby Ball Model of SMPR is presented as a useful and memorable framework for the discipline. The differences between SMPR and Sport Marketing have been clarified and the key role that SMPR plays in Sport Communications has been emphasised in the two case studies, both of which demonstrate how cricket has recently utilised SMPR with great success both in the United Kingdom and in India.

KEY TERMS

Marketing Public Relations (MPR)   All public relations functions which are used to support the marketing goals of an organisation.

Corporate Public Relations (CPR)   Those public relations activities that define the corporation's relationships with its non-customer publics, e.g. business–business communication.

Sport Marketing Public Relations (SMPR)   SMPR is the parts of 'sport public relations that are most focussed towards marketing-relevant activities' (Hopwood, 2007, p. 306). The whole range of sport communication tools and techniques can be used to achieve SMPR objectives. However, the key to successful SMPR is being able to successfully encourage publics and other intermediaries (including the media) to communicate the SMPR message on the sport organisation's behalf.

Sport Marketing   Sport marketing consists of all the activities designed to meet the needs and wants of sport consumers through exchange processes.

DISCUSSION QUESTIONS

1. For any sport organisation of your choice, identify how that organisation implements SMPR using The Rugby Ball Model as your theoretical basis.

2. Critically evaluate the differences between SMPR and Sport Marketing and give some examples of different Sport Communication incidences in which each could be implemented to good effect.

3. Conduct some further research into Marketing Public Relations (MPR) and Corporate Public Relations (CPR) and consider how both types of Public Relations can be further applied within the sport context.

GUIDED READING

Ferrand, A., McCarthy, S., 2009. Marketing the Sport Organisation: Building Networks and Relationships. Routledge, Abingdon.

Giannini Jr., G.T., 2009. Marketing Public Relations. A Marketer's Approach to Public Relations and Social Media. Pearson Education Inc., Upper Saddle River, NJ.

Harris, T.L., 1993. How MPR adds value to integrated marketing communications. Public Relations Quarterly 38 (2), 13–18.

Hopwood, M.K., 2007. Sport public relations. In: Beech, J., Chadwick, S. (Eds.), The Marketing of Sport. Pearson Education Limited, Harlow.

Kotler, P., Mindak, W., 1978. Marketing and public relations: should they be partners or rivals? Journal of Marketing 42 (10), 13–20.

RECOMMENDED WEBSITES

See this article from Jacobs on Karen Brady – a woman for all football seasons <http://www.ft.com/cms/s/0/438fbd2a-8dbf-11dd-83d5-0000779fd18c.html>.

Indian cricket page at Cricinfo.com – <http://www.cricinfo.com/india/content/team/6.html>.

The world of Twenty20 Cricket – <http://www.cricket20.com/>.

REFERENCES

Ferrand, A., McCarthy, S., 2009. Marketing the Sport Organisation: Building Networks and Relationships. Routledge, Abingdon.

Giannini Jr., G.T., 2009. Marketing Public Relations. A Marketer's Approach to Public Relations and Social Media. Pearson Education Inc., Upper Saddle River, NJ.

Grunig, J.E., Grunig, L.A., 1998. The relationship between public relations and marketing in excellent organisations evidence from the IABC study. Journal of Marketing Communications 4, 141–162.

Harris, T.L., 1993. How MPR adds value to integrated marketing communications. Public Relations Quarterly 38 (2), 13–16.

Hopwood, M., 2007. Sport public relations. In: Beech, J., Chadwick, S. (Eds.), The Marketing of Sport. Pearson Education Limited, London, pp. 292–331.

Jacobs, E., 2008. A woman for all football seasons. FT.com. Retrieved on 5 August 2009 from: <http://www.ft.com/cms/s/98314b2a-8bd8-11dd-8a4c-0000779fd18c, dwp_uud=f38b8.html>

Kotler, P., Mindak, W., 1978. Marketing and public relations: should they be partners or rivals? Journal of Marketing 42 (10), 13–20.

L'Etang, J., 2006. Public relations and sport in promotional culture. Public Relations Review 32 (4), 383–394.

Mullin, B.J., Hardy, S., Sutton, W.A., 2007. Sport Marketing, third ed. Human Kinetics, Champaign, IL.

Pickton, D., Broderick, A., 2005. Integrated Marketing Communications, second ed. Pearson Education Limited, Harlow.

Roberts, K., 2009. Loyalty beyond reason. SportBusiness International 146, (July) 29–30.

CHAPTER 5

Sport Social Responsibility

James Skinner
Griffith University

Learning Outcomes

Upon completion of this chapter the reader should be able to:

- Define the concept of Corporate Social Responsibility (CSR)
- Describe the relationship between CSR and Sport Social Responsibility (SSR)
- Define the concept of Sport Relationship Management (SRM)
- Detail aspects of SSR that give sport teams and franchises a competitive advantage
- Address those areas of SSR that have current relevance or which are in need of action

---

CHAPTER OVERVIEW

This chapter sets out to describe the concept of Corporate Social Responsibility (CSR) and its application to the business of sport. Increasingly, sport teams and franchises operate as a business, with the inherent responsibilities as a business to stakeholders, investors, sponsors and the community at large. Therefore, there is now, more than ever before, increasing expectation that sport teams and franchises assume greater responsibility for their operation and the impact of their operations on their community, their fans and the physical space in which they operate. The concept of Sport Social Responsibility (SSR) derives from an increasing awareness that the business of sport does not operate within a vacuum where only the team, the spectators and the fan base are affected by the operation of the sport.

Environmental concerns about the operation of sport, for example, are indicative of wider social concerns about the impact of business on the environment at large. This chapter discusses particular issues in relation to SSR and through two case studies looks at how sport managers can use public relations and communications practices to deal with these issues and the impact this can have on the operation of the sport as a business.

CORPORATE SOCIAL RESPONSIBILITY (CSR)

The World Business Council for Sustainable Development (2000, p. 6) has defined CSR as 'the continuing commitment by business to behave ethically and contribute to economic development while improving the quality of life of the workforce and their families as well as the local community and society at large'. Not all definitions of CSR are as all-encompassing. Heath and Ryan (1989, p. 34) found that some companies defined CSR as simply as 'performing good deeds,' whilst others believed that creating a code of ethical conduct was essential to achieve an acceptable level of CSR. However, there has emerged a consensus within these definitions that corporations must be accountable not only to shareholders in the form of economic returns, but also to stakeholders (Carroll, 2000; Clarkson, 1995). CSR has also been referred to as the continuing commitment by businesses to meet or exceed stakeholder expectations (Carroll, 2000), and further to take greater account of their social, environmental and financial footprints (Zadek, 2001). Within these definitions, however, there is a consensus that corporations must be held accountable, not only to their shareholders in the provision of economic or financial returns, but also to stakeholders (Carroll, 2000; Clarkson, 1995).

The concept of CSR evolved from a more general concept of social responsibility, which can be traced back to the early twentieth century and to the philanthropic actions of such business tycoons as Carnegie and Ford. Carnegie and Ford, like many wealthy Americans, believed that they had a responsibility to give back a portion of their wealth to improve social conditions. Whilst not a major force throughout the first half of the twentieth century, social responsibility and the more defined concept of CSR became more significant in the 1960s and 1970s with the rise of social or public activism and a greater public awareness of the impact of corporations on society at large. With this increasing awareness, segments of society began to question the actions and responsibilities of corporations and the role they should be playing in social issues (Clark, 2000).

Noted economist Friedman (1962) argued that the primary responsibility of business was to ensure economic advantage to their shareholders. Any other expenditures outside the limited ambit of profit maximization could be considered a mismanagement of funds. Friedman's strict stance on the responsibility of business, however, was not unilaterally accepted. Archie Carroll was instrumental in developing CSR theory with this three-dimensional model of corporate performance. Carroll's (1979, p. 499) model was not designed to repudiate or discredit Friedman's theory but rather to detail 'the social responsibilities of businesses in a more exhaustive manner'.

Carroll's (1979) model of CSR identified four categories that he believed formed the basis of CSR: economic, legal, ethical and discretionary. He agreed with Friedman (1962) in part in that he believed that economic responsibility was paramount. In order to benefit society, a company must be profitable. Both the shareholders of a company and society at large will benefit when a company is profitable. Legal responsibility is of slightly lesser significance – but just as clear-cut – because all businesses must follow the rules and regulations created for the good of everyone. The ethical category meanwhile is not so clear. Carroll did state, however, that society clearly expects businesses to go above and beyond what is merely legal. Finally the discretionary, or as it is sometimes referred to the philanthropic or altruistic, category is one that is not mandated but rather a voluntary attempt for businesses to address social issues. Altruistic responsibility involves a business 'giving back' time and/or money to society through charitable activities or donations. It is depicted in CSR literature that the theory entails a 'social contract' between business and society optimizing the positive effects whilst minimizing the negative (Quazi, 2003).

SPORT AS BUSINESS

Is sport a business? The relevance of sport in today's society is so great that it inevitably attracts sponsors, media and a range of economic interests. Sport is no longer just a vehicle for entertainment but is becoming one of the major players in national and international markets (Sachs, 2002).

That said, however, there are some marked differences in the operation of sport as business compared to a standard business model. The exploitative star power of elite athletes, for example (Walker, 2007), whose marketability is utilized perhaps even more successfully by non-sport-related businesses in some cases than by the actual sport that the athlete represents. The CEO of any major multinational corporation does not have the same marketability. Sport teams have connections to their local, regional and national communities in ways that a major non-sport business cannot. The business of sport also crosses international boundaries and both unites and divides fans (consumers) in ways distinct from the majority of business sectors.

Sport teams and in particular sport franchises, like other businesses, must operate at and generate a profit in order to be successful. In most cases being successful equates to being able to continue operating. This success is to a large extent dependent on community support for the team – be it locally, regionally or nationally. Sport teams and franchises also have varying management and ownership models – teams in the major US Leagues, for example, may be owned by a single individual, a group of partners or even a multinational corporation. These varying ownership structures may create a differing approach to the issue of who influences CSR within the organisation.

SPORT SOCIAL RESPONSIBILITY (SSR)

SSR subsumes the basic concepts of CSR and adapts them to the business of sport in its various interactions in the local, national and global communities.

SSR is of increasing importance for sport teams, franchises and organisations. As sport becomes a global commodity with an increasing influence across a range of markets, individual teams, franchises and organisations are becoming increasingly interdependent on the very consumer/fan base that initially elevated them to this position. The sporting public, as a major subset of the general public, is more socially aware than it has been in the past, with the first decade of the twenty-first century playing host to a range of corporate misdeeds by companies such as Enron and Merrill Lynch (Walker, 2007).

Despite the emergence of different frameworks with which to approach CSR since Carroll's (1979) model, it is that model with which I will approach the following discussion of SSR. Economic, legal, ethical and discretionary or philanthropic responsibilities are the four categories of CSR identified by Carroll.

Economic responsibility

Companies have a responsibility to earn a profit. And a sporting team or franchise operating as a business is no exception. Friedman (1962) sees economic responsibility as the primary consideration of business, and the free market society that predominates the current global community would agree with this basic premise. Professional sport teams and franchises are no different, and therefore they also aim to earn a profit, and often in the process can impact on the economic development in their city or region. Although sport teams themselves are generally not major employers, the economic effects of a professional sport team can have a large impact on a city. Sport fans spend money – by purchasing tickets, buying merchandise associated with the team and associated costs such as food, parking and even accommodation when fans travel to sporting events.

Sport franchises differ from traditional business in that revenue forms the basis of their value, as opposed to the cash flow and assets on which traditional business determines its value. Lee and Chun (2002) see the revenue that underpins the value of professional sport team and franchises generated by the buying and selling of goods (tickets, merchandise, broadcasting rights, advertising), services (the staging of major events with associated activities such as food concessions, parking) and labour (the players, managers, coaches, etc.).

Professional sport teams and franchises have different operating structures, and this can affect how the team operates financially. In the National Basketball Association (NBA), National Hockey League (NHL) and Major League Baseball (MLB) and Australian Major League Baseball (AMLB) approximately 20% of the teams are owned by corporations. In the National Football League (NFL), however, only one team is owned by a corporation, with 23 of the 32 teams being owned by small partnership groups (Extejt, 2004). When a single owner or a small group of owners is making decisions on a sport team or franchise's financial future and responsibilities, the decision-making process is substantially different from that of a traditional business operation which is most likely owned by stockholders and managed by a CEO and board of directors who are responsible to the stockholders for the outcome of any decisions that are made. Extejt further discusses the discretionary power of sport managers/team owners and how they may choose to redirect revenue or even forego revenue in certain circumstances for the good of the team, the franchise or the fans. The discretionary power to determine CSR in these circumstances, says Extejt, is significantly greater than that of a CEO or board of directors of a traditional business who are still bound by the stricter definition of CSR in relation to business profit making.

Legal responsibility

Carroll's (1979) definition of legal responsibility is that society expects business to follow those rules and regulations established by governments and regulatory authorities in the same way that the rest of society is expected to comply with those same rules and regulations.

Professional sport teams and franchises, like traditional businesses, are legally mandated to follow federal and state regulations or run the risk of penalty. The extent to which sport teams and franchises are constrained, however, differs from country to country, and these differences can be seen particularly in the operation of professional sport leagues in Europe, the United States and Australia.

Unlike more traditional industries, the sport industry in North America and Australia is often allowed by government to pursue what are effectively anti-competitive practices (Szymanski, 2003). This occurs because there is tacit agreement that a variety of restrictive practices are essential for the sport league to sustain its public interest and long-term viability. It has been argued that a completely unregulated sport league will be unsustainable since a few clubs will use their superior fan and revenue base to capture the best players and dominate the competition. This argument claims that, whilst the resulting conduct may be anti-competitive (or a restraint of trade), it is not unreasonable, nor is it against the public interest (Ross, 2003). Consequently in North America and Australia free market capitalism is limited. In North America and Australia it is argued that sport leagues perform poorly under competitive or free market conditions, and some form of self-regulation is essential to produce the outcome of uncertainty that attracts fans, sponsors and media interests (Szymanski and Kuypers, 1999). Ultimately, however, the primary beneficiaries of this regulation could be perceived as the leagues themselves. By contrast in Europe there is almost no intervention. Ensuring competitive balance is difficult as European Union anti-trust legislation is applied to sport as it is to any other industry. European law makes sporting competitors as economic competitors, treating each team as an economic unit (Edwards and Skinner, 2006).

Sport law has become a discipline in and of itself. Cole (2001) attributes this phenomenon to the fact that sport produces million-dollar deals in media usage, player contracts and league revenues. These high stakes can create legal issues within the sport industry. Anti-trust laws are perhaps the most important in the sport legal matrix, as they produce fair competition in each league. Other legal issues include gambling, trademark rights, contract laws and players following laws, including the use of illegal substances. When players participate in illegal activities, the individual is held legally responsible rather than the organisation itself, yet the player's activities often will reflect upon the team. Teams often turn to reputation management tactics in these situations, including increasing philanthropic activities.

Ethical responsibility

Carroll (1979, p. 500) defined ethical responsibilities as going beyond economic and legal responsibilities and following 'additional behaviors and activities that are not necessarily codified into law but nonetheless are expected of business by society's members'. Despite this definition, it can be difficult to define exactly what society expects. As society changes, so do the values or ethics espoused by that society change (Levy, 1972). Sport as an important microcosm of society has witnessed a changing environment of expectations and values. In most instances the values espoused by the sport team or franchise are clearly representative of their major stakeholders – the fans – and society in general, although at times sport teams and franchises will appear to be playing 'catch up' in relation to acceptable player behaviour both on and off the field. There are also other instances where sport teams, franchises and major international organisations such as the International Olympic Committee (IOC) will take a harder line than that generally expected in society, but in general respected by society – an example being a zero tolerance for performance-enhancing drugs, use of alcohol and violence against women, and so on.

For a sport team, franchise or organisation to be seen as following their ethical responsibilities, the director/manager/owner/administrator of that team, franchise or organisation must be seen to be behaving ethically. This ethical behaviour cascades down through the ranks to each player, member or affiliate. If any member of the organisation behaves in an unethical way, whether it is through mismanagement of funds, illegal gaming practices or punching another athlete on the field of play, the entire organisation is viewed as unethical.

Ethical responsibilities may be hard to define, but it is easy to see when an organisation has not been ethical. In today's age of corporate scandals, companies are called to set the standards high or their ethics are often called into question. Sport, as an international business, faces the same scrutiny. MLB in the United States, for example, received negative coverage when several of its major players tested positive for using performance-enhancing substances. This forced the offending team's administration to put a tougher anti-drug policy into place in order to appear more ethically responsible.

Another example of ethical responsibility is 'Green Sport Business' in which environmental concerns are placed at the core of the business practices of sport organisations. Until recently sport managers have typically accorded minimal attention to the environmental crisis. This is surprising as 'the right to a clean environment' (Johnson, 1995) is crucial for the realization of international human rights. Johnson further argues that 'these rights are important to understand because the environment is the foundation to which all things derive life' (p. 112). The concept of 'Green Sport' recognizes the essential importance of sport teams, franchises and organisations adopting eco-friendly strategies in the planning, marketing and staging of all levels of sporting events.

Just as the United Nations structure depends on its foundational integrity, international human rights depend on a healthy environment. Other groups have made the connection between the environment and human rights. For example, Shelton (2002) suggests that the Stockholm Declaration of 1972 is the most widely accepted international environmental norm. It asserts:

> *Man (sic) has the fundamental right to freedom, equality and adequate conditions of life, in an environment of a quality that permits a life of dignity and wellbeing, and he bears solemn responsibility to protect and improve the environment, for present and future generations.*

(p. 1)

> *Principle 1 of the Stockholm Declaration establishes a foundation for linking human rights and environmental protection and many of these ideals are contained in the 2001 Nagano Declaration of Sport. It states that a firm commitment be given to "upholding the principles of sustainability in sport activities as well as in their daily practices, and to promoting these principles on a global scale, so as to help ensure that our planet Earth is given a sporting chance."*

(pp. 2–3)

There are several agencies involved in the specific development of sport and the environment. Edwards and Skinner (2006) looked at how the United Nations Environment Program (UNEP) works with major sport organisations, including the Olympic Movement and the world Federation of the Sporting Goods Industry, to ensure that major sport events and sport goods are 'green'. The UNEP Sport and Environment Strategy has three core objectives. These are: (1) to promote the integration of environmental considerations into sport; (2) to use the popularity of sport to promote environmental awareness and (3) to promote the development of environmentally friendly sport facilities and the manufacture of environmentally friendly sport goods.

Perhaps the most significant development in recent years has been the adoption of the environment as the third pillar of Olympism along with sport and culture (Edwards and Skinner, 2006). Central to the UNEP 'Sport and Environment Strategy' is the recognition that sport is environment. One core issue is reducing waste. For example, the mercury used to make flashing lights work in children's shoes was dissipated into the air and water once the shoes were thrown away, with the mercury magnified in the food chain and being linked to harmful effects to children and the marine environment. Nike then introduced a 'ReUse-A-Shoe' program to cut waste and numerous sport have introduced environmental guidelines, codes of conduct and environmental criteria for hosting events to minimize waste (Edwards and Skinner, 2006).

Examples of environmentally friendly sport guidelines are evident in mountain biking. The International Cycling Union (UCI) created a series of

'International Environmental Guidelines' to be used at all stages of development of major mountain biking events. The Green and Gold website (http://www.greengold.on.ca/toolkit/index.html) provides guidelines that can be used as criteria for evaluating major event bids, the organisation of events and post-event analysis.

Currently the most serious global environmental threats include climate change, overpopulation, deforestation, desertification, depletion of the ozone layer and species and habitat loss. Ozone layer depletion, habitat loss and climate change have or are already having an impact on the way we conduct sport (Edwards and Skinner, 2006).

Some of the effects of environmental change and the depletion of the stratospheric ozone layer are already apparent, evidenced by the increased awareness of the need for sun protection products, including sport equipment and clothing that provide protection from harmful UVB radiation. This has potential impacts on the practice of outdoor sport.

Climate change as well is likely to call into question where certain sport can be practiced and if it can be practiced at all. Also, the increasing development of the planet's remaining natural areas – forests, wetlands, prairie, coastlines and other green spaces – means that habitat in its original state is diminished in size, number and quality. Many low-altitude ski resorts face economic hardship and even ruin as a result of global warming (Edwards and Skinner, 2006). In the case of golf and field sport played primarily on green turf any global warming will make even more intensive irrigation necessary. In the competition for scarce water resources, sport facilities may find it difficult to manage potential restrictions.

The environmental component is central to Green Sport Business as a major component of the ethical considerations of CSR/SSR for four reasons. First, understanding the environment is necessary as human rights encourages sport policy makers to consider the larger ramifications of environmental legislation, development and interaction. Second, changes in the environment that occur as a result of economic and political transition must be considered to properly measure the costs and benefits of the transition. Third, sport events activities that contribute to environmental degradation need to be scrutinized. Finally, sport managers may be faced with scheduling problems associated with climate change. It is possible that many sport events in the near future will have to consider ozone depletion placing sport in a potentially vulnerable position.

'Green Sport Business' (Smith and Westerbeek, 2004) expands on the concept of 'green sport' to associate environmentally friendly and ethically desirable aspects of CSR/SSR with an economically desirable profit maximization view of CSR/SSR. With an increasing awareness that environmental sustainability is essential for the future of the human race, Green Sport Business has the potential to also work to the financial advantage of sport. Brands which market to sporting teams, fans and other stakeholders can capitalize on the growing awareness of the dangers of environmental damage, by focusing on and promoting those aspects of the sport or sport-related product that are 'green' (Dingle, 2007). Smith and Westerbeek suggest that environmental sustainability and awareness is not only making sporting events more marketable, but is also attracting corporate sponsors who are keen to leverage public approval to enhance their corporate reputation. They suggest an increasing global awareness of the importance of environmental sustainability for the future of the human race has the potential to work to the financial advantage of sport and sport-related products. By promoting those aspects of the sport or sport-related product that are 'green', the sport public relations and communications manager or corporate sponsor can capitalize on this growing awareness of the dangers of environmental damage (Dingle, 2007).

The sport public relations and communications manager can also implement ethical CSR/SSR objectives within their promotional strategies by engaging in socially responsible marketing. Some researchers argue that brand marketing should also be used as a tool for social progress, promoting increased consumer awareness of important social issues and working as a tool to influence consumers in a positive way (Fan, 2005; Flores, 2001; Ind, 2003).

Discretionary or philanthropic responsibility

Philanthropic responsibility is another part of social responsibility, and hence part of CSR/SSR. In general terms, philanthropic responsibility includes making cash donations to causes or non-profit organisations, in-kind donations, such as free tickets, sponsorship of community events, and active employee volunteerism. Along with promoting an eco-friendly profile, this category is one of the most important to sport teams because, in order to succeed financially, each team is dependent on the local community to purchase tickets and other team goods (Extejt, 2004).

Virtually all professional teams participate in some kind of philanthropic activities. In the United States most professional sport leagues themselves require that their athletes be involved in the community. The collective bargaining agreement in the NBA, for example, requires each athlete to make at least five individual and five team appearances at community functions (Extejt, 2004). In addition to professional franchises, the sport industry also makes contributions through individual player or owner donations. For example, Michael Jordan donated $2 million to a Boys & Girls Club in

Chicago that was named after his father ('Jordan Makes Contribution', 1996). Similarly, George Steinbrenner, the owner of the Yankees, donates his own money to several causes, such as the Silver Shield Foundation in NY and the Gold Shield Foundation in Florida (Bernard, 1998).

CASE STUDY 5.1: Super Bowl XL – The National Football League (NFL) and CSR

Babiak and Wolfe (2006) discuss community outreach initiatives associated with the running of the 2006 Super Bowl XL (SBXL) in Detroit. These initiatives focused on the ethical and discretionary aspects of social responsibility, that is, activities consistent with societal expectations as well as activities beyond those expectations. They identify a number of CSR areas which cross each of Carroll's CSR dimensions, such as the treatment of employees, product safety, community welfare, environmental issues, as well as education and health concerns.

The Super Bowl attracts more viewers and creates more revenue than any other single sport event. It is more than just a game to the NFL and the communities that host it. Increasingly, organizing (host) committees, non-profit organisations and local governments in cities that are awarded the game use the event as a catalyst to address pressing social issues (Kott, 2005, cited in Babiak and Wolfe, 2006). The opportunities that a mega-event such as the Super Bowl affords a community for hosting the game in terms of economic, social, and political benefits are considerable. In a reciprocal fashion, the NFL is becoming progressively more invested in CSR initiatives in an effort to establish itself as a socially conscious organisation, one based on the twin pillars of football and the community (Tagliabue, 2006, cited in Babiak and Wolfe, 2006).

Among the most pressing issues facing Detroit immediately prior to the hosting of SBXL were poverty, crime and poor education (Babiak and Wolfe, 2006). Financial hardship had led to the closing of local community centres as well as reductions in the numbers of firefighters and police. Given the many social problems facing Detroit, there were many opportunities for SBXL CSR initiatives to positively impact the city. The SBXL Host Committee spent $18.5 million to attract and stage the game (Rovell, 2006, cited in Babiak and Wolfe, 2006). Estimated economic impact of SBXL on the deflated Detroit economy was approximately $250 million (Babiak and Wolfe, 2006; Walsh, 2006).

In order to prevent being perceived in a poor light, and/or to do the 'right' thing, the NFL and Host Committee may engage in CSR-related efforts to proactively address the concerns of critics and thus comply with societal expectations. As a result a number of 'ethically' related outreach activities were planned around SBXL – including addressing environmental concerns and ensuring fair business practices and opportunities for underrepresented groups. A number of discretionary CSR activities were also implemented by the NFL and the Host Committee, many of which were beyond the core competencies of the NFL's business: education, culture, infrastructure and charitable events and contributions. It was estimated that the charitable events and functions alone raised approximately $8 million.

CSR has been viewed as an effective public relations tool for corporations to enhance their reputation and build brand image and customer loyalty, as well as to positively influence society (Lewis, 2003). For the NFL, particularly with an event of the magnitude of the Super Bowl, engaging in CSR-related activities may help to soften some of the criticism surrounding the event (i.e., cost constraints on who is able to attend; issues of who really benefits from such mega-events; effects on the underprivileged, particularly the homeless). Doing the 'right thing', in an environment where corporations are increasingly criticized for unethical activity, may ward off backlash and contribute to the NFL's reputation as an entity that cares, and thus may enhance its image.

Continued

Babiak and Wolfe (2006) suggest that sport organisations cannot ignore CSR, regardless of whether they are motivated by financial considerations or by altruistic or philanthropic considerations. Whilst they say that the NFL's motivations for their CSR activities in relation to the Super Bowl cannot be determined to be either strictly financial or altruistic, it is clear that the NFL benefits in very practical ways by the generation of favourable publicity and by the establishment of an emotional bond with its customers – the fans.

SSR AS A SOURCE OF COMPETITIVE ADVANTAGE

Competitive advantage is that advantage over competitors gained by offering consumers/supports/fans greater value, either by means of lower prices or by providing greater benefits and service. CSR/SSR can deliver competitive advantage to a sport team, franchise or organisation in a number of different ways, most of which concern the ethical and philanthropic applications of CSR/SSR in order to generate positive perceptions of, and support for, sport teams, franchises and even mega-events.

As previously mentioned, CSR can generate long-term profits for business through positive brand perceptions, which can lead to an increase in consumer support for particular companies. This ultimately leads to a greater demand for products (Juholin, 2004; Quazi, 2003; Schiebel and Pochtrager, 2003). Sport, as business, looks to those same aspects of CSR/SSR, and the business-savvy sport public relations and communications manager aims to utilize all weapons in their arsenal to generate positive images and perceptions of their sport, team or event in order to market, advertise and stage an event (mega or otherwise) that captures the interest, loyalty and spending power of the major stakeholders (fans, advertisers and corporate sponsors). This is achieved by establishing a connection between the team, franchise or organisation and the major stakeholders on an intrinsically ethical and values-based level.

SSR AS A COMPONENT OF SPORT RELATIONSHIP MANAGEMENT

SRM can be defined as the process of fostering good relations with stakeholders – including supporters, fans, athletes, managers and the wider community in order to build loyalty and increase revenue. The sport manager, depending on their scope of responsibility within their team, franchise or organisation, can be in the unenviable position of having to balance the necessity of ensuring financial viability with the pressures of complying with societal expectations of legal, ethical and philanthropic responsibilities.

There are, as discussed earlier, a number of ways in which the sport manager can utilize aspects of CSR/SSR to establish and foster a good relationship with major stakeholders. Some of these practices are designed purely to generate profit, but most will aim to build long-term loyalty to the team, franchise or organisation by establishing a 'connection' with stakeholders by projecting an image of themselves which is perceived to be a desirable social representation (Ferrand and Pages, 1999). This can also be seen as promoting the sport, team or event as a 'brand'. The IOC is a well-known example of an international sporting organisation implementing a competitive brand marketing strategy (International Olympic Committee, 2006) in order to emphasize values such as friendship, unity, solidarity and universality (Payne, 1996), reinforcing their position in the global sporting community.

It is not only the sport manager who recognizes the importance of CSR/SSR in building relationships with stakeholders that can ultimately have long-term financial benefits. Corporate entities have recognized the opportunities accorded by sporting sponsorship in order to promote their brands to specifically targeted audiences and create stronger connections with existing consumers (May and Phelan, 2005; Simmons and Becker-Olsen, 2006). Sponsorship is an established business practice in which both the sponsor and the beneficiary of that sponsorship receive some benefit (usually financial) from the association. In sport sponsorships, the corporate sponsor links into the profit maximization view of CSR/SSR by aiming to increase recognition of their product and ultimately profits, by direct (and sometimes indirect) association with an athlete, team, franchise or event (Quester and Thompson, 2001). Smith and West-erbeek (2007) offer a different view of the sponsorship of sporting programs, believing that it is purely a business investment, not a genuine display of social responsibility. CSR, they believe, is ideally 'a genuine attempt to return benefits of successful business back into the community' (p. 7).

CASE STUDY 5.2: SSR as a Means of Re-establishing the Club/ Community Nexus in England

Breitbarth and Harris (2008) discuss the development of football in England in relation to CSR. The economic downturn of the 1980s with resultant social problems such as the rise of organized crime, increased football hooliganism in addition to increasing urban decay can be seen as the stimulus for CSR in English football (Moon, 2005, as cited in Breitbarth and Harris, 2008). In this context, CSR can be as an interchangeable concept with SSR. The 1990s saw football rapidly transforming into a business as the lucrative pay TV market changed the nature of the football-viewing public, and clubs increasingly saw the value of promotion and marketing in increasing not only the fan

Continued

base of the club but also in providing a much needed financial boost. Clubs were floated on the stock exchange as managers realized the importance of raising revenue to ensure their survival in an increasingly competitive market.

Issues around the changed nature of clubs and media control and viewer access to games increasingly moved football further on to the public agenda and began prompting calls for independent regulation of certain aspects of the game (Sutcliffe, 2000; Taylor, 2000). Debate around these issues was so widespread and impacted so greatly on society in general that in 2003 it was discussed in the House of Commons resulting in official recognition that a number of these critical issues were of sufficient enough concern to warrant official oversight. Major concerns included issues around governance, the treatment of supporters, football hooliganism and football related crime in general, racism, as well as the financial divide between football's elite, medium- and small-sized clubs.

Concern over the above problems was so great that it prompted the Football Association (FA) as well as individual clubs to join forces in order to establish strategies to deal with them. Stakeholder-driven CSR activities were identified as an effective method to address football's relationship to society and its traditional grassroots – the clubs and the fans. These CSR strategies have included various campaigns, programmes, schemes and charities designed to re-establish the traditional connection between the football clubs and their communities. The FA itself strongly believes that football has a unique place in British society and can act as a power for good off the pitch in a number of policy areas and has stated on CSR that 'we also think that the Government can and should use the power of football to this effect' (The FA, as cited in Breitbarth and Harris 2008, p. 193).

Professional clubs have implemented CSR strategies and hence become valuable players in social development (www.bitc.org.uk) and regional economies and urban regeneration (Sandy et al., 2004). Organized crime and hooliganism in and around football stadiums were seen as social consequences of the urban decay that affected many of England's major urban centres in the 1980s (Sudgen, 2002; Moon, 2005). By initiating CSR-driven strategies to combat some of these issues, football itself could be seen as a public agent working to help resolve such problems in a win–win partnership with local communities (House of Commons, as cited in Breitbarth and Harris, 2008). The 'Football in the Community' program was one of a number of programs enabling clubs to work hand-in-hand with their local communities to provide a range of essential services, including educational schemes, that provided positive inputs and modelling strategies.

Such strategies have the potential to leverage and use the power of professional clubs to create economic value within the community as well as dealing with some societal issues by engaging community involvement. Arsenal Football Club run literacy and numeracy programs in after-school, holiday and curriculum-time classes (Arsenal, 2005), and with racism at the top of the international and national agenda, the club is engaged in anti-racism campaigns. The government call for football as a partner (Pendry, 2000) in community development offers professional football clubs the opportunity to engage with the public agenda at the same time as addressing its own organisational goals by implementing self-enlightened CSR strategies that bring the game of football back to its traditional roots within the English community.

SUMMARY

Sport teams, franchises and organisations are increasingly operating on a global scale with the ensuing economic, legal and ethical considerations that come with operating as a business. With the economic benefits derived from the globalization of sport come the inherent responsibilities as a business to stakeholders, investors, sponsors and the community – be that community local or international. Society now expects that sport teams, franchises and organisations assume greater responsibility for their operation and the impact of their operations on their community, their fans and the physical space in which they operate. Sport managers and corporate sponsors alike cannot ignore CSR, regardless of whether their initial motivation is purely financial. Whilst sport managers, be they the CEO of a large franchise or manager of a small team, have an over-riding consideration to ensure that their team or organisation remains financially viable in order to remain in operation, they cannot ignore the legal, ethical and philanthropic components of CSR. This is not only because society is beginning to expect it, but also because the implementation of CSR-driven strategies can also impact positively on their communities, stakeholders and ultimately on themselves.

KEY TERMS

Corporate Social Responsibility A voluntary approach that a business enterprise takes to meet or exceed stakeholder expectations by integrating social, ethical and environmental concerns together with the usual measures of revenue, profit and legal obligation.

Sport Social Responsibility Where a sport team or franchise operates as a business, it also assumes economic, legal, ethical and discretionary considerations as part of its operation.

Competitive Advantage An advantage over competitors gained by offering consumers/supporters/fans greater value, either by means of lower prices or by providing greater benefits and service.

Sport Relationship Management The process of fostering good relations with members of the sporting community – including supporters, fans, athletes, managers and the wider community in order to build loyalty and increase revenue.

Green Sport Business Primarily concerned with the environmental impact of sport and has arisen from society's demand of sport organisations and franchises to add value to society, rather than use its resources for economic gain only.

DISCUSSION QUESTIONS

1. Identify some potential benefits that a sporting organisation or franchise can offer to the wider community by following the principles of SSR.
2. Research a major sporting organisation such as the IOC or the Federation Internationale de Football Association (FIFA). Does the

organisation espouse values and conduct commensurate with the concept of SSR? Does the sporting organisation have a published code of conduct or operation, and does this code go far enough in the current climate of community expectations of major sporting organisations?

GUIDED READING

Edwards, A., Skinner, J., 2006. Sport Empire. Meyer & Meyer Sport, Oxford. This book provides an excellent overview of the globalization sport and the emerging issues that confront the sport manger in the twenty-first century. Chapter 10 on 'Crisis Empire' is particularly relevant to the content of this chapter.

RECOMMENDED WEBSITES

Australian Centre for Corporate Social Responsibility – <http://www.accsr.com.au/>. Quick Silver Foundation – <http://www.quiksilverfoundation.org/>.

REFERENCES

Arsenal, 2005. Annual report 2004/5. Retrieved on 28 March 2008 from: <http://www.arsenal.com.>

Babiak, K., Wolfe, R., 2006. More than just a game? Corporate social responsibility and Super Bowl XL. Sport Marketing Quarterly 15, 214–222.

Bernard, H., 1998. Smith, Steinbrenner and Webb to receive 1998 Frederick Douglass awards. New York Beacon 5 (13), 34.

Breitbarth, T., Harris, P., 2008. The role of corporate social responsibility in the football business: towards the development of a conceptual model. European Sport Management Quarterly 8 (2), 179–206.

Carroll, A.B., 1979. A three dimensional model of corporate performance. Academy of Management Review 4 (4), 497–505.

Carroll, A.B., 2000. Ethical challenges for business in the new millennium: corporate social responsibility and models of management morality. Business Ethics Quarterly 10 (1), 33–42.

Clarkson, M., 1995. A stakeholder framework for analyzing and evaluating corporate social performance. Academy of Management Review 20 (1), 92–116.

Clark, C.E., 2000. Differences between public relations and corporate social responsibility: an analysis. Public Relations Review 26 (13), 363–381.

Cole, E.K., 2001. Applying a legal matrix to the world of sport. Michigan Law Review 99 (6), 1583–1607.

Dingle, G., 2007. Sport in a carbon-constrained twenty-first century. Bulletin of Sport and Culture. Victoria University Sport and Culture Group. March, No. 27.

Edwards, A., Skinner, J., 2006. Sport Empire. Meyer and Meyer Sport, Oxford.

Extejt, M.M., 2004. Philanthropy and professional sport teams. International Journal of Sport Management 5 (3), 215–228.

Fan, Y., 2005. Ethical branding and corporate reputation. Corporate Communications 10 (4), 241–257.

Ferrand, A., Pages, M., 1999. Image management in sport organisations: the creation of value title? European Journal of Marketing 33 (3–4), 387–402.

Flores, C.A., 2001. Socially Challenged: the Corporate Struggle with Responsibility. Unpublished Masters Dissertation Auburn University, Alabama.

Friedman, M., 1962. Capitalism and Freedom. University of Chicago Press, Chicago.

Heath, R.L., Ryan, M., 1989. Public relations' role in defining corporate social responsibility. Journal of Mass Media Ethics 4 (1), 21–38.

House of Commons, 2003. Current issues in football. Research paper 03/02, January 7.

Ind, N., 2003. Beyond Branding. Kogan Page, London.

International Olympic Committee, 2006. Retrieved 19 March 2009 from: <http://www.olympic.org/uk/organisation/movement/index_uk.asp>

Johnson, B., 1995. Human rights and the environment. Human Ecology 23, 111–123.

Juholin, E., 2004. For business or the good of all? A Finnish approach to corporate social responsibility. Corporate Governance 4 (3), 20–31.

Lee, S., Chun, H., 2002. Economic value of professional sport franchises in the United States. The Sport Journal 5 (3), 1–10.

Levy, C., 1972. The context of social work ethics. Social Work 17, 95–101.

Lewis, S., 2003. Reputation and corporate responsibility. Journal of Communication Management 7 (4), 356–365.

May, G., Phelan, J., 2005. Shared goals: sport and business in partnerships for development. The Prince of Wales International Business Leaders Forum.

Moon, J., 2005. An explicit model of business–society relations. In: Habisch, A., Jonjker, J., Wegner, M., Schmidpeter, R. (Eds.), Corporate Social Responsibility Across Europe. Springer, Berlin, Germany, pp. 51–65.

Nagano Declaration of Sport, 4 November 2001. Adopted by the Fourth IOC World Conference on Sport and the Environment. Nagano-City, Japan.

Payne, M., 1996. Sport organisation marketing. In: European Master in Sport Organisation Management Research Seminar. 13 December, IOC, Lausanne.

Pendry, T., 2000. Partners for progress. In: Hamil, S., Michie, J., Oughton, C., Warby, S. (Eds.), Football in the Digital Age. Mainstream Publishing, Edinburgh, pp. 214–219.

Quazi, A.M., 2003. Identifying the determinants of corporate managers perceived social obligations. Management Decisions 41 (9), 822–831.

Quester, P.G., Thompson, B., 2001. Advertising and promotion leverage on arts sponsorship effectiveness. Journal of Advertising Research 41 (1), 33–47.

Ross, S., 2003. Competition law as a constraint on monopolistic exploitation by sport leagues and clubs. Oxford Review of Economic Policy 19 (4), 569–584.

Sachs, W., 2002. Environment and Social Justice. Heinrich Boell Foundation, Berlin.

Sandy, R., Sloane, P.J., Rosentraub, M.S., 2004. The Economics of Football – An International Perspective. Palgrave Macmillan, London.

Schiebel, W., Pochtrager, S., 2003. Corporate ethics as a factor for success – the measurement instrument of the University of Agricultural Sciences (BOKU). Supply Chain Management 8 (2), 116–121.

Shelton, D., 2002. Human rights and environmental issues in multilateral treaties adopted between 1991 and 2001. Background paper no. 1. Report of the Joint UNEP-OHCHR Meeting of Experts on Human Rights and the Environment. Retrieved on 21 June 2009 from: <http://www.unep.ch/glo/glo%20pages/hr_env%20experts%20meeting%20report%20(revised).pdf>

Simmons, C.J., Becker-Olsen, K.L., 2006. Achieving marketing objectives through social sponsorships. Journal of Marketing 70 (4), 154–169.

Smith, A., Westerbeek, H., 2004. The Sport Business Future. Palgrave MacMillan, New York, NY.

Smith, A., Westerbeek, H., 2007. Sport as a vehicle for deploying corporate social responsibility. The Journal of Corporate Citizenship 25 (1), 43–54.

Sudgen, J., 2002. Scum Airways – Inside Football's Underground Economy. Mainstream, Edinburgh.

Sutcliffe, G., 2000. Why football needs an independent regulator. In: Hamil, S., Michie, J., Oughton, C., Warby, S. (Eds.), Football in the Digital Age. Mainstream Publishing, Edinburgh, pp. 264–268.

Szymanski, S., 2003. The Economic design of sporting contests. Journal of Economic Literature 41, 1137–1187.

Szymanski, S., Kuypers, T., 1999. Winners and Losers: The Business Strategy of Football. Viking, London.

Taylor, R., 2000. Why football needs a regulator. In: Hamil, S., Michie, J., Oughton, C., Warby, S. (Eds.), Football in the Digital Age. Mainstream Publishing, Edinburgh, pp. 47–54.

The World Business Council for Sustainable Development, 2000. Corporate social responsibility: making good business sense. Retrieved 24 August 2009 from: <http://www.wbcsd.org/web/publications/csr2000.pdf>

Walker, M.B., 2007. Assessing the Influence of Corporate Social Responsibility on Consumer Attitudes in the Sport Industry. Unpublished Doctoral Dissertation. Florida State University, Florida.

Walsh, T., 2006. Super boost for Detroit. Detroit Free Press. Retrieved on 24 March 2009 from: <http://www.highbeam.com/doc/1G1:143285148/Detroit+Free+Press+Tom+Walsh+column%7eC%7e+Super+Bowl+boost+for+Detroit.>

Zadek, S., 2001. The Civil Corporation: The New Economy of Corporate Citizenship. Earthscan, London.

CHAPTER 6

Community Relations and Engagement

Paul Kitchin
University of Ulster

Rob Lewis
London Metropolitan Business School

Learning Outcomes

Upon completion of this chapter the reader should be able to:

- Understand the importance of community engagement for sport organisations
- Discuss the importance of cause-related sport marketing to non-sport organisations
- Discuss the development of sport community involvement in the public relations opportunities that can arise

---

CHAPTER OVERVIEW

All sporting organisations depend on a range of stakeholders spread across disparate locations. The first idea that strikes us about community is that it is primarily local. However, as some professional sporting organisations are known around the world, community is a term that can be extended to many regions and international communities. Sport organisations' focus on these newer communities has led some to prioritise areas of potential lucre over traditional communities. Rein et al. (2006) stated that in an essentially crowded marketplace the importance of re-connecting with fans through engagement is vital to long-term success. By considering community needs as a central part of our business strategy the function of Sport Public Relations and Communications (SPRC) is to aid the organisation in reaching out and engaging the community to create positive relationships for the sport organisation.

This chapter will discuss the importance of community to sport organisations and the vital role that SPRC plays; in doing so it will address the following areas. First the chapter will briefly examine the work of sporting organisations engaging in the community and how they are using these initiatives to create positive relations. The chapter will then consider the rise of *ethical consumerism* that is in tune with increasing corporate community activities, in particular cause-related marketing (cause-RM). This part will examine objectives, benefits and issues surrounding the use of cause-RM with particular attention to initiatives with sporting organisations. Many of these sporting organisations have limited resources in which they need to operate the SPRC.

The case study example will highlight the work of a UK-based sporting charity and their efforts to use SPRC to communicate the community work they perform. Following the case the chapter will conclude with a brief discussion on the implications for the developments in the area of community relations and engagement.

SPORT IN THE COMMUNITY

Sporting organisations rely on their local communities for supporters, participants and employees. With the increasing professionalisation and commercialisation of elite sport, many organisations now attract these human resources from further afield. However, keeping in touch with the local community has a number of benefits. The clubs get to 'give something back' to the community that established them, they can generate goodwill through this involvement that can form political capital, they can keep in touch with local issues and needs and through the use of high-profile players they can deliver positive messages through the cluttered communication environment. Breithbarth and Harris (2008) highlight this as a way that sporting organisations can also begin to shape the public agenda on matters of importance to the sport.

Professional sporting clubs like the Indianapolis Colts, Saracens Rugby Union Football Club, the Urawa Red Diamonds and the Cincinnati Bengals amongst others offer *community-based initiatives* for healthy living, education, inclusion and matters concerning the environment. Hopwood (2007) provides an analysis of the potential for positive SPRC from the operations of the community programme at Newcastle Falcons. The key points being that the managers of the programme maintain the balance between operating the community initiatives while also managing to communicate their good work to their publics.

The SPRC benefit of this engagement has not yet been given adequate attention in academic research, however, from personal communication the authors know of some community managers who bemoan the fact that their good community work is less newsworthy than what one of their star players had for breakfast, and not just with the media but with their own SPRC people. This has presented the SPRC function with an important challenge, to take these community engagement activities and build on more than local relations and head towards more extensive positive public relations.

With increasing consumer interest in international affairs, many sport organisations are looking abroad to assist in international development opportunities. The National Basketball Association (NBA) operates their 'Basketball without Borders' programme in developing nations such as China, India and parts of Africa. The International Olympic Committee (IOC) has adopted care for the environment as one of the fundamental pillars of Olympism, their guiding philosophy, while the International Cricket Council (ICC) and Barcelona Football Club have entered into an agreement with the United Nations Children's Fund (UNICEF) to develop AIDS awareness programmes in Africa and the Caribbean. These organisations are engaging in issues that concern their local, regional and international stakeholders. The effective use of SPRC allows sporting organisations to stay in touch with disparate stakeholder groups and picking up on wider developments in the consumer market such as ethical consumerism and cause-RM.

CASE STUDY 6.1: Community Engagement and 'Cricket for Change'

Cricket for Change (C4C) is a sporting charity that operates from its headquarters (HQ) in South London. The charity was formed in 1981 as part of the Action Sport initiatives in response to the social unrest that troubled inner-city areas throughout England. Through the sport of cricket they attempt to engage with young people and to bring opportunities and change to their lives. The dynamics of this sport charity are rather interesting as although it can be classified as a cricket organisation it fits into the game's delivery model by providing niche services to a number of key target groups; namely, young people from housing estates and young people with a disability (C4C, 2008).

The work delivered by the charity focuses on a number of key areas:

- *Inner-city work*: The group developed a game played on the back streets of Pakistan for the urban environment. The game *Street-20* involves very few pieces of equipment and takes place on concrete pitches at housing estates and local sport centres. In

Continued

2008 the game was re-branded as *StreetChance* and integrated into the *Chance to Shine* initiative.

- *Hit the top*: This programme focuses on developing pathways into cricket for young people who have visual, physical and learning impairments. The programme provides a similar pathway to the England and Wales Cricket Board (ECB)'s elite development programme and can lead participants to international representation for England.

- *Women and girls programme*: C4C provides a focus club for women and girls' cricket offering pathways to elite play through links with their Ladies Cricket Club, the tenant of the Cricket Centre HQ (based in Wallington, South London).

All of the above programmes take a non-traditional approach to cricket and they have developed through the work the charity has done over the past three decades. Although the focus may appear to be cricket the development of non-sporting skills and abilities are also very important; it is this focus that creates their niche. However, over the recent past C4C has also developed a series of international programmes.

International work: C4C engages in international work in many countries in regions such as Israel and Palestine, the Subcontinent, the West Indies, Cuba and Central America and also Africa. This work focuses on not just delivering cricket programmes but training coaches to deliver these programmes once the C4C staff head back to their London HQ.

Leading the organisation is CEO Tom Rodwell and Programme Director Andy Sellins. A team of coaches and management assistants make up the full-time team who work with a Board of Trustees. The stakeholders that the organisation deals with are varied, ranging from local schools and businesses, to foreign governments. Despite this large network the charity operates on 'a shoe string' and does not have a great amount of funds to spend on marketing and promotion. To counter this lack of resources the charity focuses on the development of SPRC as it offers a distinct difference to the traditional marketing function.

According to Rodwell, SPRC is important but an area that leaves much room for improvement. To get around this problem C4C uses a pragmatic approach, all of the staff share the SPRC function. Rodwell describes the team as an 'ideas factory', where their ability to innovate and deliver value to their stakeholders is central to their mission. Although from a management perspective this makes the control of SPRC difficult, as it relies heavily on the enthusiasm and commitment of staff. If the staff are not committed and not passionate this strategy would not work. An example of this challenge is to engage participants who require a demonstration of commitment and enthusiasm from programme leaders in order to take part:

> *running sport programmes in schools is easy as the kids have to be there, whereas what we do, we turn up on an estate and if they (young people) are not interested they won't come. We have to make it interesting, you have to care about what you are doing.*
>
> (Personal Communication: T. Rodwell, 22 October 2008)

Both Rodwell and Sellins believe that the relationship with traditional cricketing authorities is complex. Through years of working with the ECB, the Cricket Foundation and the County Crickets Boards (Counties) that operate in London (Essex, Kent, Surrey, Middlesex) they have achieved a position where '*we are partners in action but essentially… we are tolerated*'. Managing this relationship is one of C4C's toughest SPRC challenges. Most external funding bids for sport require approval at the national authority level. At the national level they deal with the ECB. This approval (or '*tick*') is needed for many of their significant initiatives, such as extending their HQ to include an indoor training centre. C4C needs to communicate similar aims to that of the ECB and in the past, due to lack of SPRC focus, this has not always been the case. Where disagreement arises the relationship must be carefully managed, essentially through either interpersonal communication or by continually generating goodwill by ensuring that they can assist whenever and wherever the ECB requires it.

Rodwell believes that although the network is interdependent, the Counties view C4C as a competitor. This is true even though the primary focus of the Counties is on developing elite cricketers, whereas for C4C it is clearly not. Apart from Middlesex who have large urban areas, necessitating a good fit between themselves and the charity, other Counties take a different approach. All of the Counties need C4C to provide mandated services but if C4C were to make more of their work (i.e. increase the publicity through SPRC) within the Counties, Rodwell feels that this might destabilise the relationship further.

The most significant development for the charity in their recent past was taking advantage of an opportunity that arose through the *Chance to Shine* initiative and the use of stakeholder management to increase their profile. *Chance to Shine* is a programme from the Cricket Foundation, the charity arm of the ECB. The aim of *Chance to Shine* is to get cricket back into schools, particularly those run by the government. The C4C team realised that the mechanics of the programme were ideally designed for suburban and country schools with green expanses at their disposal, but not for the urban environment. Their competence in delivery within these urban environments allowed Rodwell and Sell-ins to push the message to the Cricket Foundation to deliver the modified *Street-20* in urban schools and estates. They redesigned the *Street-20* game to fit into cricket coaching sessions aligned with wider *Chance to Shine* goals. The charity's existing links with the Metropolitan Police allowed them to access the Home Office's Positive Futures team, a government organisation that specialises in young people's inclusion needs. With the weight of the combined group of partners they were able to attract a blue chip sponsor.

Barclays Bank is one of the leading banks in the UK. However, it was their *Spaces for Sport* programme, started in 2004, that warranted them attention in sport management circles in the UK. *Spaces for Sport* was a *Corporate Social Responsibility* (CSR) initiative of *Barclays in the Community* that provided financial support for the construction of sporting facilities, with additional revenue funding for 3 years to establish sustainable sporting programmes – to revise your understanding of CSR refer to Chapter 5. This revenue assistance differed considerably from other funding sources. By 2008 over 500,000 disadvantaged people have had the opportunity to benefit from their investments (StreetChance, 2008).

The partners launched the programme in 2008, and it now operates in 10 London boroughs (local councils), selected for the range of pressing youth issues. The delivery aspects suit C4C well. It aims to provide in- and out-of-school cricket training for ages 8–18 delivering a total of 5000 units of delivery (e.g. 200 children participating for 25 hours). The key benefit to C4C is not only the funding which is significant but it also allows them to use SPRC methods to highlight their good work.

Establishing links with international governments also arises in an ad hoc fashion. When Rodwell spoke at Canning House[1] where he presented C4C's work in Cuba, he found that the audience were very interested in the work that C4C had done. Out of the meeting came the contact with the Panamanian Embassy to discuss opportunities to work internationally. The beauty of sport is that discussions do not always have to take part around boardroom tables. In this instance, a trip to Lord's to see a match and have a meal was able to establish a relationship which later resulted in a Presidential offer to deliver their disability programme in Panama. This unconventional approach to public/stakeholder relations used assets that all sporting organisations could probably have access to within their existing networks. Furthermore, the staging of cricket matches involving celebrities and press officers of stakeholders is another way of delivering positive messages while enhancing relationships between C4C and its publics.

In the future one of the main challenges for the charity in the use of SPRC is to make them look bigger than they are. Rodwell fears that if partners realise how small they are they might be put off. The international work allows them to do this as the scope belies their small organisational size. However, the international work comes at a price. Formerly funded by UK Sport and the Home Office, the arrival and subsequent attention on the 2012 London Olympics has seen UK Sport focus all

---

[1] A Latin American, Hispanic Council based in London.

Continued

its attention on achieving Olympic success. With the withdrawal of UK Sport funding, the task of choosing working partners is vitally important for the charity. However, their international work is now establishing links with countries abroad and has opened up new partnership opportunities, so although these programmes use considerable resources the SPRC benefits to the charity are clear.

Finally Rodwell believes that if C4C can continue to demonstrate success then there will always be interest in their work and therefore funders available. He feels that as CSR budgets are smaller than marketing budgets they may be less likely to be cut, especially if organisations need to demonstrate that they are in touch with the community. Hence, although the SPRC function can be improved, successful links with organisations such as Barclays will increase the likelihood of their being approached for further involvement in community engagement activities. Furthermore, if C4C can tap into the power of new media (further discussion of this is taken up in Chapter 11) they could aim to counter the constant issues of traditional media awareness and attention and wrest control of their SPRC function through the use of these technologies to communicate with their stakeholders.

This case study aimed to highlight the PR issues and challenges faced by a sporting organisation operating amongst a range of stakeholders. Although C4C is unique to the cricketing hierarchy it still demonstrates that small organisations struggle to prioritise the public relations function. However, it is clear that when the organisation uses its SPRC networks it leads to significant developments and new opportunities for engagement with partners, potential funders and media agencies.

ETHICAL CONSUMERISM

The term ethical consumer generates significant attention in the traditional and academic press. Strong (1996, p. 5) characterised ethical consumers as those individuals whose 'buying behaviour reflects a concern with the problems of the third world'. However, while the terminology of ethical consumer is current in the literature the type of consumer has been around for many years. Ethical consumers can be seen as an extension of Webster's (1975, p. 188) *socially conscious consumer*. Webster defined this type of consumer as an individual who:

> *Takes into account the public consequences of his/her private consumption or attempts to use his or her purchasing power to bring about social change.*

Some of the areas of concern to these consumers include:

■ Environmental issues – reducing carbon emissions by decreasing consumer and product travel along with recycling and reductions in general waste,
■ Fair trade and the maintenance of real wages in foreign labour markets,

- Ethical finance and investment and
- Animal testing and many others (Co-operative Bank, 2006).

The focus of ethical consumerism has shifted from this third-world perspective to a more comprehensive view of thinking globally and acting locally. More consumers are now focusing on ensuring that local needs are addressed in an attempt to concurrently address wider issues. The role of all organisations in providing programmes of corporate responsibility has extended from the commercial sector to other sectors of the economy (Crowther and Rayman-Bacchus, 2004).

Dawkins and Lewis (2003) developed a consumer typology of the ethical consumers and identified three key groups that lead action in the market. This typology is highlighted in Table 6.1.

Dawkins and Lewis (2003) felt that the latter two groups were more likely to talk ethically than consume ethically. This has been supported by a body of research and the authors feel that this is positive news for the SPRC function. It means that the opportunities for engaging customers in conversation about issues important to them are available. By engaging in this fashion the sport organisation has a clear ability to build relationships through these discussions. The potential of the market is growing as nearly a third of all consumers are categorised into these groups. Furthermore, as growing numbers of consumers are interested in ethical–organisational activities they may be willing to engage in communication on the matter. According to the Co-operative Bank (2006), the number of ethical consumers is growing each year and the value of this market has increased by 81% in the last 5 years.

Many countries are witnessing increasing numbers of ethical consumers. Although a vast body of research exists in the UK the rise in ethical

Table 6.1   Dawkins and Lewis' Typology of Ethical Consumption (2003)

Category	% of pop.	Description
Global watchdogs	5%	The 'hardliners' who purchase on ethical criteria, they belong to high social grades and are aged 34–54.
Conscientious consumers	18%	These consumers purchase ethically when they can, as long as value for money and quality is not compromised. They tend to discuss the issues more than act.
Brand generation	6%	These consumers purchase ethically but are heavily influenced by brands. This group is typically from mid-social grades and a third of this group is under 25.

Adapted from Dawkins and Lewis (2003).

consumerism is not just restricted to this region. In many western countries these needs are gaining more and more public and media attention. For instance, the environment is the fifth biggest issue facing the Canadian population, while HIV/AIDS is the third highest in South Africa (Ritchie, 2007).

CAUSE-RELATED MARKETING

At the same time, the emergence of ethical consumerism has seen the development of cause-RM. Cause-RM is a facet of CSR which views the organisation as having a wider responsibility than just its employers and shareholders. The use of CSR to support SPRC has been discussed in Chapter 4, hence this chapter will focus on one particular aspect of CSR activity, Cause-RM, with an emphasis on the SPRC benefits firms entering such initiatives can achieve. Cause-RM is a collection of marketing initiatives that generally adhere to Varadarajan and Menon's (1988, p. 60) definition:

> *The process of formulating and implementing marketing activities that are characterized by an offer from the firm to contribute a specified amount to a designated cause when customers engage in revenue-providing exchanges that satisfy organisational and individual objectives.*

The explicit financial nature of this definition has softened into a more current definition which states:

> *A commercial activity by which business and charities or causes form a partnership with each other to market an image, product or service for mutual benefit.*
>
> (BITC/Research International, 2004)

These definitions separate cause-RM from other forms of corporate community activities. This tool differs from philanthropic giving in that it is not altruistic as it aims to achieve some form of bottom-line advantage. It differs from traditional commercial sponsorship as while they share a transactional ethos they differ through the primary focus on an external cause (Seitanidi and Ryan, 2007). Central to cause-RM is the role and importance of the consumer in the initiative. The consumer also seeks a benefit from taking part in the campaigns to satisfy their own consumption needs (Hawkins et al., 2001; Mintel, 2003).

Cause-RM can be used to achieve a range of SPRC benefits that aid the corporate organisations that support the various initiatives. These can include, but are not limited to:

- Gaining national visibility
- Enhancing corporate image
- Thwarting negative publicity
- Pacifying customer groups
- Increasing brand awareness
- Increasing brand recognition
- Enhancing brand image
- Reinforcing brand image (Varadarajan and Menon, 1988)

Mintel (2003) highlights a number of types of cause-RM including product link-ups, non-sales oriented cause-RM initiatives and sponsorship. An overview of cause-RM can be seen in Table 6.2. These types of cause-RM programmes can be identified through the following characteristics:

Type 1. Product link-ups: These campaigns involve a link between the purchases of products that have an allocation of their sale prices directed to a cause. These deals can be short term or long term in nature. General Motor's support of breast cancer research by entering into a deal with the Women's National Basketball Association (WNBA), which allocates a percentage of ticket prices towards the cause, the Live Strong Campaign by Nike and the Lance Armstrong Foundation (McGlone and Martin, 2006) are examples. Affinity marketing schemes provide a benefit to consumers by allocating a percentage of their everyday spending to good causes. Moreover, Nedbank of South Africa provides a percentage of each credit card transaction towards worthy causes.

Type 2. Non-sales oriented: Sport organisations and athletes support programmes that share similar aims or concerns. The National Football League (NFL) clubs link with the various homeless charities that see them assist in the collection of non-perishable foodstuffs for those in need. No financial transaction occurs but the sport organisation still lends its support, staff and through this, raises its media profile.

Type 3. Contemporary sponsorship: Contemporary sponsorship is seen more as a partnership that focuses on more than simply commercial exchange (Seitanidi and Ryan, 2007). This type of sponsorship is less commercially oriented but generally involves a corporate organisation that

Table 6.2	Examples of Sport Cause-Related Campaigns		
Cause	**Sporting Organisation/Event**	**Cause Partner**	**Type**
AIDS/HIV	International Olympic Committee	UNAIDS	2
Animal protection	Various Athletes	WildAid – When the Buying stops the Killing Can Too	2
Breast cancer research	Cricket Australia	The McGrath Foundation	2
Children (health)	AFL	QANTAS	3
	DCSF Schools	J. Sainsbury's	1
Children (safety)	The Football Foundation	National Society for Prevention of Cruelty to Children	2
Children (education)	Cincinnati Bengals	Marvin Lewis Community Fund	2
Community development	Boston Red Sox – *Lindos Suenos*	Various	2
Homeless	Street League UK	St Mungo's	3
Hunger	National Basketball Association	Campbell Soup, National Association of Letter Carriers	2
Recycling	National Sport Council – Nepal	Resolve International	2

Source: Authors.

enters into a sponsorship agreement with a cause supported by a charity or a sporting organisation. Some examples include the St Jude Classic golf tournament formerly supported by FedEx (Irwin and Lacowetz, see further reading) or Flora's former sponsorship of the London Marathon (Mintel, 2003).

CASE STUDY 6.2: Getting It Right, Getting It Wrong

Many non-sport organisations have launched cause-RM programmes to support initiatives to prevent unhealthy eating and declining physical activity, particularly in young people. Two such programmes have been J. Sainsbury's 'Active Kids' and Cadbury's 'Get Active!' campaigns. The success, or otherwise, of these initiatives provides interesting lessons for cause-RM planning and activation.

Supermarket chain Sainsbury's Active Kids programme was initiated in 2006 aiming to drive sales growth and attract new customers. It allowed customers to collect vouchers that could be exchanged for sporting equipment, coaching sessions and sport kit to be used in local schools. By operating this initiative local Sainsbury's stores formed a valuable network through their local primary schools, enhancing their community presence. The supermarket chain generates good publicity from the network, puts equipment into schools that need it, has won Business in the Community Awards for the initiative and is also seeing increases in sales (BITC, 2008). Sainsbury's even drives local competition by publishing a leader board at its stores to highlight the most successful schools.

In 2003 Cadbury's, the chocolate manufacturer, launched a voucher scheme initiated to address increasing levels of inactivity in young people. By exchanging chocolate bar wrappers schools could purchase sporting equipment. Although both schemes were sales oriented the Cadbury's programme proved a public relations nightmare. Despite assurances from the company that children would eat the chocolate regardless of promotions (and therefore why not allow it to contribute some sport equipment) the sheer volume of wrappers required to earn one volleyball (320 wrappers) could not allow that message to be delivered in any positive fashion.

The differences between each cause-RM initiative are actually quite small but the consumer perception of each cause differs significantly. There exists a growing body of research that documents how well thought-out cause-RM improves not only the profile and image of these causes, but also the images consumers hold towards these corporations (Stipp and Schiavone, 1996; Webb and Mohr, 1998). Therefore getting it wrong can damage the reputation of the organisation. Understanding how customers perceive cause-RM initiatives and what can be done to manage them effectively is important for SPRC practitioners.

Like most consumer behaviour theory interest in cause-RM and ethical consumerism is influenced by internal and external factors. The research in both these areas has contrasting views on what motivates consumer support. One view is that self-perception theory, where an individual's actions impact on their self-perception necessitates that 'doing good, means feeling good'. Therefore participating in good causes and a desire to consume ethically bring intrinsic benefits to the consumer (Vaidyanathan and Aggarwal, 2005). Alternative theories such as social identity theory and interpersonal influence are externally oriented motivations for participation in causes. Bearden et al. (1989) quite negatively concluded that we consume in a way so as to enhance our view with significant others we seek to impress, while conforming to wider societal expectations. Pragmatically if the authenticity of the issue or cause is genuine and important, the focus of motivation is essentially irrelevant, as it is the thought (or indeed action) that counts.

Consumer attitudes and beliefs have been positively influenced by organisations supporting good causes. Generally speaking, younger people (Cui et al., 2003) and women (Kropp et al., 1999; Irwin et al., 2003) tend to be more supportive of these initiatives but as cause-RM increases so do consumers' positive associations. For the SPRC function this is an important factor because communicating our care for, and engagement with, the community can generate goodwill, support and reinforce the legitimacy of the organisation. However, issues are being raised concerning the accuracy of relying on intentions as there currently exists a gap between what consumers say they believe (attitudes and beliefs) and what they actually do (actions) (Barone et al., 2000; Carrigan and Attalla, 2001; Cui et al., 2003; Webb and Mohr, 1998).

Research on intentions and ethical consumerism in Belgium found that consumers reported high attitude and belief scores, but when these consumers were required to pay more for ethical products, only those who exhibited strong 'watchdog' traits would actually contribute (De Pelsamcker et al., 2005). Likewise, when consumers in the UK were asked if unethical business practices had any impact on purchase decisions the results were surprising. Consumers were found to be selectively ethical, ranking certain issues such as animal welfare over third-world labour practices (Carrigan and Attalla, 2001). In Finland consumers stated difficulty in picking ethical companies from those who were not, while the high price of certain ethical products also reduces their willingness to purchase an item (Uusitalo and Oksanen, 2004).

MANAGEMENT IMPLICATIONS FOR CAUSE-RM

There are important considerations that SPRC staff should take into account regarding the management of cause-RM. With regards to pricing, an important strategic factor, when deals are initiated it is good practice to ensure that there is no increase in the price of the item, especially if there is no increase in quality. Research has proved that when prices increase so too does consumer scepticism and they begin to doubt the motives of the partner or do not purchase the product at all (Barone et al., 2000; Cavill & Co., 2001; Endacott, 2004; Webb and Mohr, 1998). Ensuring that cause involvement is seen as authentic is vital to encourage consumer support and trust to spur action. It is clear that sporting organisations should carefully consider the nature of such deals and the SPRC function should develop a response to any potential negative consumer responses. Such authenticity can be developed through the following strategies: providing an appropriate fit between the sponsor and the cause, developing significant length of involvement and finally utilising SPRC to assist in expressing genuine motives.

Appropriate fit: The fit between the organisation and the cause must create an appropriate match in the minds of various stakeholders. Consumer confidence in the legitimacy of the deal is lost when this does not occur (Garcia et al., 2003). In the Cadbury's example few would argue with the good cause of helping schools to access more sporting equipment, however, to require the purchase of chocolate, no matter how everyday the purchase may be, led to significant pressure being placed on the manufacturer. This does not mean that in practice any products that lack healthy credentials can be involved in sporting practices, as seen by the close association between McDonalds and the English F.A., but each party must use their public relations functions to ensure that the links portray an appropriate message. The appeal of McDonalds to young children is undoubted but McDonalds works hard to get the message of 'balanced diet' across. Nevertheless getting the fit right is important as Pracejus and Olsen (2004) found that close-fit cause-RM initiatives can lead to up to 10 times more value accruing to the cause than the alternative.

Developing a significant timeline: Generally, the association between an organisation and a cause has been found to be most effective when the partnership is developed over the long term. Organisations that go for short-term initiatives have their motives questioned by consumers (Cui et al., 2003; Ellen et al., 2006; Vaidyanathan and Aggarwal, 2005; Webb and Mohr, 1998). Hence long-term engagements are therefore preferable for sport and their causes as it demonstrates to consumers that each party is committed to the cause. Flora's sponsorship of the London Marathon 1996–2009 is an example of such a long-term partnership.

Express genuine motives: The association needs to be managed, leveraged and communicated as thoroughly as possible. BITC/Research International (2004, p. 9) terms this as *'live and breathe the relationship'*. The importance of successful partnership management creates stronger bonds between the organisations involved in the cause (Seitanidi and Ryan, 2007). This is analogous to most partnerships, as this has received significant attention by sport organisations to their business networks. Consumers have greater trust for what they perceive to be more symbiotic relationships (Barone et al., 2000; Ellen et al., 2006; Schimmel et al., 2007). By communicating these factors through the SPRC function the intention is to help these causes address the lack of consumer understanding of who is an ethical company (Uusitalo and Oksanen, 2004). Also in the event of unethical practice perceived to be arising, a strategy for dealing with any negative publicity is deployed. This was seen in Cadbury's case when the manufacturer called in their sporting ambassadors, such as Paula Radcliffe and Darren Gough (English Cricketer), to try and limit the adverse publicity.

CASE STUDY 6.3: Arsenal in the Community

For over 25 years Arsenal have been engaging in community work, originally in London and now further afield. Their programmes focus on four key areas: sport, education and training, social inclusion and diversity. Two areas of focus for this example are an educational programme called the Arsenal Double Club and Arsenal Kickz, a social inclusion programme.

Operating since 2002, the *Arsenal Double Club* is an educational programme that develops skills in Key Stage 2 and 3 of the (UK) National Curriculum by placing students with mentors. Initially the programme focused on developing literacy and numeracy skills in school hours and then the addition of an out-of-school sport programme in football or hockey. The success of the programme saw the curriculum expanded to include other subjects such as science and languages. Programme assistant Samir Singh is keen to have the full range of national curriculum covered by the programme in the future. The programme has been so successful that the community team have entered into a deal with the Department for Children, Schools and Families (DCSF) who are looking to deliver the programme nationally. Using the international playing talent at Arsenal is an innovative way to encourage students to engage with foreign languages, an area of concern for the DCSF. In 2007, Manuel Almunia (the Arsenal goalkeeper) was present at the launch of the language programme (which now covers French, German and Spanish), this endorsement from the players, who even take part in DVD learning materials, demonstrates to young people the importance of educational attainment and the opportunities it can provide. This is supported by the European Commission and promotes the club as an innovator in the field of educational engagement and has achieved awards for the Club.

Continued

Arsenal Kickz is a social inclusion programme developed with the Metropolitan Police, which has been running since 2006. It involves placing coaches, who deliver free sporting sessions to young people aged 10-19, in the community. The programme has developed from football for all groups, to programmes for women and girls, and in 2007 to boxing sessions with a local boxing club. Support from their local borough and an investment of £80,000 for Dennis Berg-kamp's (former Arsenal player) testimonial match has resulted in the upgrading of local leisure facilities which could hopefully lead to wider regeneration of the local area.

One of the real strengths of the department is the training and development of their staff, some who have progressed from participant involvement in the programme themselves. However successful the programme has been, there is still a need to leverage these efforts further through the SPRC process.

SUMMARY

Sport has been involved in community relations and engagement activities for many years. However, few sport organisations have truly released the potential of leveraging these activities to their various publics through the SPRC function. With the rise of ethical consumerism and an increase in the use of cause-RM by organisations, it is important that these activities are highlighted as central to the sport organisation's purpose.

Many managers within sporting organisations seek to access traditional media to 'spread the word' on their good work. The case study on C4C highlighted how one organisation is dealing with the SPRC function with limited resources. However, as the reader will see in Chapter 11 there are new ways that organisations can engage with their publics. The challenge in the future for this area is to do two key things. The first is to demonstrate innovation and creativity in the planning of community relations and engagement activities. The second is to investigate the way of utilising the SPRC function through a range of existing and emerging media to highlight the success of these activities.

KEY TERMS

Ethical Consumerism Those individuals whose 'buying behaviour reflects a concern with the problems of the third world' (Strong, 1996, p. 5).

Cause-Related Marketing A commercial activity by which business and charities or causes form a partnership with each other to market an image, product or service for mutual benefit (BITC/Research International, 2004).

Community-Based Initiatives Organisational activities that aim to work with and/or enhance provision of services in local communities.

Socially Conscious Consumer   Webster defined this type of consumer as an individual who: takes into account the public consequences of his/her private consumption or attempts to use his/her purchasing power to bring about social change (p. 188).

DISCUSSION QUESTIONS

1. Why would Barclays Bank be interested in working with a small charity like C4C?
2. Why is sport particularly well suited to cause-RM initiatives?
3. How would you refocus the SPRC activity for the Cadbury's *Get Active* campaign to reduce negative associations?

GUIDED READING

The reference list contains many useful sources of information relevant to the topic, however, the authors recommend three sources in particular:

The FedEx St Jude Classic Golf Tournament has been running since 1986 (incidentally it started its association with St Jude Children's Research Hospital in 1970 while the tournament itself began in 1958). Research by Irwin and Lacowetz (and others) has covered a range of consumer related and business-to-business benefits for the tournament presentation sponsor FedEx. This collection of articles is providing an interesting longitudinal study of cause-RM sponsorship, which readers may want to investigate further. Lachowetz, T., Irwin, R., 2002. FedEx and the St. Jude Classic: an application of a cause-related marketing program (CRMP). Sport Marketing Quarterly 12, 114–116.

Readers interested in learning more about the community engagement activities of the former G14 Clubs should look to Community Engagement: Insights into the Contribution of European Club Football by Business in the Community which can be found at <http://www.bitc.org.uk/resources/publications/community_engagement.html>.

Readers interested in the English Premier League's community engagement activities can likewise be directed to <http://www.premierleague.com/page/CommunityPL/0,,12306,00.html>.

RECOMMENDED WEBSITES

Street-20, Cricket for Change –< http://uk.youtube.com/user/Cricket4change>.
   Sainsbury's Active Kids campaign –< http://www.sainsburys.co.uk/activekids>.
   Arsenal in the Community –< http://www.arsenal.com/community>.

REFERENCES

Bearden, W.O., Netemeyer, R.G., Teel, J.E., 1989. Measurement of consumer susceptibility to interpersonal influence. Journal of Consumer Research 15 (4), 473–481.

BITC/Research International, 2004. Brand Benefits. Research International, London.

BITC, 2008. Sainsbury's – Active Kids. Retrieved 12 June 2008 from: <www.bitc.org.uk/resources/case_studies/afe_1343.html>.

Breithbarth, T., Harris, P., 2008. The role of corporate responsibility in the football business: towards the development of a conceptual model. European Sport Management Quarterly 8, 179–206.

Barone, M.J., Miyazaki, A.D., Taylor, K.A., 2000. The influence of cause-related marketing on consumer choice: does one good turn deserve another? Journal of the Academy of Marketing Science 28 (2), 248–262.

C4C, 2008. About us. Retrieved 11 November 2008 from: <www.cricket4change.org.uk>.

Carrigan, M., Attalla, A., 2001. The myth of the ethical consumer – do ethics matter in purchase behaviour? Journal of Consumer Marketing 18, 560–577.

Cavill & Co., 2001. Heart and sold: Australian consumers speak from the heart on cause-related marketing. Retrieved 11 November 2008 from: <http://www.cavill.com.au/pages.asp?area=24&page=55>.

Co-operative Bank, 2006. The Ethical Consumerism Report 2007. Co-operative Bank, Manchester.

Crowther, D., Rayman-Bacchus, L., 2004. Introduction: perspectives on corporate social responsibility. In: Crowther, D., Rayman-Bacchus, L. (Eds.), Perspectives on Corporate Social Responsibility. Ashgate, London, pp. 1–20.

Cui, Y., Trent, E.S., Sullivan, P.M., Matiru, G.N., 2003. Cause-related marketing: how generation Y responds. International Journal of Retail and Distribution Management 31, 310–320.

Dawkins, J., Lewis, S., 2003. CSR and stakeholder expectations: and their implications for company strategy. Journal of Business Ethics 44, 185–193.

De Pelsamcker, P., Driesen, L., Rayp, G., 2005. Do consumers care about ethics? Willingness to pay for fair-trade coffee. Journal of Consumer Affairs 39, 363–384.

Endacott, R.W.J., 2004. Consumers and CRM: a national and global perspective. Journal of Consumer Marketing 21, 183–189.

Ellen, P.S., Webb, D., Mohr, L., 2006. Building corporate associations: consumer attributions for corporate socially responsible programs. Journal of the Academy of Marketing Science 34, 147–157.

Garcia, I., Gibaja, J.J., Mujika, J., 2003. A study on the effect of cause-related marketing on the attitude towards the brand: the case of Pepsi in Spain. Journal of Non-profit and Public Sector Marketing 11, 111–135.

Hawkins, D.I., Best, R.J., Coney, K.A., 2001. Consumer Behavior: Building Marketing Strategy, eighth ed. Irwin McGraw-Hill, New York, NT.

Hopwood, M., 2007. Sport public relations. In: Beech, J., Chadwick, S. (Eds.), The Marketing of Sport. Pearson Education Limited, London, pp. 292–331.

Irwin, R.L., Lachowetz, T., Cornwell, T.B., Clark, J.S., 2003. Cause-related sport sponsorship: an assessment of spectator beliefs, attitudes, and behavioural intentions. Sport Marketing Quarterly 12, 131–139.

Kropp, F., Holden, S.J.S., Lavack, A.M., 1999. Cause-related marketing and values in Australia. International Journal of Nonprofit and Voluntary Sector Marketing 4, 69–80.

Mintel, 2003. Cause-related marketing – UK – May 2003. Mintel International.

McGlone, C., Martin, N., 2006. Nike's corporate interest lives strong: a case of cause-related marketing and leveraging. Sport Marketing Quarterly 15, 184–187.

Pracejus, J.W., Olsen, G.D., 2004. The role of brand/cause fit in the effectiveness of cause-related marketing campaigns. Journal of Business Research 57, 635–640.

Rein, I., Kotler, P., Shields, B., 2006. The Elusive Fan. Irwin-McGraw-Hill, New York, NY.

Ritchie, J., 2007. Cause related marketing. The Marketing Site. Retrieved 11 November 2008 from: <http://www.themarketingsite.com/live/content.php?Item_ID=181>.

Seitanidi, M.M., Ryan, A., 2007. A critical review of forms of corporate community involvement: from philanthropy to partnerships. International Journal of Nonprofit and Voluntary Sector Marketing 12, 247–266.

Stipp, H., Schiavone, N., 1996. Modelling the impact of Olympic sponsorship on corporate image. Journal of Advertising Research 36, 22–28.

StreetChance, 2008. Partners. StreetChance. Retrieved 11 November 2008 from: <http://www.streetchance.co.uk/partners>.

Strong, C., 1996. Feature contributing to the growth of ethical consumerism – a preliminary investigation. Marketing Intelligence and Planning 14, 5–13.

Schimmel, K.E., Clark, J.S., Irwin, R., Lachowetz, T., 2007. What communication methods work well for sport events? An analysis of the FedEx St. Jude Classic. International Journal of Sport Management and Marketing 2, 301–315.

Uusitalo, O., Oksanen, R., 2004. Ethical consumerism: a view from Finland. International Journal of Consumer Studies 28, 214–221.

Webb, D., Mohr, L., 1998. A typology of consumer responses to cause-related marketing: from sceptics to socially concerned. Journal of Public Policy and Marketing 17, 226–238.

Webster Jr., F.E., 1975. Characteristics of the socially conscious consumer. Journal of Consumer Research 2, 188–196.

Varadarajan, P.R., Menon, A., 1988. Cause-related marketing: a coalignment of marketing strategy and corporate philanthropy. Journal of Marketing 52, 58–74.

Vaidyanathan, R., Aggarwal, P., 2005. Using commitments to drive consistency: enhancing the effectiveness of cause-related marketing communications. Journal of Marketing Communications 11, 231–246.

CHAPTER 7

Sport Volunteerism

B. Christine Green, Laurence Chalip
University of Texas at Austin

Learning Outcomes

Upon completion of this chapter the reader should be able to:

- Describe the ways that public relations can be used to recruit volunteers
- Define and identify the ways that public relations helps to retain volunteers
- Detail ways in which volunteers can be used to promote the sport organisation
- Address the key challenges to the effective use of volunteers in public relations

---

CHAPTER OVERVIEW

This chapter sets out to describe the symbiotic relationship between public relations and successful volunteer programs. Public relations efforts can enhance the profile and image of a sport organisation, making it easier to attract and retain volunteers. At the same time, volunteers can be invaluable sources for sport organisations to get their stories to the public. The chapter begins with an examination of the role of public relations in the recruitment and retention of volunteers. It then discusses ways that volunteers can promote stories about the sport organisation. It ends by considering the challenges in depending on volunteers to deliver a sport organisation's public relations.

THE NEXUS BETWEEN PUBLIC RELATIONS AND VOLUNTEERING IN SPORT

Like other businesses, sport organisations depend on media to get their story to the public. Unlike other businesses, for sport organisations, public relations (rather than advertising) serves as the central hub for integrated marketing communications (Favorito, 2007). It is not just that sport can be news; it is that sport's significance to its audience depends on it being news. Sport organisations require a high public profile – one which suggests not merely that sport is important, but one which demonstrates its ongoing value to people and their communities. That is why successful sport organisations maintain a proactive public relations unit. In the United States, this unit is often called 'sport information' or 'community relations'.

The public relations function can assist in the recruitment and retention of volunteers. Public relations can enhance the profile of sport organisation and its volunteer program, thereby attracting volunteers. Public relations also affects public perceptions about the sport organisation, thereby affecting the degree to which volunteering for the organisation is attractive.

Additionally, volunteers can contribute to a sport organisation's public relations effort in two ways. The first derives from the fact that volunteers can themselves provide a useful basis for promoting stories about the sport organisation to the media. For example, in 2000 the British Olympic Association (BOA) partnered with Griffith University to design, implement and staff a volunteer program for the British Olympic Holding Camp prior to the Sydney Games. The story was covered by print and broadcast journalists. Both the BOA and Griffith University benefited from the coverage. Coverage of volunteer programs and the volunteers themselves can benefit the sport organisation, and also benefits the volunteer program as a whole. The second way that volunteers can assist the organisation's public relations is to help get stories to the public. In this capacity, volunteers become part of the overall public relations function.

The remainder of this chapter describes the ways by which sport organisation's public relations and its volunteer program can be interwoven. This chapter begin by considering the role of public relations in the recruitment and retention of volunteers and then move on to the ways by which volunteers can enhance the overall public relations program.

RECRUITING VOLUNTEERS

There is a substantial array of opportunities for people to volunteer their time to community organisations. Consequently, organisations compete to attract quality volunteers. Public relations plays a key role in helping sport organisations to make the volunteer opportunities they offer attractive (Ellis, 2002). This occurs in two ways: by shaping public perceptions of the sport organisation and by directly promoting the organisation's volunteer program.

The more significant and prestigious the organisation is perceived to be, the more desirable it becomes to be associated with it. The more talk there is about the sport organisation (whether that talk is positive or not) the more significant it appears to be, and talk is mobilised and sustained by stories that appear in local media (e.g. newspapers, magazines, television, radio, the Internet) about the sport organisation and/or its people. The more positive the talk, the more prestigious the organisation appears, and that can also be shaped by media.

Thus, the sport organisation's overall public relations effort plays a vital role in the overall volunteer program. The volunteer program depends on the quality of the overall public relations effort in order to make it attractive for people to volunteer. The organisation's public relations establishes the background conditions which make volunteering attractive (or unattractive). Consequently, those responsible for managing the volunteer program have an ongoing stake in the quality of the organisation's public relations and should make every effort to contribute wherever possible.

More significantly, the kinds of stories and messages that have been communicated to the public through the overall public relations program set the tone for each volunteer recruitment campaign. Any communications, whether through advertising or public relations, will capitalise upon what people already know or believe about the sport organisation. As a result, it is useful to review the stories and messages that have been communicated through the organisation's public relations in the months leading up to any effort to recruit volunteers.

Stories about the sport organisation during the time that volunteers are being recruited will be particularly important. This is particularly important for major sport events such as the Olympic Games and World Cup competitions. These events typically need 50,000 or more volunteers to fill a broad array of roles. Recruitment efforts begin more than a year prior to the event. As a result, volunteers may have to wait many months to hear the results of their application. Public relations can play a significant role in maintaining their enthusiasm over this time. Positive stories about the Organising

Committee and the event can remind potential volunteers of their initial attraction to volunteering. Volunteer-specific public relations can enhance this further. Social networking sites such as MySpace and Facebook are increasingly being used to build excitement and commitment amongst volunteers during the selection period. For example, the 2010 Vancouver Winter Olympic Games have at least one official Facebook group and several created and administered by the volunteers themselves. Volunteers (and potential volunteers) use the site to share their excitement. For example, one selected volunteer wrote:

just finished my creating team training too! i did it yesterday.. it was amazing,! im gonna be in charge of one of the NOC's.. any one else've been at that type of volunteering training? and i guess they select you by the way you behave there, or your enthusiasm.. who knows, at least I know that in my section of volunteers there's supposed to be 800 elected, and we are about 1000, so only 20% is going to be kicked out.

Others use the site to encourage those who have not yet been selected:

if you haven't received a call yet, don't lose hope – they need 25,000 volunteers for games-time. they do however look at your skills based on your application and area where you'd like to get involved (customer service, ceremonies, opening and closing, technology, etc). Also, they take your responses from the telephone interview they conduct before you get your invitation to the "creating team 2010" session. Be prepared to support your choices in the functional area you select. The questions they ask when you do the phone interview as well as at the orientation will determine if you are called back for a sport event. the sport event will give you a chance to shine for games time! Enjoy the experience at your sport event, meet tons of people get to know what you're going to be doing by 2010. ACCEPT WHATEVER POSITION THEY OFFER!

In addition to maintaining volunteers' interest in the organisation, past and current stories may suggest bases for appealing to volunteers. Reports about the sport organisation which make it appear significant or prestigious can be emphasised. Where appropriate, one or more specific details from a recent story can be noted to strengthen the link between the appeal for volunteers and what has recently been written about the organisation.

Public relations plays a vital role whenever appealing to recruit volunteers. The very fact that the sport organisation seeks volunteers can be the basis for a news story. There are many things the public will want to know and around which specific news stories can be created. For example, why are volunteers needed? What do volunteers enable that paid staff cannot? How does this help the sport organisation? How does it help the community? What work will volunteers be doing? How will they be trained? When will they work? What will be required of them? What will volunteers gain from the experience? What have past volunteers gained? Questions like these enable multiple stories to be created for the media.

As in any public relations effort, the key challenge is to make it all interesting to the public – even those who may have no desire to volunteer. Remember that reporters must entertain their audiences, as well as inform them. So, the public relations task when recruiting volunteers is to help reporters find an angle on the volunteer program that will appeal to their readers, listeners or viewers.

While volunteers are being recruited, it is also useful to keep the volunteer recruitment drive in the news. One story is not enough. Work with reporters to find ongoing things to report. There are a lot of possibilities, such as the status of the volunteer recruitment effort, new developments in the volunteer program or feature stories profiling interesting volunteers (old and new).

Volunteers come to the sport organisation for a variety of reasons (Dolcinar and Randle, 2007; Finkelstein, 2009), so profiles of volunteers should highlight an array of different benefits that they perceive themselves to be obtaining. In some cases, volunteers are seeking something that will specifically benefit themselves. For example, they may seek relevant work experience or training in a relevant skill. Others might want to expand their social networks or want to help a family member who benefits from the organisation. Others may be seeking a particular kind of experience. They might enjoy feeling that they are on the 'inside' of something important. They might feel that sport is a refreshing escape from their everyday world. Others may choose to volunteer because they value what the sport organisation contributes to those with whom it works or to the community as a whole.

The wide array of motivations for volunteering is important when creating or promoting feature stories about volunteers. Although volunteers are often popularly cast as altruists, many (usually most) volunteer for other reasons. In order to make volunteering attractive to as wide an array of potential volunteers as possible, stories should feature an array of different benefits that volunteers feel they are getting. Some stories might feature a volunteer who is excited about the skills being strengthened or obtained or a volunteer whose social networks have been enhanced by volunteering. Other stories might feature the quality of the immediate experience of volunteering – the sense of being on the inside or the refreshing escape from the mundane. There could also be stories about volunteers who are excited about the contribution their work makes to the sport organisation's clientele or community. By creating and publicising volunteer profiles that highlight different benefits from volunteering, the appeal of volunteering is widened.

Features like these are often popular with local media, particularly because they can be held and then reported on slow news days. This is not the case, however, with news about the volunteer program. On busy news days or when the news about the volunteer program is not sufficiently significant (to the media audience) to warrant a separate story, it could nonetheless be embedded elsewhere. For example, local sport columns are good places to embed a short paragraph or two. Similarly, the volunteer program and its recruitment efforts can be noted in news releases about other happenings in the sport organisation or they can be mentioned whenever the sport organisation hosts a news conference on other aspects of the program.

The recruitment effort can also be made newsworthy by creating news about it. Hiring an interesting new manager for volunteers or partnering with a local educational institution to train volunteers can each be basis for news releases and (depending on the profile of the manager or the institution) news conferences. Similarly, having volunteers to write letters to the paper, Blog or phone into local (call-in) talk shows to ask a question or say something about the volunteer program can create attention. Even a question or statement seemingly about another topic can create discussion. For example, 'Don't you think the impressive volunteer support for this event will impress tourists who come here?' Or, 'I made a lot of new friends when I volunteered to organize clinics for the sport club'.

In summary, volunteer recruitment builds upon the public profile that the sport organisation has built for itself through its public relations. Volunteer recruitment also provides an added context for public relations about the sport organisation. In particular, volunteer recruitment should be supported by a planned and coordinated public relations program specifically designed to promote recruitment of volunteers.

CASE STUDY 7.1: Special Olympics International

Special Olympics International, like many sport organisations, would not function without the hard work of their more than 750,000 volunteers. However, unlike some sport organisations, Special Olympics recognises that its volunteers are motivated by a wide range of potential benefits. They embed their communications with messages to appeal to multiple motives, such as enjoyment, skill mastery, professional networking, learning, transforming lives (both the athletes' and the volunteers'), the desire to help others and/or the community and interest in building one's own social network. This wide range of benefits ensures maximum appeal, thus attracting a large, diverse pool of potential volunteers. Further, volunteers and volunteer opportunities are featured elements of their public relations.

The website (http://www.specialolympics.org) includes photo displays of volunteers, links to volunteering, testimonials from volunteers, as well as stories about volunteers and their interactions with athletes. Media releases at local and regional levels often feature stories about volunteers. These stories create goodwill for the organisation and its events and often inspire others to get involved. Their volunteers are often changed by their experience with Special Olympics and offer emotional testimony about their experience. One volunteer explained her experience this way, 'The Special Olympics athletes and other people I have met along the way have shaped my life in such a dramatic way. I found strength in them that I could not discover in anyone else. As I helped them, they changed me.' Special Olympics volunteers also function in traditional public relations roles. They may take on a spokesperson role in the community, speak in schools, develop fundraising campaigns and public relations events and communicate with the media. In short, Special Olympics International is a leader in creating a symbiotic relationship between its volunteers and its public relations.

VOLUNTEER RETENTION

Sport organisations make an investment in their volunteers. Volunteers are not free. Training volunteers, rewarding volunteers, managing volunteers and providing support to volunteers each cost time and resources. Further, programs and events may depend on the services that volunteers provide. Consequently, retaining volunteers is vital (Wittich, 2002).

As in the case of recruitment, volunteer retention depends significantly on the sport organisation's overall public relations effort. The public climate for volunteering depends in large measure on the ways that the organisation is perceived. Volunteers prefer to work for organisations about which they are proud. Consequently, the organisation's ongoing public relations campaign matters a great deal to its volunteer program.

Clearly, then, the volunteer manager needs to monitor the ongoing public relations effort and the ways that the organisation is perceived in the community. This applies not merely during a sport season or during an event, but during the off-season and before an event has even taken place. The tasks of managing a sport program or putting on a sport event begin long before the sport's season or the event takes place. In fact, this is one of the times that volunteers are most crucial. Yet, it is also a time that the sport organisation's public relations effort may be slow or even inactive. News releases may not be forthcoming; the organisation's website may not be updated (particularly during the off-season); feature stories may not be promoted.

The off-season or pre-event period (particularly well in advance of an event) are challenging times to promote the sport organisation, but it is nonetheless vital that volunteers' enthusiasm for their work be maintained. Consequently, this is a particularly important time to find ways to promote the sport organisation. It is useful to brainstorm with staff and volunteers to identify important matters that might be made interesting to the public. Those can then be developed into news releases, feature story ideas, Blogs and Internet postings (the organisation's website should be updated regularly.) Milestones are a particularly appropriate basis for news stories, mentions in local sport columns or discussions on local talk radio programmes (particularly sport talk radio programmes). This is also an excellent time for feature stories about current and past volunteers. The kinds of stories used during volunteer recruitment are also relevant for volunteer retention, as ongoing stories about the sport organisation's volunteers can also help to raise morale by building the prestige associated with volunteering. As feature story ideas are forthcoming, the relevant media should be queried in order to solicit their interest in writing and publishing or broadcasting those stories. Particularly interesting or high-profile volunteers might themselves be promoted to appear on talk shows.

During a major sport event or a season of competition, much of the reporting has to do with things beyond the sport competition itself (Reinardy and Wanta, 2009). Reporters endeavour to provide colour through the sidebars and backgrounders that they write. Editors seek such stories to build reader, listener and viewer interest and to fill space. The volunteer program provides an ideal context for sidebars and backgrounders. Stories about the work that volunteers are doing, the contribution their work makes to the event or the season and the way the volunteer program works can each provide useful backgrounders. Similarly, feature stories about particular volunteer or groups of volunteers can provide useful sidebars.

News about the volunteer program can also be created as a means to foster volunteer retention. Given the importance of volunteers to sport organisations, most provide various forms of reward and recognition. Rewards and recognition (whether before or after the event or the season) can be useful means to create a sense that something newsworthy is happening. Too often, sport organisations limit their rewards and recognitions to private ceremonies or simple tangible gifts. In fact, rewards and recognitions can become news, especially when they are bestowed with some pomp and circumstance (and preferably with good photo opportunities). Even if the press does not attend an awards event, the sport organisation can create a story by taking pictures or video and by providing the information necessary for a news story (including a transcript if an audio or visual recording is being provided). This is how many such events find their way into local media.

Rewards and recognition ceremonies can be made even more attractive to media if they include a famous guest or speaker. A well-known athlete, entertainer or politician may make the event something that the media particularly wants to cover. Even if the guest or speaker becomes the focus of the story, this is also an opportunity to promote the volunteer program. Yet, regardless of whether there is someone high profile in attendance or not, positioning rewards and recognition as newsworthy enhances the prestige of volunteering and can help retain volunteers for the future.

In summary, the sport organisation's public relations program sets the tone for the climate within which programs to retain volunteers must be planned and organised. For this reason, the public relations program during off-season or pre-event periods are particularly important. The volunteer program and its volunteers each provide potential stories to flush out stories during those otherwise slow periods. During an event or a season, the volunteer program can be the basis for sidebars and backgrounders. The volunteer program's rewards and recognition systems can also be the basis for creating news about the volunteer program. Together, these public relations efforts help to foster an environment that is conducive to retaining volunteers.

USING VOLUNTEERS TO PROMOTE STORIES ABOUT THE SPORT ORGANISATION

So far, we have seen that the sport organisation's overall public relations effort plays a vital role in establishing the conditions under which volunteers are recruited and retained. We have also seen that the volunteer program can enable substantial numbers of stories in its own right. This aspect of the volunteer program also enables it to help promote the sport organisation.

Clearly, stories about the organisation's volunteer program and about its volunteers add profile to the sport organisation. So, just as it is useful to think about the ways that public relations can serve the volunteer program, it is also useful to consider means by which the volunteer program can serve the sport organisation's public relations. Of course, most of the techniques and opportunities described so far are as relevant to the sport organisation as they are to the volunteer program. However, there are additional means by which the sport organisation can make use of volunteers to extend its public relations.

One of the simplest means is to use volunteers to represent the organisation to the community (Hardy et al., 2006). Many sport organisations maintain a speakers bureau as a way to foster and strengthen connections with the community. Speakers can cover topics about the organisation itself, such as its history, operations or future plans. Speakers can also represent the organisation while giving talks to schools (e.g. stay-in-school talks), charities (talks having to do with important causes) or community organisations (e.g. anti-drug talks). These are often done by athletes or coaches because they are often well enough known to be popular with the public. Nevertheless, appropriately trained and prepared volunteers can also represent the organisation as public speakers. The volunteer's credibility can be enhanced if they are given a job title that sounds impressive. Alternatively, if the volunteer is already well known in the community for other reasons (e.g. they are a high-profile executive or public figure), then they will be an attractive speaker. The key objective is to recruit and train volunteers, in part, to represent the sport organisation publicly. Indeed, their presentations can themselves become occasions for additional news coverage that is favourable to the sport organisation.

A related technique is for the sport organisation to form a partnership with a particular cause or charity (Lachowetz and Gladden, 2003). This is known as 'cause-related marketing'. The sport organisation typically provides speakers, volunteers and incentive opportunities to support events designed to promote the charity, its cause and its fundraising. The sport organisation benefits from the partnership as a result of the added positive profile its partnership with the charity enables, as well as its consequent access to the charity's community networks. Cause-related marketing is another way that sport organisations make their value to the community visible and tangible. Volunteers play a vital role in cause-related marketing by undertaking tasks required to implement and maintain the relationship. Of course, their work for the partnership is itself a potential basis for positive stories about the sport organisation.

CASE STUDY 7.2: Football Fans Against Sexual Assault

In an unusual twist, football fans in Australia struck out on their own to create a grassroots, volunteer-led organisation called, 'Footy (now Football) Fans against Sexual Assault' (FFASA). The group began in 2004 in response to an increasing incidence in sexual assault allegations against elite players in two of the most popular football codes: the National Rugby League (NRL) and the Australian Football League (AFL). While the public relations efforts of the teams and players were focused on managing and minimising the attention focused on these incidents, FFASA was intent on change. Not by highlighting the bad behaviour of players, but by raising public awareness of the positive practices, role models and efforts by players, teams and leagues to acknowledge and prevent gender violence. Their main promotional tactic to achieve this goal took the form of the 'Purple Armband Games' (PAG).

PAG (www.purplearmband.org) are sport competitions in which the players wear purple armbands. According to FFASA:

> Purple Armband Games aim to make it socially acceptable for the silent majority of men and women to speak out against violent and abusive behaviors towards women. In sport, armbands are a symbol of grief and respect. Purple is the colour for women's rights. By donning a purple armband, the wearer: makes a statement of respect for women; acknowledges the grief caused by sexual assault; stands against gender violence and abuse.

The first teams to wear the purple armbands were the Women's State of Origin teams for Queensland and New South Wales and the NRL's Brisbane Broncos and Manly Sea Eagles. Since the first PAG in July of 2004, over 850 men's and women's teams at all levels and in a variety of sport have donned the armbands to support the initiative.

PAG at all levels of sport have been incorporated into the public relations efforts of a wide range of sport organisations. FFASA provides sample loudspeaker announcements to use during competitions and purple armband banners to be incorporated into clubs' websites. Stories about the PAG have appeared in local and regional news and have been published in club newsletters.

What began with a small group of fans now claims an online community of over 1100 members. These volunteers continue to work in and for sport organisations at all levels to publicise and build support for its cause. FFASA maintains a website, an email list and an online newsletter. Each is key to the success of their public relations efforts. For example, FFASA sent a newsletter to all members of its email list after the first PAG in the NRL (Dimitrov, 2008). The newsletter encouraged recipients to 'send a message of support to the teams. Tell them what this stance means to you as a footy fan, woman, parent or concerned person'. Hundreds of supportive emails were sent to the teams. In short, FFASA's efforts work. What began as a volunteer effort separate from the teams, leagues and athletes has now been embraced by those entities and incorporated into their own public relations. This is a win–win situation for all involved.

In summary, the volunteer program can enhance the sport organisation's relations with the public. Stories about the organisation's volunteer program enhance the reach and frequency of its media presence. Volunteers can also enrich the organisation's speaker's bureau, thereby enabling greater outreach to the community. Cause-related marketing, which may rely extensively on volunteers, also provides substantial opportunities for additional positive media coverage.

VOLUNTEERS IN PUBLIC RELATIONS

The favourable public profile enjoyed by most sport organisations does a great deal to facilitate effective public relations. Nevertheless, many sport organisations (particularly small event organisations and clubs competing outside top level leagues) do not enjoy substantial or significant media attention. Even many leading sport organisations do not fully exploit the array of media opportunities that are afforded to them. The problem is twofold. First, many sport organisations lack sufficient staff to undertake the kinds of intensive and creative public relations that would be required to create and then capitalise on media opportunities. Second, sport organisations often under-estimate their media potential and the work required to capitalise on that potential. Consequently, the staff time and energy devoted to media relations in sport organisations is often inadequate.

Volunteers can play a useful role by providing the staff time and energy required to undertake an adequate public relations campaign. The tasks of planning and executing media relations can be supported or independently executed by volunteers. In fact, many sport organisations assign media relations to volunteers. However, the result is not always what was desired.

Public relations is a skilled activity. Amongst the many skills a practitioner needs to have are skills at: planning and managing stories, querying editors, working with reporters, nurturing relations with community organisations, creating and disseminating news releases and fact sheets, running news conferences, preparing and publishing media guides, creating and maintaining an effective website, building and updating files, managing media at events, etc. Unless the volunteer has a media or public relations background, it is unlikely that they come to the organisation with any of these skills. Even if they have such a background, they may lack specific required skills. From the outside, public relations for sport may look easy, but that appearance is deceptive. The job requires appropriate training and experience.

For that reason, it is not appropriate simply to assign one or more volunteers to the public relations function (cf. Fisher and Cole, 1993). The first task required is to assess the volunteer's skills, particularly writing and speaking skills, as well as the volunteer's knowledge of media operations and the various tasks required in public relations. Some volunteers may simply lack the requisite communication skills for any but the most mundane tasks. Those whose communication skills warrant it can then be trained for the job.

Journalists, editors and producers may be somewhat forgiving of a volunteer's lack of polish, but only to a limited degree and for a very short period of time. Journalists face deadlines and the demands of editors and their public. They do not have time, energy or inclination to accommodate the naïve missteps of well-intentioned volunteers. Consequently, the volunteer's training needs to cover the procedures and skills required to do whatever tasks will be required to complete the jobs to which they have been assigned.

This is no small task. These days, public relations professionals undergo a substantial volume of specialist training. Journalists and administrators of community organisations have come to expect a degree of professional acumen from those with whom they deal. Volunteers who do the sport organisation's public relations work must be trained sufficiently to execute their tasks with a degree of professionalism. No volunteer (unless already a trained public relations professional) should be assigned to deliver or support the sport organisation's public relations unless the organisation has arranged for them to be trained to do so.

The curriculum required to provide that training will depend to some degree on the context and needs of the sport organisation. Nevertheless, the training needs to be designed by persons with suitable expertise. In some cases, it may serve the sport organisation's interests to invest the resources required to have a training package developed. On the other hand, the need to train might itself be the basis for recruiting volunteers. Local practitioners and/or academics with the relevant expertise might be recruited to design and deliver the training necessary. The key point to bear in mind is that the sport organisation's public relations is so important that only adequately trained and skilled personnel (even if they are volunteers) should be assigned to the task.

The volunteers who support or independently deliver the sport organisation's public relations must be managed and evaluated. The function is too important to leave to chance. If there is not a public relations officer on paid staff to handle the management of the volunteers, then an employee from elsewhere in the organisation who is familiar with public relations basics should be assigned that role. The expectations and lines of communication for the volunteer need to be established, and a suitable job description should be formulated and agreed, including expectations for relations between the volunteer and paid staff. In particular, procedures should be put into place to coordinate the messages being created and sent by volunteers such that they are consistent with the goals and overall marketing objectives of the organisation. Finally, methods and procedures for evaluating the volunteer's performance need to be spelled out and then implemented.

There is an added risk here. Volunteers are not paid staff. They have volunteered their leisure time to work for the sport organisation. Yet, when they play a role in the sport organisation's public relations, they can have a pivotal impact on the organisation's relations with the public. For that reason, volunteers who work in public relations must be held to a standard comparable to that of professional staff who would be working in the same job. Some volunteers may welcome that responsibility; others might find it to be incompatible with the quality of volunteer experience they seek. Consequently, this is a matter for review and frank discussion with the volunteer as selection, training and job assignment proceed.

In summary, in order to be effective, the sport organisation's public relations effort often requires more staff support than the organisation can afford. Volunteers can fill the gap by providing public relations services. However, the tasks of public relations require skilled planning and execution. Consequently, when a sport organisation seeks to support its public relations function with volunteers, thoroughly planned procedures must be put into place to select appropriate volunteers, train them adequately, manage them and evaluate their performance.

MAKING IT PAY

We have seen that the relationship between the sport organisation's public relations and its volunteer programs should be a symbiotic one. The challenge is to enable the symbiosis. In order to do so, the public relations program and all other marketing initiatives need to send complementary messages. The image that the organisation communicates to the public should be consistent, whether it comes from advertising, sales, customer service or public relations. This is called 'integrated marketing communications', and it can optimise the impact that public relations has on the sport organisation's brand equity.

The challenge is that each facet of contact with the public is executed by different individuals often from different departments of the sport organisation. Integrating the marketing communications across individuals executing different functions is challenging even when all are paid staff operating within the same department. However, as the functions become more substantially dispersed, the coordination challenge becomes all-the-more challenging. When some (or all) of the individuals who contact the media or the public are volunteers, the challenge is amplified.

In order for volunteers to contribute to the overall integration of marketing communications, they need to understand the image that the sport organisation seeks to portray. Volunteers are often outside the channels of communication directed at paid staff, and their position in the organisation can be less well-established precisely because they are volunteers rather than paid staff. Consequently, they need to be made aware of the overall objectives of the organisation's marketing communications, as well as the position it seeks to establish in the public mind. This requires that they be included in relevant communications that have been directed to paid staff, and it requires that training of volunteers familiarise them with the organisation's overall communication objectives.

The relations between volunteers and paid staff are also important in this regard. It is not uncommon for there to be a palpable status difference between volunteers and paid staff. This can affect morale and volunteers' execution of their responsibilities. In so doing, it can undermine the public relations objectives associated with volunteers' services to the public and to media. Consequently, it is useful for training of paid and volunteer staff to address the expected responsibilities of staff and volunteers – not merely to the organisation, but also when working together.

In summary, volunteers must communicate and demonstrate values and information that are consistent with the sport organisation's overall values and objectives. This requires that the training of volunteers covers those values and objectives and that volunteers be included in communications to paid staff that address, reinforce or modify those values and objectives. Training and management of volunteers and paid staff should also clarify the nature of working relationships that are expected between volunteers and staff.

SUMMARY

Public relations can play a significant role in attracting and retaining volunteers in sport. Public perceptions of a sport organisation as significant, prestigious and worthwhile can stimulate a desire to volunteer as a way of associating oneself with an organisation. A well-crafted image can make it easier to recruit new volunteers and to solidify the commitment of existing volunteers. Further, a successful volunteer management system or even a recruitment campaign can provide newsworthy publicity for a sport organisation, particularly during periods when there is little to report about the sport itself. Lastly, volunteers can be trained to serve the public relations function of a sport organisation, yet this is not without challenges.

Sport organisations' volunteer programs are too often under-resourced, and too often relegated to positions of low status and poor influence within the organisation. Yet most sport organisations could not succeed without the support of volunteers. Similarly, sport organisations too often under-resource the public relations function and relegate it to low status and influence. Yet, public relations plays a core role in moulding the public's perceptions and consequent support of the sport organisation. The most successful sport organisations do not make these mistakes. When public relations and volunteer programs are given pride of place and are constructed to be synergetic, the sport organisation will thrive.

KEY TERMS

Altruistic   The performance of an act that is beneficial to others for no personal benefit to oneself. Volunteers who donate their time with no expectation of personal benefit are said to be altruistic.

Cause-related Marketing   A commercial activity by which business and charities or causes form a partnership with each other to market an image, product or service for mutual benefit (BITC/Research International, 2004).

Integrated Marketing Communications   An approach that seeks to have all of an organisation's marketing and promotional activities coordinated such that they project a consistent, unified image to its publics. It requires centralised messaging to ensure that everything an organisation says and does communicates a common theme and positioning.

Motivation   The set of reasons that determines one's willingness to engage in a particular behaviour such as volunteering.

Recruitment   The process of attracting, screening and selecting individuals for a vacancy in a volunteer-based sport organisation or event.

Retention   The ability to keep volunteers within an organisation.

Sidebar   A term for information placed adjacent to an article in a printed or web publication. A sidebar is graphically distinct from the article, but is contextually related.

DISCUSSION QUESTIONS

1. Identify the potential benefits that your sport organisation or event can offer to potential volunteers. Use two to three key benefits to develop a core message that can be used to recruit volunteers for your organisation or event. Design a public relations campaign based on your core message.

2. Use a social networking site to search for sport volunteer groups. Analyse the effectiveness of the site for attracting and retaining volunteers. Analyse its effectiveness in creating or maintaining a positive image for

the sport organisation or event. What elements can be created or enhanced by the organisation? Which are dependent on volunteers themselves? What recommendations would you make to the sport organisation to take advantage of the site? Why?

3. Develop a story idea based on some aspect of the volunteer program (an interesting volunteer, a milestone in the program, the need for volunteers, etc.). To whom will you pitch the story? Why would the reporter be interested? How will you tailor your pitch to the specific reporter/publication/media?

4. Outline a volunteer training program that will prepare volunteers to assist with the public relations efforts of a sport organisation.

GUIDED READING

Working with Volunteers in Sport (2006) by Graham Cuskelly, Russell Hoye, and Christopher Auld is a good introduction to managing volunteers in sport contexts ranging from local clubs to national sport organisations and major events such as the Olympic Games. The text is predominantly Australian, but provides relevant examples from throughout the world.

The article, Sport Volunteers: Research Agenda and Application (1998) by B. Christine Green and Laurence Chalip published in Sport Marketing Quarterly discusses the recruitment and retention of volunteers as a marketing task. The efficacy of marketing strategies to attract new volunteers and keep existing volunteers is examined. Examples are included.

RECOMMENDED WEBSITES

Volunteerism Worldwide Hub – <http://www.worldvolunteerweb.org/>.
Volunteering in Australia – <http://www.ausport.gov.au/participating/volunteers>.
Special Olympics – <http://www.specialolympics.org/volunteers.aspx>.

REFERENCES

BITC/Research International, 2004. Brand Benefits. Research International, London.

Dimitrov, R., 2008. Gender violence, fan activism and public relations in sport: the case of "Footy Fans Against Sexual Assault". Public Relations Review 34, 90–98.

Dolcinar, S., Randle, M., 2007. What motivates which volunteers? Psychographic heterogeneity among volunteers in Australia. Voluntas: International Journal of Voluntary and Nonprofit Organizations 18, 135–155.

Ellis, S.J., 2002. The Volunteer Recruitment (and Membership Development) Book, third ed. Energize, Philadelphia, PA.

Favorito, J., 2007. Sport Publicity: A Practical Approach. Butterworth-Heineman, Burlington, MA.

Finkelstein, M.A., 2009. Intrinsic vs. extrinsic motivational orientations and the volunteer process. Personality and Individual Differences 46, 653–658.

Fisher, J.C., Cole, K.M., 1993. Leadership and Management of Volunteer Programs: A Guide for Volunteer Administrators. Jossey-Bass, San Francisco, CA.

Hardy, S., Barcelona, R., Hickox, R., Lazaro, C., 2006. Image isn't everything. Athletic Business 30 (5), 50–56.

Lachowetz, T., Gladden, J., 2003. A framework for understanding cause-related marketing programs. International Journal of Sport Marketing and Sponsorship 4, 313–333.

Reinardy, S., Wanta, W., 2009. The Essentials of Sport Writing and Reporting. Routledge, New York.

Wittich, B., 2002. Keep Those Volunteers Around. Knowledge Transfer, Fullerton, CA.

CHAPTER 8

Crisis Communication and Sport Public Relations

Allan Edwards, Wayne Usher
Griffith University

Learning Outcomes

Upon completion of this chapter the reader should be able to:

- Define crisis management
- Describe the trends within crisis management research
- Discuss the application of crisis communications strategies within a sport environment
- Understand the need to develop sport-specific approaches to crises

CHAPTER OVERVIEW

Much has been written regarding crisis management (Fearn-Banks, 1994; Gonzalez-Herrero and Pratt, 1995) and public relations (Cutlip et al., 2000; Fearn-Banks, 1994; Gonzalez-Herrero and Pratt, 1995). Most of the crisis management literature deals with case studies on how an organisation handled a crisis and what lessons were learned from the situation, yet few specifically deal with sport crises (Hopwood, 2005). The first major crisis in modern sport occurred in 1919 in US Major League Baseball, close to 50 years after its establishment in 1871. Eight players on the Chicago White Sox conspired with gamblers to throw the World Series; this crisis would go on to be known as 'the Black Sox' scandal. Despite crises in sport existing for almost a century it is only recently that crisis management has emerged as an important area of sport public relations. A review of the current literature reveals that little attention has been directed towards addressing how a sporting organisation should manage a crisis. Therefore, this chapter examines the concept of crisis management and crisis communication within sport public relations and within a wider sporting organisational context.

CRISIS MANAGEMENT

Kreps (1986) defines crisis management as the use of public relations to minimise harm to the organisation in emergency situations that could cause the organisation irreparable damage. A more elaborate definition from a multi-disciplinary perspective is given by Pearson and Clair (1998) as the systematic attempt by organisational members with external stakeholders to avert crises or to effectively manage those that do occur. Crisis management intersects with several disciplines, such as psychology, mass media, communications, public policy, reputation (image) management, risk management, public relations, strategic management, ethical discourse, relationship management, stakeholder management and international relations. According to Del Rio (2007) the crisis management literature falls into two main categories:

1. Dealing with crisis management from a 'naturalist perspective' (crises are products of social and cultural interactions).
2. Dealing with crisis management from a 'positivist perspective' (theories can be structured and tested empirically).

These categories shall now be briefly discussed.

NATURALIST PERSPECTIVE

Loosemore (1999) says that a naturalistic approach considers that reality is constructed and maintained over time by people and that it does not exist in a rigid, stable sense. Hearit and Courthright (2003) see crises as dynamic social constructions that are both created and resolved terminologically, based on the assumption that all perspectives of reality, from scientific discourse to crisis communication, are socially constructed through communication. From this perspective, assessment of an event as a crisis is jointly constructed by the participation of multiple actors in the social exchange, be they organisations, media, special interest groups or consumers – all of whom offer discourse as the instrument by which they participate.

A separate arm of the naturalistic literature deals with the issue of organisational sense-making. Weick (1993) argues that sense-making is about such things as placement of items into frameworks, comprehending, redressing surprise, constructing meaning, interacting in pursuit of mutual understanding and patterning. Weick adds that the basic idea of sense-making in organisations is that reality is an ongoing accomplishment that emerges from efforts to create order and make retrospective sense of what has occurred. Weick's analysis is concerned primarily with the identification of the sources and structures of organisational resilience.

In summary, the naturalist approach helps us to understand the environment, context, processes and social interactions that may take place during a crisis event.

POSITIVIST PERSPECTIVE

The crisis management positivist approach has been examined from a number of perspectives and has identified six approaches to crisis management, these being: (1) risk management approach, (2) governance approach, (3) stakeholders' approach, (4) public relations approach, (5) reputation management approach and (6) combined crisis management approach (Loosemore, 1999). An overview of some of these approaches is presented and discussed below.

Risk management approach

Risk management focuses on the importance of identifying and monitoring factors that may generate a crisis. Risk management models also help organisations to identify media and communications management strategies to alleviate the impact of a crisis event.

Risk communication is another branch of risk management where there have been a number of studies aimed at linking risk and crisis management. Chess (2001) sees risk communication as a means to increase legitimacy after a crisis. In summary, the risk management approach offers a number of solid strategies to prevent a crisis.

Table 8.1	Four Approaches to Public Relations and Managing Crisis
Approach	**Summary**
1. Crisis response strategies	The recent literature on crisis management tends to combine a positivist approach shaped by naturalist assumptions like limiting research results to cultural and social settings (Taylor, 2000).
2. Reputation management approach	Reputation management is a public relations practice used to enhance or maintain an organisation or brand image (Harris, 1998). Public relations departments that practice reputation management are there to build or maintain a positive image for an organisation (Fearn-Banks, 1996; Harris, 1998).
3. Media crisis management	Crisis communications is the actual verbal and written communication between the organisation and the publics prior, during and after management of a crisis. The communications are designed to enhance the organisation's image and minimise the damage from the negative occurrence (Fearn-Banks, 1994).
4. Planning for crisis	Planning for crisis involves identification and analysis of strategies that prevent crises events ever occurring.

Public relations approach

In relation to crisis management, public relations scholars have focused traditionally on four areas (Table 8.1), these being: (1) crisis response strategies (broadly known as crisis communication), (2) reputation management approach, (3) media crisis management and (4) planning for crisis.

PUBLICS

An important key in any crisis communication situation therefore is 'the identification, monitoring, and analysis of trends in key publics' opinions that can mature into public policy and regulative or legislative constraints' (Seeger et al., 2001, p. 156). As has been previously discussed in previous chapters, publics are essentially the groups of people who can have an effect upon or are affected by an organisation. Publics are responsible, whether knowingly or not, for granting legitimacy to an organisation and, thus, make an organisation dependent upon the approval of each given category of publics (Metzler, 2002). Metzler identified the four categories of publics that an organisation must keep in mind. The first category is the 'enabling publics', which control allocations of authority and resources and offer regulatory functions. The second category is the 'functional publics', which supply inputs to and receive outputs from the corporation. The third category is the 'normative publics', which incorporate norms for the corporation and represent publics that share similar interests with the corporation. The fourth category is the 'diffused publics', which reflect unorganised publics who may be subject to the consequences of the corporation's activities and 'general publics'.

In general, but even more so during a crisis, an organisation has goals, interests and agendas. The same can be said of publics. This fact can 'guide the discourse toward certain issues and away from others' (Metzler, 2002, p. 322). For example, a public might be trying to maintain or enhance its own legitimacy, might have other agendas that it is trying to further through the dispute or might need the approval of one public to enhance its efforts with another. An example of this is provided in the Broncos Rugby League Club case study which follows.

CASE STUDY 8.1: Brisbane Broncos Rugby League Club

In August 2008 the Australian Rugby League faced a crisis when the Brisbane Broncos, one of the best known teams in the National Rugby League (NRL) competition, were embroiled in a series of alcohol-fuelled crises. Three players came under police investigation for alleged sexual assault and phone videotaping of a sexual encounter in a toilet at a Brisbane nightclub. Days later, it was revealed that the team (and Australian) captain had been reported to police for assault at another nightclub.

In response to the controversy, the Broncos chief executive Bruno Cullen appeared to appease the publics who felt concern about the image of the team. In response to this public pressure he held an emergency meeting with staff and team coach and leaked his club's new anti-alcohol guidelines to the major Brisbane newspaper, 'The Courier-Mail'. Cullen's decision appeared to be designed to appease governing agencies (enabling publics), the press (functional publics), the fans (normative publics) and the general public (diffused publics). The club also used diversion similar to that described by Bruce and Tini (2008). While not condoning the behaviour of the players, the club linked their behaviour to the wider societal issues of drink culture in Australian society. In this way the Broncos attempted to indicate that alcohol problems at the club were symptomatic of society and that because society had failed to curb alcohol abuse the club would take responsibility to ensure that policies were put in place to protect both the players and image of the club. The Murdoch media that have a controlling influence on the NRL competition came out in support of the Broncos stance. The success of diversion as a crisis strategy in this case supports the argument that sport public relations could focus on building quality relationships with key publics rather than concentrate on the technical communication practices which are frequently utilised in non-sport crises (Hopwood, 2005; Ledingham, 2006).

MAIN TYPES OF CRISIS COMMUNICATIONS STRATEGIES

The main types of general crisis communications strategies that have been areas of inquiry are 'apologia' and 'image repair discourse theory'. These strategies shall now be discussed.

Apologia

Apologia seeks to defend an organisation's or an individual's alleged offensive actions while re-establishing organisational legitimacy. In cases of organisational or individual transgressions, the accused typically use apologia. Hearit (1999, p. 300) states that ritual is at the root of why organisations or individuals issue apologia, as 'doing so fulfils public expectations along with completing the cycle of charge, guilt and restoration'. Apologia does not involve an actual apology, but rather, a defence (Hearit, 1996). It defends behaviour and denies accusations of wrongdoing, followed by attempting to differentiate the organisation or individual from the charges. Hearit (1996) defines three categories of apologia strategies that are commonly used: (1) 'mortification', which is an admission of guilt; (2) 'victimage', which is essentially scapegoating in order to direct the blame elsewhere and (3) 'transcendence', which entails defending one's actions through appearing to be morally above reproach.

Hearit (1996) also examined a form of apologia, 'counter kategoria-apologia', whereby organisations use disassociation and wage counterattacks on their accuser(s). The aim of disassociation is to separate an accused organisation or individual from charges and claim that the charges are but an appearance and do not represent reality. 'Counter kategoria-apologia' is made up of three approaches: focusing on other issues, wherein a statement such as 'the real travesty here is …' might be made (this approach is seen to validate notions of guilt); challenging the validity of charges and seeks to redefine, wherein a statement such as 'the charges are groundless and those who have factual knowledge of the case know this' and challenging the ethics of the accuser (Hearit, 1996).

Image repair discourse theory

Benoit (1997) is the originator of the 'image repair discourse theory'. This theory is predicated on the fact that image is essential to organisations and individuals. Once an organisation is held responsible for an act that is viewed to be offensive, the need for image restoration exists. It makes no difference whether or not the accused is actually responsible. All that matters is that publics view the accused as responsible. Five strategies make up the rhetoric or image repair discourse and each of these strategies has a set of positions within them. The first strategy is denial, which consists of simple denial (the act did not occur or the accused did not commit it) and blame shifting (identifies the real culprit). The second strategy is evasion of responsibility, which consists of provocation (responding to an earlier offence), defeasibility (the organisation had no control over the act), accident (the accused had no intent for the act to occur) and good intentions (the good intentions of the accused went bad). The third strategy is that of reducing offensiveness, which consists of bolstering (discusses positive attributes of the accused to offset offensiveness), minimisation (suggests that severity of the act was exaggerated), differentiation (puts act of accused in context with worse acts perpetrated by others in the past to argue that it pales in comparison), transcendence (puts act of accused in a broader moral context so as to make it appear as though ends justify means), attacking accusers (undermines accuser's credibility) and compensation (accused provides a form of remuneration for victim). The fourth strategy is a corrective action, which repairs damage caused by the offensive act and proposes steps to ensure that the act will not happen again. The fifth and final strategy is mortification, which communicates responsibility for the offensive act, an apology is made and forgiveness is asked for (Benoit, 1997).

SPORT PUBLIC RELATIONS APPROACHES

Frederick (2007) examined the media coverage of the brawl that occurred between the Indianapolis Pacers and the Detroit Pistons on the night of November 19, 2004, at the Palace of Auburn Hills in Auburn Hills, MI, USA. Video of the brawl was replayed numerous times on television in the days that followed, so that the brawl became a 'media event'.

Most journalists adopted NBA commissioner David Stern's framing of the brawl. Stern placed some of the blame on the fans, but the majority of the blame on the Indianapolis Pacer players, and specifically, on player Ron Artest, who received a season-long suspension. Frederick (2007) proposed that Stern's decision to deal such a severe punishment to Artest appeared to be designed to appease white corporate sponsors and white audiences, who began to feel threatened by the hip-hop culture the league once embraced.

Churchill (2006, p. 6) suggests that recent times have seen 'an upward spiralling, and almost chaotic, trend in player-related incidents and legal troubles' and that these incidents have 'made many fans upset at the NFL for its lack of control and subsequent negative image'. He suggested that public relations practitioners for the NFL, individual teams and the Associated

Press all play a role in branding the NFL's image. As a consequence methods of reporting these negative occurrences from each team's public relations department have had an effect on how fans perceive the NFL. He added that not everyone gets news from the same source. New technologies such as Internet, digital television, satellite radio and older media such as radio and print continually feed information to the public. These new and older methods of communication are as influential towards opinion formation as the message itself. He found that information about bad news or controversial issues with players from all or some of these sources was leading to the public formation of negative opinion concerning the NFL and its image of a family sport and pastime.

Gonzalez-Herrero and Pratt's (1996) model has been recently studied as an approach that could be utilised in sport public relations to deal with sport-related crises, and this model will now be discussed.

GONZALEZ-HERRERO AND PRATT: CRISIS MANAGEMENT MODEL

Gonzalez-Herrero and Pratt's (1996) 'Integrated Symmetrical Model for Crisis Communications Management' identifies that a crisis has four distinct phases through which it may progress. These four phases are described by Gonzalez-Herrero and Pratt (1996) as a 'crisis's biological life cycle'; displaying such growth phases as (1) birth, (2) growth, (3) maturity and (4) death. With proper intervention or management, "a crisis can be aborted, never grow to maturity or anything in between" (Gonzalez-Herrero and Pratt, 1996). The aim of interventional strategies should be to shorten the life expectancy of any crisis (by way of avoiding negative media coverage or its recurrence) and 'to engage in reputation-enhancing, socially responsible activities' (Gonzalez-Herrero and Pratt, 1996, p. 25).

The three underlying principles that are required for the model to be effective are identified as being: (1) issues management, (2) planning–prevention and (3) implementation. Gonzalez-Herrero and Pratt (1996) also state that research plays a vital role in every phase of the crisis management model and should be aimed at determining its publics' attitudes towards issues or situations. With this knowledge, the organisation may better tailor its course of action in an attempt to shorten the crisis' life expectancy.

Phase one: issues management

Throughout this phase the organisation identifies any potential issue or crisis and aims to deter its onset (Gonzalez-Herrero and Pratt, 1996). This is achieved by scrutinising the immediate environment for any public trends or for effects on competitors, which may in turn affect the organisation. Strategies include collecting and analysing data in an attempt to prevent or redirect a crisis before it can take place.

Phase two: planning–prevention

Gonzalez-Herrero and Pratt (1996) conceptualise the planning–prevention phase as an organisation recognising that a crisis is about to take place or that an issue might change quickly with intensity. This phase is the beginning of a crisis that takes an organisation by surprise. The recognised crisis has gone beyond management and thus demands a proactive policy to be set into motion. In addition, management needs to assess the 'dimensions of the problem, degree of control the organisation has over the situation and the options the company can choose from in developing a specific crisis plan' (p. 28).

Gonzalez-Herrero and Pratt (1996) indicate that there are four identifiable strategies which need to be taken into consideration when a crisis has entered into the planning–prevention phase, these being (1) the reanalysing of the organisation's relationships with its stakeholders, (2) preparing a contingency plan, designating members to a crisis management team, (3) identifying the company spokesperson and determining the message and (4) targeting media outlets needed to implement the plan. These 'pre-crisis strategies' either tend to identify and analyse strategies that prevent crises events ever occurring or tend to analyse specific type/s of organisations that seem to own/develop/have certain characteristics that help them to cope better in crisis situations.

Phase three: the crisis

During this third phase, Gonzalez-Herrero and Pratt (1996) maintain that the organisation attempts to prevent negative publicity, while communicating corrective actions the organisation is taking to handle the situation. Simplified, the third phase involves the company's response to 'The Crisis'. In addition, company messages and strategies should be directed at affected stakeholders and third-party support, from an expert, should be obtained and an internal communications plan should be implemented.

Kauffman (2005) states that effective crisis communication is needed if a situation is to be defused or eliminated. Consequently, if done correctly, it can sometimes bring an organisation a more positive reputation than before the crisis occurred (Kauffman, 2005). However, if an organisation fails to respond to a crisis in the correct manner, a bad situation can be made worse. Arpan and Pompper (2003, p. 293) suggest that 'tell it all and tell it fast is the general rule for all crises'. The crisis response strategies focus mainly on the development and framing of messages to the stakeholders including internal staff (Coombs and Holladay, 2001), timing response strategies, a combination of message development and the most efficient implementation of time (Gonzalez-Herrero and Pratt 1996; Lagadec, 1993).

Coombs (1996) suggests that the following strategies should be used when dealing with the media and when discussing crises:

1. Tell the story: start early, repeat it often and be consistent. Define messages concisely. Plan to communicate key messages first.
2. Avoid speculation.
3. Improve the message as more information becomes available; be open-minded and responsive to new information.
4. Avoid stonewalling or resorting to 'no comment' responses – the truth will eventually come out.
5. Never make comments 'off the record'; assume everything will be used. Avoid giving your personal opinion.
6. Keep calm; focus on the issues and avoid taking questions personally or becoming emotional.
7. Tell the truth. Admit mistakes and move on.
8. Strive for proactive responses. Turn negatives into positives; try to neutralise a hostile situation.
9. Use language that shows you care and demonstrates you are trying to put the matter right.
10. Respond quickly to media requests.
11. Speak in sound bites. Speak in short, simple sentences that are believable, and organise your message in a succinct and provable manner.
12. Be aware of verbal and non-verbal communication. Maintain eye contact and always be aware of your body language.

Phase four: the post-crisis

Following a crisis, the organisation needs to evaluate the crisis plan's effectiveness; incorporating feedback to improve it for future crises while also developing a communications strategy to undo the damage caused by the crisis (Gonzalez-Herrero and Pratt, 1996). To determine if the level of crisis management/plan has been effective, the organisation needs to monitor its multiple publics' general perceptions and feelings about the crisis and the organisation as a whole. Fundamentally, the organisation needs to continue to inform the media of the status of the situation until it has completely subsided.

Gonzalez-Herrero and Pratt (1996) believe that public relations practitioners should practice reputation management as a type of preventative public relations, so that a crisis will be minimised when it does occur. Gonzalez-Herrero and Pratt agreed that internal preventative strategies should be developed and maintained if organisations are to effectively manage crises and implement the above-mentioned crisis management strategies. They suggest that as part of crisis management, organisations should be practicing reputation management on a continuous and ongoing basis.

CASE STUDY 8.2: Professional Sport Leagues: USA

In a comparative historical analysis of three major professional sport leagues, Oakes (2006) examined how Major League Baseball (MLB), the National Basketball Association (NBA) and the National Football League (NFL) use crisis communications strategies to handle the threats to their organisational legitimacy that transpire when a crisis occurs. Oakes found that there were two factors that dictated crisis communications strategies used by each party. The first factor was Metzler's (2002) four publics for whom each message or action was intended – governing agencies (enabling publics), the press (functional publics), the fans (normative publics) and the general public (diffused publics). The second factor was the restraint of risk, which involves the conflicting mindsets of public relations, which seeks to establish organisational credibility, and the law, which seeks to establish organisational liability.

Oakes (2006) examined three major crises between 2000 and 2005. In 2005, Rafael Palmeiro of Major League Baseball's (MLB) Baltimore Orioles tested positive for anabolic steroids after an impassioned testimony before a House Government Reform Committee investigating steroids in professional sport just 5 months prior. In 2003, Kobe Bryant, of the National Basketball Association's (NBA) Los Angeles Lakers, was accused of raping an employee of a hotel where he was staying in Eagle, CO, USA. In 2000, Ray Lewis, of the National Football League's (the NFL) Baltimore Ravens, was accused of murder after leaving a Super Bowl party in Atlanta, GA, USA. These crises posed problems not only for the individuals who caused them, but also for the organisations of which they are members.

Using Metzler's (2002) four publics (enabling, functional, normative and diffused publics) approach he identified: regulatory and/or governing agencies (enabling publics), the press (functional publics), the fans (normative publics) and the general public (diffused publics). Oakes (2006) suggests that each league was indebted to enabling publics. For instance, MLB did not deal with its steroid problem so Congress, in order to save baseball from itself subpoenaed players and executives and threatened to take over the sport if the MLB did not do the right thing.

Once an organisation is publicly viewed as responsible for an act that is offensive, the need for image restoration exists. Responsibility for an offensive act need not be proven, as public perception is all that matters. Thus, the leagues used image repair discourse in the form of corrective action, in both words and deeds. Commissioner Bud Selig, on behalf of MLB, proposed a tougher steroid policy and then acted upon that proposition at the end of the season. Commissioner Paul Tagliabue also spoke of the fact that the NFL's policy on violent crime had become stricter. However, the NBA made no comments regarding any

Continued

corrective action that was going to occur. In fact, the NBA challenged the notion that corrective action needed to occur. The NBA used counter kategoria-apologia in order to challenge the validity of the charges being made about the culture of sexual assault within the NBA and the perception that nothing was being done about it.

In the context of the teams within each league, the enabling public was the league to which they belonged. Teams were careful of what they communicated to each league because each league could have penalised each team for its actions, and also its words. It was all the more important for each team to say the right thing at the right time. Each team employed the strategy of 'apologia' in the form of bolstering. This strategy was used across the board at the onset of each crisis, as teams spoke of each player's shining reputation throughout the past in order to strengthen their present and future image.

For each of the players, the enabling publics were both their team and the league in which they played, but they also had legal systems to worry about. Bryant and Lewis were also scrutinised by enabling publics that consisted of the police and court systems. As a result, they all used the strategy of 'image repair discourse' in the form of a simple denial and evasion of responsibility for the charges brought against them. However, Palmeiro and Bryant also used 'apologia' in the form of mortification, they made an admission of guilt and asked for forgiveness. Apologia was used by Palmeiro and Bryant because it carried out the expectations of enabling publics in that both players took some level of responsibility for their actions by completing the cycle of charge, guilt and restoration.

Oakes (2006) concluded that the cases of Rafael Palmeiro, Kobe Bryant and Ray Lewis suggest that the most important crisis communication strategy of all is truth. The lack of truth caused each crisis to branch out and sprout new issues other than those in existence at the onset.

SUMMARY

Crisis sport public relations is a new and evolving concept within sport. In relation to crisis management, public relations scholars have focused traditionally on four areas (Table 8.1), these being: (1) crisis response strategies (broadly known as crisis communication), (2) reputation management approach, (3) media crisis management and (4) planning for crisis. The main types of general crisis communications strategies that have been areas of inquiry are 'apologia' and 'image repair discourse theory.' It is proposed that Gonzalez-Herrero and Pratt's (1996) 'Integrated Symmetrical Model for Crisis-Communications Management' may provide a starting point for crisis management within the sport context. It is argued nevertheless that to effectively and professionally manage sport crises we need to generate new theoretical models appropriate to the sport context. Case study analysis of sport crises responses provides an initial approach, which could inform these new models. Much more work in this vital area of sport public relations and communication is required.

KEY TERMS

Apologia   Seeks to defend an organisation's or an individual's alleged offensive actions while re-establishing organisational legitimacy.

Crisis Management   The use of public relations to minimise harm to the organisation in emergency situations that could cause the organisation irreparable damage (Kreps, 1986).

Image Repair Theory   Is based on the assumption that maintaining good public image is essential to sport organisations and individuals (Benoit, 1997).

Naturalist Perspective   Considers that reality is constructed and maintained over time by people and that it does not exist in a rigid, stable sense (Loosemore, 1999).

Positivist Perspective   A view that sees reality as an inert amalgam of facts, which can be released by the right methodology (Loosemore, 1999).

Publics   Are essentially the groups of people who can have an effect upon or are affected by an organisation. Publics are responsible, whether knowingly or not, for granting legitimacy to an organisation and, thus, make an organisation dependent upon the approval of each given category of publics (Metzler, 2002).

DISCUSSION QUESTIONS

1. Discuss the strengths and weaknesses of the Gonzalez-Herrero and Pratt's crisis management model as it applies to crises in sport.
2. Discuss the view that the success of diversion as a crisis strategy bolsters the argument that public relations should focus on building quality relationships rather than on technical communication practices.
3. Discuss the key elements of the crisis communication process that should be included in a sport crisis management plan.

GUIDED READINGS

Pfahl, M.E., Bates, B.R., 2008. This is not a race, this is a farce: Formula One and the Indianapolis motor speedway tyre crisis. Public Relations Review 34, 135–144. This paper identifies that during a crisis, an organisation must respond to the situation in both public and private ways.

RECOMMENDED WEBSITES

Image Repair Discourse – <http://web.missouri.edu/~benoitw/image_repair.html>.

REFERENCES

Arpan, L., Pompper, D., 2003. Stormy weather: testing "stealing thunder" as a crisis communication journalist. Public Relations Review 29 (3), 291–308.

Bruce, T., Tini, T., 2008. Unique crisis response strategies in sport public relations: Rugby league and the case for diversion. Public Relations Review 34 (2), 108–115.

Benoit, W.L., 1997. Image repair discourse and crisis communication. Public Relations Review 23, 177–186.

Chess, C., 2001. Organisational theory and the stages of risk communication. Risk Analysis 21 (1), 179–188.

Churchill, J., 2006. The Power of the Message: A Study of Media Influence on the Development of Public Opinion. Unpublished Master's Thesis. Rowan University, Glassboro, New Jersey.

Coombs, W.T., 1996. Communication and attributions in a crisis: an experimental study in crisis communication. Journal of Public Relations Research 8 (4), 279–295.

Coombs, W.T., Holladay, S.J., 2001. An extended examination of the crisis situations: a fusion of the relational management and symbolic approaches. Journal of Public Relations Research 13 (4), 321–340.

Cutlip, S.M., Center, A.H., Broom, G.M., 2000. Effective Public Relations. Prentice-Hall, Upper Saddle River, NJ.

Del Rio, V., 2007. High-Profile Crisis Management in Australian and New Zealand Organisations. PhD Thesis. Faculty of Economics and Commerce. Unpublished doctoral dissertation. University of Melbourne, Victoria, Australia.

Fearn-Banks, K., 1994. Crisis Communications: A Casebook Approach. Lawrence Erlbaum Associates, Hillsdale, NJ.

Fearn-Banks, K., 1996. Crisis Communications: A Casebook Approach. Mahwah, New Jersey: Lawrence Erlbaum Associates, Inc.

Frederick, B., September 2007. This ain't NASCAR': Framing the Pacers–Pistons brawl. Unpublished doctoral dissertation. University of Colorado, Colorado, pp. 776, dai:A 68/03.

Gonzalez-Herrero, A., Pratt, C.B., 1995. How to manage a crisis before – or whenever – it hits. Public Relations Quarterly 40 (1), 25–29.

Gonzalez-Herrero, A., Pratt, C.B., 1996. An integrated model for crisis communication management. Journal of Public Relations Research 8 (2), 79–105.

Harris, T.L., 1998. Value-Added Public Relations: The Secret Weapon of Integrated Marketing. Chicago, Illinois: NTC Business Books.

Hearit, K.M., Courthright, J.L., 2003. A social constructionist approach to crisis management: allegations of sudden acceleration in the Audi 5000. Communication Studies 54 (17), 79.

Hearit, K.M., 1996. The use of counter-attack in apologetic public relations crises: the case of General Motors vs. Dateline NBC. Public Relations Review 22, 233–248.

Hearit, K.M., 1999. Newsgroups, activist publics, and corporate apologia: the case of Intel and its Pentium chip. Public Relations Review 25, 291–308.

Hopwood, M.K., 2005. Public relations practice in English county cricket. Corporate Communications: An International Journal 10 (3), 201–212.

Kauffman, J., 2005. Lost in space: A critique of NASA's crisis communications in the Columbia disaster. Public Relations Review 31, 263–275.

Kreps, G., 1986. Organizational Communication. Longman, NY.

Lagadec, P., 1993. Preventing Chaos in Crisis: Strategies for Prevention, Control and Damage Limitation. McGraw Hill, London.

Ledingham, J.A., 2006. Relationship management: a general theory of public relations. In: Botan, C.H., Hazelton, V. (Eds.), Public Relations Theory II. Lawrence Erlbaum Associates, Mahwah, NJ, pp. 465–483.

Loosemore, M., 1999. A grounded theory of construction crisis management. Construction Management and Economics 17 (1), 9–19.

Metzler, M.S., 2002. The centrality of organizational legitimacy to public relations practice. In: Heath, R.L. (Ed.), Handbook of Public Relations. Sage Publishing, Thousand Oaks, CA, pp. 323–333.

Oakes, M., 2006. The Crisis Communications Strategies of the Three Major Professional Sport Leagues: A Comparative Historical Analysis. Unpublished Master's Thesis. University of Nevada, Reno.

Seeger, M.W., Sellnow, T.L., Ulmer, R.R., 2001. Public relations and crisis communication: organizing and chaos. In: Heath, R.L. (Ed.), Public Relations Handbook. Sage, Thousand Oaks, CA, pp. 155–166.

Taylor, M., 2000. Cultural variance as a challenge to global public relations: a case study of the Coca Cola scare in Europe. Public Relations Review 26, 277–293.

Weick, K.E., 1993. The collapse of sensemaking in organizations: the Mann Gulch disaster. Administrative Science Quarterly 38 (4), 628–652.

CHAPTER 9

The Public Relations Role of Fans and Supporters' Groups

Maria Hopwood
Leeds Metropolitan University

Everywhere we go people want to know who we are, where we come from…

Learning Outcomes

Upon completion of this chapter the reader should be able to:

- Consolidate their understanding of sport public relations and communication
- Understand and appreciate the role that fans and supporters' groups play in sport public relations and communication
- Think about fans and supporters as a strategic sport public relations and communication tool
- Appreciate that sport business would cease to function without the support of fans and supporters

---

CHAPTER OVERVIEW

In this chapter we will be looking specifically at the role that fans and supporters play in sport public relations and communication. Fans and supporters are the highly visible representation of sport public relations and communication as they are the living and breathing representation of sport – the heart and soul. Fans and supporters are the lifeblood of any sport organisation. Without their support, the sport organisation would arguably cease to exist and function. For the astute sport organisation, fans and supporters are a key public relations tool. They only say good things about the sport organisation and they support it through thick and thin. Even more importantly, they are likely to pass on their passion for the sport organisation to their children and others. For this reason and others, fans and supporters' groups are extremely important brand ambassadors for any sport organisation and, consequentially, are an extremely powerful sport public relations and communication resource.

THE PUBLIC RELATIONS POWER OF FANS AND SUPPORTERS' GROUPS

In order to begin to think about the role that fans and supporters play in sport public relations and communication look at yourself. Which team do you support? How do you express your commitment to that team? Do you purchase merchandise? Are you a season ticket holder? Do you travel around the world in support of your team? Have you created a scrapbook around your team? Have you got pictures of your team posted on your bedroom wall? Do you seek out friends who support the same team as you? If you can answer 'yes' to any of the above then *you* come into the category of fan and supporter and *you* are an example of sport public relations and communication in action.

Sport fans are a hugely important public relations mechanism for sport organisations. They take on the role of 'brand ambassadors' in a way that is envied by many other consumer-oriented organisations. The love of sport engenders a distinct brand loyalty which is hard to replicate in any other consumer product. The die-hard sport fan will follow their team through the good times and the bad; they will never stop supporting their team because it is in their blood. They associate themselves with the qualities of their team; in fact their whole identity is merged and blended with their team. How many other consumer products can say the same about their following?

Fans and supporters' groups are therefore highly significant when we talk about sport public relations and communication. Perhaps more than any other aspect of sport public relations and communication they are the most visible and persuasive form of communication because of their enthusiasm and their innate ability to communicate their sporting passion. It makes sense, therefore, for sport organisations to tap into this limitless resource as a public relations and communication technique.

During recent years, fans and supporters' groups have become one of the most visible aspects of sport public relations yet according to some researchers, this particular dyad is one of the most under-utilised:

Considering the importance of the relationship between a soccer club and its supporters it is interesting to note that clubs rarely manage this relationship proactively.

(Theysohn et al., 2009, p. 303)

Fans and supporters' groups are, in my opinion, *the* most important sport public relations and communication mechanisms. I base this statement on my personal experience of being a member of cricket's Barmy Army in Antigua when England was playing the West Indies in the 2004 Test Match. The Hopwood family were there to witness Brian Lara's 400 not out and what a fantastic experience that was! We are a family of four – 50% of whom understand the game of cricket. My youngest son, Ricky, aged 20, is currently playing minor counties' cricket for Buckinghamshire and my husband is a huge cricket fan. I have become a cricket fan because it became a case of 'if you can't beat them, you join them'. My eldest son, Martin, aged 22, has absolutely no interest in sport whatsoever. He's a computer animator but he came with us to Antigua and, if you were to ask him, he would say that being a member of the Barmy Army was a brilliant experience. In his own words, 'it was fun and unpredictable' and the photograph below gives an idea of just how much fun it was especially as England won the series.

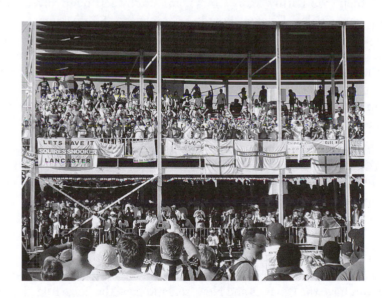

During the 2005 Ashes Series, Andrew 'Freddie' Flintoff described the crowd at the Edgbaston Test as 'the Twelfth Man' because it was their vociferous support which really lifted the team and helped them win. In the

2009 Ashes Series, Ricky Ponting, Australia's captain, said the following in a newspaper interview:

> *I have said for a long time that the Barmy Army are the best sporting crowd in the world. I don't care what sport you are talking about or what country – they are unbelievably good supporters. There is never anything untoward, it is always good light-hearted stuff, and when England have a sniff of winning the volume goes up tenfold. They add a lot to the whole experience of the Ashes.*
>
> (Ponting, 2009)

Wherever the Barmy Army travels in the world to watch England play, they create positive public relations for a sport which has traditionally not attracted the same sort of support as football. A visit to the Barmy Army website at http://www.barmyarmy.com/ will show just how much they do for the profile of the game, local communities, tourism, charity - and of course, the local hostelries! - when they are on a 'tour of duty'. Anyone can 'join', regardless of age or gender, and their Mission Statement is to 'make watching cricket more fun and much more popular' (Barmy Army.com, 2009). They have their own cricket team, which plays in local charity matches wherever they happen to be and they support cricket development through their own Barmy Army Colts team and by getting involved with the England and Wales Cricket Board's Chance to Shine scheme, which promotes the playing of cricket in state schools in the United Kingdom.

The Barmy Army originated in Australia during the 1994 Ashes Series when the supporters were christened with the name by the Australian media who thought they were wonderful but could not understand why they persisted in supporting England when they were losing all their matches. Since then, the Army has gone from strength to strength so that:

> *Such was the success of the Army that in 2007 the decision was taken to launch a full membership Scheme. But as the Army evolves over time, the ethos remains the same; to be passionate about England, passionate about cricket and passionate about fun and to welcome everyone to our particular gang whether they join us for a day, a week or a lifetime.*
>
> (BarmyArmy.com, 2009)

As a result of the success of the Barmy Army other sporting nations, particularly Australia and New Zealand, have created their own versions. The Australians have the Fanatics and New Zealand have the Beige Brigade, both of whose websites are worth a visit to see how they are used for sport public relations and communication purposes. The Fanatics differ from the Barmy Army in that they support Australia at *all* national and international sport occasions as do the Beige Brigade when following New Zealand. On their website at http://www.beigebrigade.co.nz/, the Beige Brigade has their slogan which is 'It's about passion not fashion' which really sums up the public relations function of fans and supporters' groups. These groups are all about creating and developing relationships whilst, at the same time, promoting their sport and their national identity. If embraced by sport governing bodies, teams and organisations, they can provide an excellent ambassadorial and publicity role which is priceless.

THEORETICAL APPROACHES

Of course, it is not only cricket which has colourful, noisy and highly visible fans. All sport does and some of the world's football (soccer) fans and supporters' groups are some of the most highly visible, unfortunately, not always for the right reasons. In a 2009 article in the *International Journal of Sport Marketing and Sponsorship* entitled 'Official Supporters' Clubs: the untapped potential of fan loyalty', Theysohn et al.'s research amongst 439 supporters club members of the German national team has produced some interesting findings which, though related specifically to relationship marketing strategies and customer loyalty programmes, are directly relevant to sport public relations and communication. The relational approach to public relations posited originally in 2000 by Ledingham and Bruning in their seminal text *Public Relations as Relationship Management: A Relational Approach to the Study and Practice of Public Relations*, and discussed elsewhere in this text, is completely directed towards creating long-term, mutually beneficial relationships which can be translated to mean loyalty. Grunig and Huang writing in that same text book refer to Morgan and Hunt's 1994 definition of relational commitment, which is actually taken from the relationship marketing perspective:

> *An exchange partner believing that an ongoing relationship with another is so important as to warrant maximum efforts at maintaining it; that is, the committed party believes the relationship is worth promoting and savouring to ensure that it endures indefinitely.*
> (Morgan and Hunt, 1994, quoted in Grunig and Huang, 2000, p. 45)

Some more recent research by Finne and Groonroos (2009, p. 193) proposes that integrated marketing communication, of which public relations is an element, should be renamed relationship communication and they have devised their Relationship Communication Model which demonstrates that:

...relationship communication is not an input that is planned as such and by definition differs from some other type of communication. Instead, relationship communication is an outcome. It is the receiver who determines whether a communication message or campaign is relationship communication or not.

They define relationship communication as follows:

Relationship communication is any type of marketing communication that influences the receiver's long-term commitment to the sender by facilitating meaning creation through integration with the receiver's time and situational context. The time context refers to the receiver's perception of the history and envisioned future of his/her relationship with the sender. The situational context refers to other elements internal or external to the receiver.

(Finne and Groonroos, 2009, p. 193)

The relevance of these theoretical ideas to sport public relations and communication generally and the public relations power of fans and supporters' groups is clear. Any fan or supporter usually is a lifelong supporter of their team and is really passionate about their support and the relationship that they have with the sport entity. It makes perfect sense, therefore, that sport organisations learn to value and appreciate their fans in order to return on the not inconsiderable investment that fans and supporters' groups make to their chosen team over a lifetime. According to Theysohn et al. (2009, p. 306):

Loyalty among fans imports a broader meaning within sport than it does in non-sport industries. Loyal sport fans will generally not adopt another club or favourite player because of short-term failures.

In an article published in 1998, Clowes and Tapp (1998, p. 20) conducted research into the validity of football clubs in the English Premier League adopting a relationship-marketing paradigm to their dealings with their fans. At the time of their research, football clubs were very much focussed on using a transactional approach with their supporters, i.e. thinking of them as paying customers only and the financial gain they provided. However, their findings are still relevant today and should be considered by all sport organisations when they are dealing with their fans and supporters' groups:

■ Acquiring a new customer costs more than retaining an existing one.
■ The ongoing account costs for an existing customer are less as time goes on.

- Long-time customers tend to be less price sensitive, permitting higher prices to be charged.
- Long-time, satisfied customers are likely to provide free, word of mouth advertising.
- Long-time, satisfied customers are likely to provide additional products and services.

Some of these observations have to be treated with caution as it is the case that recent price hikes in season tickets by football clubs have alienated some of their fan base who feel they are being taken for granted. That said, though the majority of fans might complain about the cost, they are still likely to buy the season ticket rather than forego the opportunity to watch their beloved clubs.

Treatment of supporters' groups is a key element in the relational approach to sport public relations and communication. According to Bruning et al. (2008, p. 29) relationships between organisations and their publics should be founded on dialogue:

> These results also suggest that the practice of public relations needs to continue exploring techniques for personalising organisation-public interactions. Far too often relationship building activity has adopted a "one size fits all strategy". A relational approach, grounded in dialogic principles, requires that the organisation tailor communication and organisational action to specific recipients based upon relational needs.

Sport public relations and communication needs to be all about finding out what the fans and supporters' groups feel about and want from their organisation. Some sport – such as cricket – are beginning to take this approach as discussed in a previous chapter. This could well be the reason why the Barmy Army are such loyal supporters. During the time of some media criticism against the Barmy Army during the 2009 Ashes Series when Ricky Ponting and the Australian team were booed and heckled by the crowd – the Barmy Army denied they were responsible – England and Wales Cricket Board (ECB) chairman, Giles Clarke quoted in Burnton (2009) said:

> It is very important for the game to understand what the spectators want to watch, when they want to watch it and how long they want to watch it for, because we should, at all times, be reacting to the changes in society.
>
> (Burnton, 2009)

Such comments as this are important for fans and supporters' groups because they demonstrate the willingness and commitment of sport organisations to work with fans. Quite naturally, the Internet and social media have made it easier than ever for fans and supporters' groups to voice their disenchantment and this is driving the more relationally oriented focus demonstrated by organisations such as the ECB. Fan discussion forums on club websites and social networking sites such as Facebook or Twitter can be immediate and in real time and can seriously damage, or enhance, a sport organisation's reputation. Many sport organisations are turning social networking to their advantage. For example, Chelsea Football Club are on Facebook and Twitter which means that they can closely monitor – and perhaps influence – what the fans are saying. These are very powerful public relations tools because they allow sport organisations to monitor the mood of their fans and supporters' groups and, hopefully, to take action before any long-term public relations damage is done.

In these more unsettled times for sport organisations fans and supporters' groups have, according to Theysohn et al. (2009), got distinctive roles to play which are very much sport public relations and communication based. Their research with the German football fans mentioned earlier in the chapter illustrates that there are three important aspects for football clubs in having supporters clubs:

1. **They are an additional source of revenue and they can expand existing revenue streams.**

   For example, supporters' groups can be targeted with a range of different membership packages at different annual prices; they can be targeted with personalised merchandise and travel offers and they can be given Internet access to relevant reports or publications as part of that package.

2. **They offer the potential for a heightened atmosphere in the stadium on match day.**

   The case study of my experiences of being with the Barmy Army that comes towards the end of the chapter is a testament to this as is what I have written about them above. The actual match-day experience together with the atmosphere generated is crucial to the point of sale service of the sport product. Fans and supporters' groups are actively used to generate that important atmosphere by being given designated seat allocations, singing songs and anthems and wearing the team colours. All these contribute to a highly visible and impactful sport public relations and communication experience. The ECB actively supported the Barmy Army in creating this visibility during the 2009 Ashes series:

   Now it (the ECB) orchestrates loud renditions of 'Jerusalem' before each day's play and sends a van around the country to record the slurred support of vaguely coherent half-drunk people and puts footage on its website.

(Burnton, 2009)

3. **Supporters' groups allow a club to gather information about its members and potentially to discover/track criminal offences both in the stadium and outside.**

   Security at stadia has recently become a serious issue because of the incidences of violence surrounding certain games. After a riot during a recent match between the two Sicilian sides Palermo and Catania, Union of European Football Associations (UEFA) president, Michel Platini said that finding a solution to the blight of violence permeating European football was essential. During the 2006 Fédération Internationale de Football Association (FIFA) World Cup, fans were issued with personalised tickets and some fans have been prevented from travelling overseas to watch football matches by having their passports confiscated. Clearly, security, or the lack of it is a key sport public relations issue. If fans do not feel safe when they go to watch their team they will quite simply stop going.

It is quite evident that fans and supporters' groups are extremely important to the achievement of successful long-term sport public relations and communication. It is up to sport organisations to maximise the potential of this numerous and willing resource – by implementing a dialogic relational approach to their public relations and communication, it can be done.

CASE STUDY 9.1: Contemporary Sport Public Relations in Action: Cricket's Barmy Army

Picture the scene – it's mid-afternoon on Sunday 11 April 2004, the venue is the Antigua Recreation Ground and it's Day Three of the fourth and final Test match between England and the West Indies. It's Easter Sunday and the sun's beating down on the rickety, packed West Indies Oil Stand, which has become the place to be. Just before lunch, Brian Lara scored a record 400 not out and everyone in the ground, West Indies and England supporters alike, enthusiastically acknowledged his fantastic and historic achievement. It was one of those sporting moments you know you'll never forget – the emotion, the camaraderie, the 'just being there' as part of the crowd. Now England are batting and the time has come to let the players know we're right behind them. And so it begins, a chap dressed in a leopard skin toga with his face painted with the flag of St George starts the refrain with "Everywhere we go-o…" and the whole contingent of England's supporters, all around the ground, join in word-perfect. The song ends with a rousing chorus of 'Michael Vaughan's Barmy Army, Michael Vaughan's Barmy Army, Michael Vaughan's Barmy Army…' And so the chant goes on, comfortably breaking Day Two's 20 minute record and setting the benchmark for Day Four's efforts. We'd better put in some practice on the bus on the way back to the hotel.

Continued

Even if you've never actually attended an international cricket match when England are playing you're likely to have heard of the Barmy Army. If you've ever watched a televised England match, you'll most certainly have seen and heard the Barmy Army – that colourful, noisy band of supporters that adds the unique atmosphere that has become the hallmark of the modern international game. It has become something of a tradition to see the Pink Panther and Sylvester the Cat watching cricket in all the world famous cricket grounds. That those two characters have arguably become one of the most visible representations of how spectators engage with sport communicates a powerful message about the accessibility and appeal of cricket. This is what the Barmy Army is all about, but perhaps more importantly as far as cricket and sport generally is concerned, they have become an immensely powerful sport public relations mechanism, raising awareness of cricket as a form of entertainment and attracting a new and younger audience to the game whilst simultaneously debunking some of cricket's outdated stereotypes.

Public relations' role within contemporary sport business is creating a new dynamic for this communication discipline and opportunities are emerging for people who want to combine their love of sport with public relations practice. The public relations academic literature rarely refers to sport apart from in relation to sponsorship activities and completely neglects the wider potential of public relations in areas such as sport relationship management, sport community relations, sport image and identity creation and sport marketing public relations. For those who want to study sport marketing communications further, it is necessary to turn to the sport marketing literature, but even here, sport public relations has only very recently started to be mentioned, usually in terms of sponsorship and media relations, and its wider value and potential is yet to be fully realised. In their book *Strategic Sport Marketing 2/e* Shilbury et al. (2003, p. 267) view public relations as a critical component of the sport marketing communications mix and they have devoted a complete chapter to the subject because they say: 'This is an important tool for the sport marketer because of the high visibility and attractiveness of the sport product'. According to Helitzer (1999) sport administration, together with computer science, has been one of the most dynamic growth industries of the past 25 years but regarding sport as a business, at least in the UK, has been a very slow process. Having to compete on business terms, however, has meant that sport organisations are having to consider their communications strategies, amongst other things, much more critically and public relations is emerging as a vital commodity.

Having passionate supporters on your side can give sport organisations real public relations competitive advantage, particularly when they are as photogenic, media friendly and well-behaved (for the most part) as the Barmy Army. Regular visits to the discussion forum on the Barmy Army's official website at http://www.barmyarmy.com/ show that there is a constant influx of new 'recruits' to the ranks who are keen to actively display their love for cricket and to participate in the welcoming party being organised for the Australians coming over for the eagerly anticipated 2009 Ashes series. It was, after all, the Australian media via an article in the *Sydney Morning Herald* which originally coined the name 'Barmy Army' as a grudging term of respect for the hordes of touring English fans whose unstinting vociferous support for their team in the face of defeat after defeat during the disastrous 1994–1995 Ashes tour was a source of constant amazement to the Australians for whom losing at any sport particularly cricket is inconceivable.

On 30 January 2005, *The Sunday Express* newspaper ran an article on the Barmy Army in its *s:2* magazine supplement. The cover picture shows Andrew Flintoff, complete with bottle of champagne, greeting members of the Barmy Army after England's Test Match victory in South Africa. In the editorial, Paul Vale writes: 'The most famous supporters in world sport, England's Barmy Army have completely dismantled the traditions of cricket spectatorship over the past 10 years.... At a time when the five-day game of Test cricket has been losing favour throughout the world … these supporters have played a valuable role in keeping the traditional game alive.' During that same tour of South Africa, a local supporter wrote in a letter to the *Cape Times*: 'It's incredible that the same country that can spawn soccer hooligans can also produce cricket lovers whose enjoyment of the game is a pleasure for all to experience'. How's that for third-party endorsement?

And what do the players think about the Barmy Army? Well, they love them and say they can be a real boost to the team when things are flagging a bit. Matthew Hoggard reckons that they have a big effect on the team, especially when times are hard and energy levels are low, 'Sometimes, that little thing of supporters giving you that bit extra keeps you going. We really appreciate their support'. Standing next to some of the England players on the pitch at the end of the Antigua Test and watching them clap their approval of the Barmy Army and taking photos of the mass of riotous support in the West Indies Oil Stand was further evidence of what the players think.

Perhaps one of the most appealing features of the Barmy Army is that anyone can 'join', regardless of age and gender. There are no membership fees to pay, you just turn up to a match and join in with the fun – the only provisos are that you like cricket, you bring your sense of humour with you and you are prepared to have a television camera thrust in your face. The Barmy Army's Mission Statement, emblazoned on the website, is 'To make watching cricket more fun and much more popular'. So, if you want to see twenty-first century cricket at its best and most fun, spend a day in the company of the Barmy Army this summer. You don't have to paint your face, wear a wig or dress strangely, but it helps if you can take the trouble to learn the 'Barmy Army Anthem' – that's the one that starts 'Everywhere we go-o…', you'll find the words on the website. Oh, and if you find yourself standing next to a chap in a bright orange wig who answers to the name of Hogwart, say hello from me!

SUMMARY

This chapter has considered the sport public relations role of fans and supporters' groups and concluded that they are a powerful but generally much under-utilised resource by sport organisations. There is also very little in the way of literature and research around their unique role in sport public relations and communication. Fans and supporters' groups are the life and soul of sport. As demonstrated by the discussion around the Barmy Army, they are a form of entertainment in their own right and take their role as ambassadors for English cricket very seriously indeed. Fans do a great deal more than following their team. They actively get involved in community relations, wherever they are in the world, they are involved with charitable works and they develop grassroots sport, again as evidenced by the Barmy Army. Unfortunately, travelling fans often get noticed for the wrong reasons, chiefly getting drunk, fighting in the streets and rioting at football matches. Perhaps some of this behaviour could be avoided if they were given a more strategic public relations role to play in the representation of their preferred sport. The chapter has also identified some key theoretical underpinning on which such sport public relations and communication could be based. The relational approach to public relations is vitally important in this type of public relations and the critical nature of dialogue has been highlighted to demonstrate this. The new concept of relationship communication has been introduced as providing a basis for fans and supporters' groups public relations as this theory considers the essential role that time plays in relationships which is eminently important in the sport context as relationships are potentially lifelong and because of the unique nature of the sport product and the emotional element involved. Relationship communication is considered to be an outcome of the sport public relations process rather than an input as the receiver is the one who decides whether a communication message or campaign is relational. The power of social networking sites has also been considered as fans are using these as networks of communication amongst themselves and the clubs. These sites therefore have to become part of that communication world, as with the example of Chelsea Football Club. Three distinct aspects from recent research have been highlighted as important elements of sport public relations and these needs have to be considered by *all* sport organisations. The chapter concludes with a case study of my own experiences of being with the Barmy Army on their Tour of Duty to the West Indies in 2004. This case has been chosen as it gives a sense of the fantastic atmosphere which was created and because it shows just how much fun you can have as a fan carrying out your sport public relations role without even realising it.

KEY TERMS

Fans and Supporters' Groups This is taken to mean any individual or group who regularly goes to watch their chosen sport organisation.

Relational Approach to Public Relations This refers to a particular approach to public relations discussed in more depth in Chapter 3.

Relationship Communication   Is any type of marketing communication that influences the receiver's long-term commitment to the sender by facilitating, meaning creation through integration with the receiver's time and situational context.

Word of Mouth Advertising   This is a public relations technique where satisfied sport publics talk in favourable terms about their sport organisation to others thereby creating interest amongst other potential fans and supporters.

DISCUSSION QUESTIONS

1. As a sport fan or member of a supporters' group, evaluate what you consider to be *your* sport public relations role and how you might carry it out.
2. Visit the websites of the Barmy Army, the Fanatics and the Beige Brigade, all listed in the recommended websites section, and analyse each in terms of their sport public relations and communication value. Decide which one you most prefer and give your reasons for your decision.
3. Visit the social networking sites for your chosen sport organisation, if they have them, or visit those of Chelsea Football Club given in the recommended websites. What do you think of these as a sport public relations mechanism?
4. Critically evaluate how any sport organisation of your choice carries out sport public relations and communication with its fans and supporters.

GUIDED READING

Beech, J., 2007. Case 24: On tour with the Barmy Army. In: Chadwick, S., Arthur, D. (Eds.), International Cases in the Business of Sport. Elsevier Butterworth-Heinemann, Oxford.

Finne, A., Groonroos, C., 2009. Rethinking marketing communication: from integrated marketing communication to relationship communication. Journal of Marketing Communications 15 (2), 179–195.

Ledingham, J.A., Bruning, S.D., 2000. Public Relations As Relationship Management: A Relational Approach to the Study and Practice of Public Relations. Lawrence Erlbaum Associates, Mahwah, NJ.

Parry, M., Malcolm, D., 2004. England's Barmy Army: commercialisation, masculinity and nationalism. International Review for the Sociology of Sport 39 (1), 75–94.

Theysohn, S., Hinz, O., Nosworthy, S., Kirchner, M., 2009. Official supporters clubs: the untapped potential of fan loyalty. International Journal of Sport Marketing and Sponsorship 10 (4), 302–324.

If you would like to watch the Barmy Army in action, you will find them on YouTube.

RECOMMENDED WEBSITES

Cricket Supporting Fangroups – <http://barmyarmy.com>, <http://www.thefanatics.com/>, <http://www.beigebrigade.co.nz/>.

Chelsea on Twitter.com – http://twitter.com/CFCNEWS and Facebook – <http://www.facebook.com/pages/Chelsea-FC/29984399941>.

REFERENCES

BarmyArmy.com (2009). The year is 1984, the game is cricket. Retrieved 12 June 2008 from: <http://www.barmyarmy.com/about/index.php?m=history on>.

Bruning, S.D., Dials, M., Shirka, A., 2008. Using dialogue to build organisation–public relationships, engage publics, and positively affect organisational outcomes. Public Relations Review 34, 25–31.

Clowes, J., Tapp, A., (1998). From the 4Ps to the 3Rs: relationship marketing in football clubs. Managing Leisure 1 (3), 18–25.

Finne, A., Groonroos, C., 2009. Rethinking marketing communication: from integrated marketing communication to relationship communication. Journal of Marketing Communications 15 (2), 179–195.

Grunig, J.E., Huang, Y., 2000. From organisational effectiveness to relationship indicators: antecedents of relationships, public relations strategies, and relationship outcomes. In: Ledingham, J.A., Bruning, S.D. (Eds.), Public Relations As Relationship Management: A Relational Approach to the Study and Practice of Public Relations. Lawrence Erlbaum Associates, Mahwah, NJ.

Helitzer, M., 1999. The Dream Job: $port$ Publicity, Promotion and Marketing. University Sport Press, Athens, OH.

Burnton, S., 2009. England's Barmy Army prompts equally barmy reaction. The Guardian Online. Retrieved on 5 August 2009 from: <http://www.guardian.co.uk/sport/blog/2009/aug/04/england-australia-ashes-barmy-army>

Ponting, R., 2009. The Ashes: Ricky Ponting says Barmy Army are the best sporting crowd in the world. The Daily Telegraph Online. Retrieved on 5 August 2009 from: <http://www.telegraph.co.uk/sport/cricket/international/theashes/5974013/The-Ashes-Barmy-Army-are-the-best-sporting-crowd-anywhere-in-the-world.html>

Shilbury, D., Quick, S., Westerbeek, H., 2003. Strategic Sport Marketing, second ed. Allen and Unwin, Crows Nest, NSW, Australia.

Theysohn, S., Hinz, O., Nosworthy, S., Kirchner, M., 2009. Official supporters clubs: the untapped potential of fan loyalty. International Journal of Sport Marketing and Sponsorship 10 (4), 302–324.

CHAPTER 10

Cross-Cultural Sport Public Relations and Communication

Jacquie L'Etang

Stirling Media Research Institute
University of Stirling

Learning Outcomes

Upon completion of this chapter the reader should be able to:

- Define the role and scope of cross-cultural public relations (PR)
- Understand the importance of 'culture' to public relations practice
- Explain the role of public relations in cross-cultural sport practice

---

CHAPTER OVERVIEW

This chapter explains the role of public relations in contemporary complex societies and explores the opportunities and challenges that face public relations in an international context. It seeks to explain the communicative dimensions of cross-cultural sport and identify key issues for public relations practice.

In this chapter I explore the role and scope of cross-cultural sport public relations through a description and discussion of key terms, in relation to examples drawn from practice. My aim, therefore, is partly to define an area of practice and associated skill sets that may help to advance understanding of this specialist area. In tackling this subject, I outline the broad strategic and policy areas of public relations work in cross-cultural communications as well as the business and tactical level. This chapter, therefore is not solely concerned with the daily practice of public relations, but with its role in culture more broadly. In this chapter I explore how an understanding of the term cross-cultural communications and related terms can be used to understand sport public relations and communications in a particular way. My approach aims to be cross-cultural, in that I seek to highlight comparative examples of practice in a variety of different cultural contexts.

Cross-cultural issues in sport studies tend to emerge in broader discussions of globalization (Maguire, 2000; Edwards and Skinner, 2006; Hargreaves, 2002; Maguire, 2006), ethnicity (Jarvie, 2000; Grainger et al., 2006), nationalism (Allison, 2000, 2005); international politics (Riordan and Kruger, 1999); the role of international organisations (Foster, 2005; Skinner and Toohey, this volume) or in country-specific or area-studies approaches or reports of research world-wide (Coakley and Dunning, 2000).

Public relations scholars and practitioners have long been aware of the importance of global interconnectedness for their work. As leading scholar Sriramesh (2003, p. xxv) pointed out:

It is difficult to overstate the importance of a global perspective of public relations practice and scholarship, because this profession has truly become a global enterprise. I question whether there is such a thing as domestic public relations anymore because of the international outreach of organisations of all sizes and types as a result of globalization... every public relations practitioner must have a multi-cultural and global perspective to be effective.

Likewise, Tilson and Alozie (2004, p. 1) argued:

The world has become a global village. Olympic athletes are natives of one country but represent another in the Winter Games; US football players play on teams in NFL Europe...to prepare properly for a career in public relations, it is essential to globalize your education.

Literature in public relations on cross-cultural communications has tended to apply Hofstede's model of cross-cultural variants and this model will be summarized later in this chapter along with other approaches to cross-cultural communication. Key sources are Sriramesh and Vercic (2003, 2009), Tilson and Alozie (2004) and van Ruler and Vercic (2004). Some contributions within this literature are somewhat distorted by authors who seek to impose US models of practice on cultures elsewhere, but nevertheless there is useful empirical data and multi-cultural insights in all of these sources. A theoretically driven text was that of Banks (2000) who linked multi-cultural concepts with intercultural communication theory and public relations (Banks, 2000 cited in Falkheimer and Heide, 2006). These are all useful sources of cross-cultural public relations practice and demonstrate how the practice takes its character from the political economy and socio-cultural frameworks of specific cultures. Similarly, sport practice emerges from cultural and ethnic roots. At the same time, both public relations and sport have globalized dimensions and practices, which are exploited by the international business class. Some of these tensions between nationalism and globalization arise in the context of the international business of sport and public relations has the potential to play a crucial role in relationship management as well as the promotion of sport organisational interests.

PUBLIC RELATIONS IN SOCIETY: FUNCTIONAL AND CRITICAL PERSPECTIVES

Public relations is present at all political, economic, socio-cultural and technological change in contemporary, post-industrial cultures in a globalized world. The function of public relations is to establish and monitor internal and external relationships with stakeholders; to monitor the public agenda for rising issues and social concerns and to protect the reputation of the organisation. Public relations is not just promotion or media relations although these aspects are the most visible parts of the work. Public relations practitioners seek feedback from stakeholders, publics and opinion leaders and endeavour to get their organisation into relevant 'public conversations'. Public relations is a way of giving an organisation voice and identity, and it entails internal introspective work within the organisation as well as representative work outside it. It is also responsible for ensuring that the organisation thinks through the likely impact of policy on reputation, and for this reason, public relations is properly responsible for policies of corporate social responsibility. In the course of their work, public relations practitioners engage with cultural beliefs and practices, communicative action, discourse ethics, organisational cultures and climates, formation of public agendas and debates and interest-group activism. Public relations practitioners work as advocates on behalf of many different types of organisations (corporations, health boards, sport organisations, trades unions) to engage with multiple stakeholders. Within sport, public relations work is needed by international sport organisations such as the International Olympic Committee (IOC) or Fédération Internationale de Football Association (FIFA), on behalf of sport stars, sport associations, sport corporations (Nike, Adidas), sport sponsors and sport media. To summarize, public relations practice is the occupation responsible for the management of organisational relationships and reputation. It encompasses issues management, public affairs, corporate communications, stakeholder relations, risk communication and corporate social responsibility. Public relations practice operates on behalf of many different types of organisation both at the governmental and corporate levels, to small business and voluntary sectors. Public relations, whether managed or not by PR practitioners, takes place at points of societal change and resistance.

'Functional' approaches to public relations concentrate on the importance of the role to organisational effectiveness and the way in which the occupation can contribute to the achievement of managerial aims. The dominant school of thought (or 'paradigm') in the field of public relations has been the application of systems theory, which suggests that the public relations practitioner acts as a 'boundary spanner' between the organisation and its wider environment (composed of political, economic, socio-cultural and technological systems). Organisational systems have to adjust to their environments (issues and publics) and the public relations function can help them to do this. Since organisations and environments are constantly in flux, public relations not only supplies early warning systems (issues management and scenario and crisis planning); but also helps to provide stability and international integration (employee communication, corporate culture); as well as co-creating and communicating organisational mission and vision (corporate identity, corporate communications).

This normative model prescribes how public relations ought to be practised ethically and effectively based on a typology of practice drawn from the US PR historical path, which classified organisational communications into a multi-part framework: 'publicity', 'public information', 'propaganda', 'two-way asymmetrical communication' (communication which is dominated by output from the organisation but which does seek and take account of feedback of stakeholders and the wider public) and 'symmetrical communication' (a somewhat idealistic version in which the organisation is in dialogue with its stakeholders and seeks to adapt to their feedback, rather than imposing its vision upon the environment). Other themes within the dominant paradigm which are useful in evaluating the role of public relations are the following:

■ Relationship management, which focuses on refining the understanding of the relationships between organisations and stakeholder/publics;

■ Communitarian, which argues that the appropriate role for public relations is community building;

■ Rhetorical, which argues that the role of public relations as organisational rhetoric is beneficial to societies as it facilitates public debate and helps respective groups to arrive at consensus.

Critical research highlighting the role and impact of public relations in society and its links to power was developed largely in Scotland and New Zealand in the mid-1990s (L'Etang and Pieczka, 1996, 2006; Motion and Leitch, 1996) and this now includes cultural studies (the role of PR in the political and cultural economy), post-colonial and sub-altern approaches (the perspectives of alternative voices and disempowered groups) as well as rhetorical work, which explores public relations practitioners as 'discourse workers' (L'Etang, 2008). The discourse approach explores how public relations practitioners use language for strategic gain. This work connects public relations to the classical Greek Sophists who acted as argument and persuasion consultants. Post-modernism has become a focus for alternative perspectives that generate non-managerial meanings within and about organisations (Holtzhausen, 2000, 2002; McKie and Munshi, 2007). According to the most prominent US scholar, James Grunig:

> Critical scholars such as L'Etang and Pieczka (1996) and Leitch and Neilson (2001) and post-modern scholars such as Holtzhausen and Voto (2002) have derided the excellence theory as modernist, functionalist and positivist and as a theory that serves only the interests of management or organisations and not the interests of publics or society.
>
> (Grunig and Grunig, 2008, p. 330)

Thus, in considering sport communications and public relations practice in this specialist field we should not only be concerned about the effectiveness of practice on behalf of sport organisations, but also consider wider issues such as power, exploitation, ethics, for example, issues relating to children's rights, environmentalism and sustainability, relationships between the developed and developing worlds, post-colonial diasporas, cultural imperialism, the promotion and representation of certain body shapes, ageism, gender issues, racism and the impact of commercialization of sport (L'Etang, 2009).

CULTURE

Culture is the term used in English to explain shared patterns of behaviour, common values and assumptions about daily living within a particular community. Indeed, it is the 'shared-ness', which partly defines the community. Culture facilitates the operational functioning of a community. Culture is partly intangible, 'between the hyphens', defined by the deep structures and functions of a community which in themselves, partly shape the outward appearance of culture. Culture is expressed by ways of living and taken-for-granted nature of a community's daily life as well as the climate and atmosphere of a context. The mental and linguistic aspects of culture are at least, if not more important than the outward manifestations, as Barnett and Lee (2002, p. 276) pointed out:

> *Culture consists of the habits and tendencies to act in certain ways, but not the actions themselves. It is the language patterns, values, attitudes, beliefs, customs and thought patterning.*

Emphasis in this definition is given to language, because it is language, which shapes interpretive frameworks. Language is part of an overall symbol system that enacts a community through the expression of 'collective representations' that arise from the association of minds through the process of social interaction (Barnett and Lee, 2002, p. 277).

Language and symbolism are central to public relations practice since the function is responsible for the articulation of organisational views. Take, for example, the way in which different nations put forward their interests in hosting Olympic sport.

In Activity Box below are some quotes from the various Mayors whose cities were candidates for the 2012 Olympics.

Activity Box

Albertos Ruiz Gallardon
Mayor of Madrid

We are ready! We have been saying this in every forum and every time the opportunity has presented itself. We want our message to be heard loud and clear: Madrid is ready! With 70 per cent of the total sport facilities being used or being built, the Spanish capital city's project, which was very well considered by the International Olympic Committee's experts when the shortlist was announced in May, is in the advanced stages of development, and receiving high praise from many throughout the world's sport community.

We are ready because in Madrid there exists a sport consciousness and the whole community has decided to spread the shared hope that is the Olympic Games. We can feel this hope spreading through the city; we can breathe the desire to win this difficult race in which we are immersed. When you arrive in Madrid you can immediately notice that achieving our purpose in Singapore is what interests us most of all.

The Madrid Olympic Games will be the very best in Olympic history. This will be due to the fact that the athletes will be able to walk from the Olympic Village to the Stadium, the Aquatic Centre or the Olympic Pavilion; because of the short distances between the different venues, due to Madrid's high quality public transport network; and because of the hospitality of its citizens, who will make this Olympic Games unforgettable.

The Games will also leave an extraordinary legacy in Madrid, not only of very valuable sport facilities and infrastructures for its people, but also the quality of life of our inhabitants will be improved because of the planned future investments in the southern and the eastern parts of the city.

Madrid as a whole is ready because the citizens want it to be – they are the engine of this wonderful project that has been designed to win. Since the very first day of our bid we have felt the support of our people, who are Madrid 2012's biggest asset. And we have received that support not only from the local population, which is represented by the huge amount of volunteers that are currently joining us, but also from the different official institutions, the sportsmen and the businessmen alike. Without their help and support it would have been impossible to achieve our target of competing together with the best cities of the world.

The people of Madrid have been and will always remain the main asset in our candidacy. We will try not to disappoint them with our work at the helm of Madrid 2012.

Yuri Luzhkov
Mayor of Moscow

For Moscow, the Olympic and Paralympic Games are more than just a sport event. They embody the dreams of every Muscovite and every Russian. More than 90 per cent of Muscovites and 89 per cent of Russians want Moscow to host the 2012 Games. This is one of the highest levels of support ever recorded for a candidate city.

One of Moscow's main advantages is our unique Games pan – The Olympic River Concept. For the first time, the Games would be held within the limits of one city. This means that it would take just 28 minutes to get by river from the beginning to the end of the Olympic route on an Olympic fleet of special river boats.

The Olympic River encompasses the major Olympic venue – the Luzhniki Sport Complex, where the Opening and Closing Ceremonies will be held. Moscow is known to have a well-developed world-class sport infrastructure and unique experience in hosting major international sport events. In fact, Moscow already has 65 per cent of the sport events needed to host the 2012 Olympic Games. The largest venue – Krylatskoye Skating Centre – has recently been commissioned and surpasses International Sporting Federation standards. When opening Krylatskoye. Oyyavio Cinquanta, President of the International Skating Union, said there is no other venue of its kind in the world.

By 2012, 15 new major Olympic venues are to be constructed in Moscow, including new soccer stadiums Spatak and CSKA which can seat 50,000 spectators each, a sport complex in Tushino with a baseball stadium for 25,000 spectators, an athletics and a swimming arena holding 15,000 spectators.

The Olympic Village will be located 10 minutes away from the central arena of Luzhniki.

Continued

What Moscow also offers is a guarantee that construction of all of the sport venues and accommodation facilities for athletes and spectators will be finished by 2010.

Ensuring security during the Games is one of our top priorities. The overall management and responsibility for security during the Olympic Games will be entrusted to the Russian Federation Ministry of the Interior, which will coordinate the various functions performed by the Federal Security Service, Civil Defence and Emergencies Ministry and a number of other federal and municipal bodies. We plan to use the latest security technology and we will form and train new law enforcement units, providing them with the most advanced communication equipment, weapons and protections devices. We will expand road, boat, air and horse patrols. Whatever resources are needed, they will be there.

There is one more reason we believe the 2012 Games should be held in Moscow – we will give the entire world the opportunity to get to know the new Russia. Our country has transformed itself over the past decade into a vibrant democracy that embraces market ideals.

Moscow is the embodiment of the Russian soul – a true and good friend. It is a reliable partner for the International Sport Federation. Through the 2012 Olympic and Paralympic Games we will extend that hand of friendship to the whole world.

Ken Livingstone
Mayor of London

The Olympic Games is one of the greatest prizes for any city, so it is no wonder that five of the greatest cities in the world are competing to host the 2012 Olympic and Paralympic Games. All have strong claims, but none can match London's. Our bid offers the best ever Games for athletes, a social, economic and environmental boost for our city.

Our bid is centred on the Lower Lea Valley, only a few miles from the centre of London. The availability of land for regeneration here means we can create one of the most compact and inclusive Olympic Parks in history. Our plans centre on a brand new Olympic Park in East London that will include the athlete's village, main stadium, aquatics centre and seven other sport venues as well as the main press/ broadcast centre. Fifty per cent of athletes will live, train and compete in the Olympic Park and another 30 per cent will be within 20 minutes of their venues. A purpose-built village will offer space for all Olympic and Paralympic athletes, and the Games will leave a fantastic legacy of five fully funded sporting facilities for London.

The site of the main stadium in the Lea Valley is only seven minutes by express train from the centre of London, and 10 railway lines – nine of which already exist and service the Olympic Park area – will transport 240,000 people an hour to the Olympic Park. London would like to be the best ever connected Games. But famous landmarks across London will play their part too: Lords Cricket Ground, Wimbledon for tennis, Horse Guards Parade, Greenwich Park, the Millennium

Dome and Hyde Park will enable all to enjoy the Games against spectacular, world famous backdrops.

A London Olympic and Paralympic Games will be great for athletes and London. The Lower Lea is at the heart of our Thames Gateway regeneration plans. It is an area with a legacy of social and environmental decline. That is going to change. Through bringing the Games here, we will kick start regeneration, leaving legacy of parkland – the biggest in any city in Europe for 150 years.

Our bid has benefited from an excellent bid committee, led by athletes to bid for athletes, with Olympian Seb Coe as its chair. It has also benefited from wholehearted support from London's business community, including the London Chamber of Commerce and Industry, London First and the Confederation of British industry. But our biggest asset is our people. In Athens last summer, our bid really gathered pace, as Team GB surpassed expectations in the medal count, urged on by 20,000 British fans, demonstrating our country's passion for sport.

London is completing major projects – the congestion charging scheme, the Channel Tunnel Rail Extension, Heathrow Terminal 5 – the biggest construction project in Europe – on time and to budget and we can do the same for the Games.

Bertrand Delanoe
Mayor of Paris

On several occasions over the past few months, I had the great pleasure of speaking about the Paris bid to host the 2012 Olympic and Paralympic Games. Each time I passionately described the foundation of our bid – L'Amour des Jeux – and the essential values it symbolizes: fraternity, tolerance, competition in the sprit of mutual respect and a determination to win.

Indeed our ambition is to organize a Games that will blend modernity and tradition, reflecting the very foundations of Olympism. We are determined to organise an Olympics that will be visionary, ecologically-minded, ethical, democratic and completely secure.

To ensure that these Games are truly egalitarian, we will create a true chemistry between the athletes, the Olympic Family, the public and the city.

Our aim is to create a comfortable environment for the athletes and the spectators alike. This is why 80 per cent of the Olympic events will be concentrated in two competition venue clusters, each located only 10 miles away from the Olympic Village. In this spirit, for particularly symbolic competitions, we will use world-famous iconic Parisian sites, such as the Eiffel Tower and the Palace of Versailles.

In addition, we will leverage our experience gained in the reorganisation of some of the largest international sporting events of the past few years. We will set up the Optimal Accommodation and Strategic Transport Plans to ensure the best possible management of the Paris Games. As a result, everyone will be able to

Continued

enjoy the Games in a safe environment at the very heart of Paris, fully dedicated to the celebration of this spectacular event.

With future generations in mind, we have set up an ambitious goal: to ensure the sustainable success of a "green" Olympics. Indeed, a major component of this project is our clear and innovative commitment to organising the first Olympic Games to result in a neutral balance of greenhouse gas emissions. Similarly, we chose to emphasise the accessibility of all Olympic venues and transport to people with disabilities. This will be one of the event's lasting legacies.

Paris seeks the 2012 Olympics because we are convinced that the Olympic and Paralympic Games will leave an extraordinary and sustainable heritage in Paris and all of France. The Olympics in its wide scope, represents an engine of transformation for our country, serving as a historic impetus for modernisation and evolution in the national mindset.

Such broad consensus around a project is truly unprecedented in France. The Paris 2012 bid is a collective passion that unites all the democratic, sporting, economic and social forces for our country. Today, our whole nation hopes for a victory. Affirming with enthusiasm the ideals and aspiration of Olympism. Indeed, each one of us feels and shares 'L'Amour des Jeux'.

Source: *Sport Business International* (2005) Issue 99 February: 30, 34, 38, 42.

Discussion Question: Rhetorical Analysis

What do you notice about the language employed by the various Mayors? What is shared, and what is different in the approach they take? To whom are they making their appeal? What rhetorical strategies have been adopted? How convincing are they, and why? Compare and contrast the promotional approach taken. What use is made of the concept of culture in the appeals?

In broader terms, what inter and cross-cultural public relations would be necessary to support such a bid, and why? (See definitions of these terms beneath.) Who would be the key publics and what key messages might be developed and why?

Culture is 'a socially shared activity...the property of a group rather than an individual' (Nieberg, 1973 cited in Barnett and Lee, 2002, p. 276). Culture is not a term which applies solely to nation–states or ethnic groups but can be applied much more widely to organisations ('Nike culture'), to specialized activities ('sport culture', 'rugby culture', 'skateboard culture'), to generations ('youth culture') and to elite or distinct groups ('political culture', 'royal culture' 'Olympic culture'). Culture can also be enacted through online communities.

Discussion Question and Ethnographic Activity
Describe and discuss the key features of three different types of sport culture. If possible, go and observe friends participating in sport you do not play yourself and socialize with them after they have completed their activity. You might want to choose one sporting activity that is completely different to your own sporting activities (climbing or orienteering compared to ball sport), and one that is closer (football compared to rugby). Take observational notes about the way people dress, speak, behave and relate to each other.

Culture is about qualitative experiences and subjective perspectives that enable people to feel a sense of belonging to a community, as Barnett and Lee (2002, p. 277) explained:

Culture… is a group's shared collective values, attitudes, beliefs, customs and thoughts… an emergent property of how group members communicate. The meanings that are attributed to verbal symbols and nonverbal behaviours are determined by society as a whole. Culture may be taken to be a consensus about the meanings of symbols. Verbal and nonverbal, held by the members of a community. Without general agreement about the meaning of symbols, intra-group interaction would be impossible.

It is therefore culture, which distinguishes one group from another, as expressed through shared behaviours, speech and body language, rituals, discourse practices, jargon, reference points, degrees of formality or informality, social intercourse and personal relationships, atmosphere or 'climate'. Degrees of touch and physical closeness are also indicative of cultural difference, with high-contact cultures tending to be based in warmer countries and low-contact cultures tending to be in colder climates. There is also a distinction to be made between low- and high-context cultures (Hall, 1976 cited in Gudykunst and Lee, 2002, p. 36). Low-context cultures are explicit and direct, often individualistic, with meaning encapsulated in the spoken word. High-context cultures encode much of the message to be communicated in the person or physical context so that communication is indirect and subtle. Kaplan and Manners (1972) identified four determinants of societal culture:

- techno-economics (economic development and technological capacity);
- social structure (feudal, caste and class);
- ideology (worldviews, philosophies, spiritualities, religions);

- personality (child-rearing, acculturation processes in education and workplace) (Kaplan and Manners, 1972 cited in Sriramesh and Vercic, 2003, pp. 8–9).

Discussion Question

Consider how Kaplan and Manners' determinants of societal culture might affect sport practice in any particular culture. How might these cultural determinants and the sport culture that arises as a consequence affect communications practices?

Scholars have sought to define certain key determinants of culture in order that differences may be measured quantitatively. Probably the best-known framework of this sort is that of Hofstede (1984, 2001) who identified five dimensions of societal culture:

- power distance (vertical stratification of society; gap between richest and poorest);
- social mobility (ease of movement between lower and higher levels of society);
- collectivism (extent to which individual is valued over collectivity or vice versa);
- masculinity–femininity (degree to which gender influences roles);
- uncertainty–avoidance (extent to which ambiguity can be tolerated);
- long-term orientation (extent to which tradition and commitments are respected);

Other scholars have identified important dimensions such as:

- interpersonal trust
- deference to authority
- harmony (Sriramesh and Vercic, 2003, pp. 9–10).

The Chinese Culture Connection (1987) cited in Gudykunst and Lee (2002) isolated alternative dimensions of cultural variability such as:

Confucian dynamism

Ordering relationships by status and observing this order; having a sense of shame; thrift; persistence; protecting one's face; personal steadiness; respect for tradition; reciprocity.

Integration

Harmony/solidarity with others.

Human-heartedness

Patience, courtesy and kindness.

Moral discipline

Prudence, absence of greed and moderation.

Discussion Question

What evidence was there of the Chinese Culture Connection in the Beijing Olympics? Are such values apparent in the philosophy of the Asian Games?
Useful sources: <http://www.gz2010.cn/en>; <http://www.gz2010.cn/special/0078002J/sight.html>.

A number of scholars (Aw et al., 2002; Chen, 1996; Huang, 2000; Tan, 2000) have explored the notion of *Guanxi* (cultivation of interpersonal relationships) in relation to public relations frameworks and concepts, particularly the personal influence model (Sriramesh, 2009). Huang (2000) suggested that *Gao Guanxi* extends the concept of *Guanxi* towards a more instrumental networking approach. This is highly relevant in sport business, which is often described by its exponents as 'a people business'. In many Asian societies the concept of *mianzi* (face) is also relevant although this has not yet been studied within a public relations context (Sriramesh, 2009).

All of the determinants of culture mentioned above have an impact on sport practice in different cultures, in terms of what is played, how it is played, rituals, who plays (class, gender, race, age) the values that are espoused by the players and (any) spectators.

In the last 30 years or so, developed countries have seen the emergence of a very particular culture of importance to those in sport – the phenomenon of 'promotional culture'.

PROMOTIONAL CULTURE

Promotional culture was a term made famous by a book of that name by Andrew Wernick (1991), a cultural studies scholar who explored the way in which communications were becoming increasingly imbued with promotional rhetoric. Promotional culture entails a particular discourse through which organisations and individuals seek to 'sell' themselves and their vision. Wernick argued that this promotional tendency, which copied the marketing of goods in a capitalist environment, fundamentally alters the nature of that which is promoted. The ideology of the public relations academic discipline includes the belief that public relations concepts must be absorbed into the life stream of the organisation via its management, in order to ensure that the organisation is imbued with public relations concerns of reputation, relationships and, implicitly, with promotion. It is not uncommon, for example, for managers to state that they wish their organisation 'to raise the profile', but this simple statement requires the organisation to think about not just how it is, but how it would like to be seen. It is this reflexiveness that contributes to the self-conscious sense of the organisation's promotional currency. Furthermore, it is the case that the dominant paradigm in public relations has favoured a normative version of public relations practice that may respond to change in its environment by changing itself. In other words, organisational awareness of its impact, or relationship states, may lead the organisation to alter its policy, not simply because it is the right or prudent thing to do, but because such adaptation can be used in future promotion about the organisation. The same processes may be applied to individual impression management, part of personal public relations, highly relevant to celebrity PR, including sport celebrities.

Promotional culture emerges alongside the marketization of society and the commodification of talent and creativity. It is not enough to be an outstanding sport person, it is important to learn the tricks of impression management to maximize your saleability in a host of non-sport markets and sponsorships. Hence Anna Kournikova achieved financial success not solely through her tennis racket, but through her self-commodification. Sport celebrities are cultural products and they can move from one field to another, for example, Serena and Venus Williams have both designed their own jewellery, clothing and footwear. Sport stars share celebrity-space and crossing celebrity cultures, either by performing in another field, or through relationships with a star from another field can provide additional promotional opportunities. In some adventure or lifestyle sport there are tensions between the generations who espouse alternative lifestyle formations and ideologies and more recent generations who see advantage in commercial opportunities, such as those that have spun off as a consequence of the X-Games (L'Etang, 2009).

CULTURE IN PUBLIC RELATIONS

The connection between public relations practice and culture is fundamental (L'Etang, 2009). Public relations practice is discourse work and centrally concerned with the ideas and opinions of organisations, stakeholders and the broader public opinion. Within organisations public relations is involved in the 'management' of corporate culture. However, a careful distinction must be drawn between the notion of 'corporate culture', which comprises the desired values and practices which managers wish their employees to espouse; and 'organisational culture' which defines the actual values and practices of organisational members at all levels. Understanding and defining 'organisational culture' requires multi-method research described as a 'communication audit' (best described in Hargie and Tourish, 2000). The term 'corporate identity' is used to explain the organisational personality, vision and mission, whereas the term 'visual identity' describes the symbols, design and architecture which may be employed to communicate that identity.

Public relations is involved in intercultural communications between different organisations, media and international publics located in various countries. Thus the concept of culture is of central importance to the operation of public relations practice.

Public relations has been identified by some in cultural studies as one of several occupations that act as cultural intermediaries, behind-the-scenes communicators that package goods, services, organisations, experiences and identities to enhance communication. This role was described by sport studies academic, Catherine Palmer (2000) as that of 'the cultural broker'.

Public relations therefore plays a crucial role in the cultural processes in which meaning is created, modified and reinvented during processes of symbolization, representation, consumption and identity formation. In sport, public relations activity may be linked to national identity in a form of communication defined as *devotional–promotional communication* (Tilson, 2006), 'used by individuals and political or religious organisations in order to attract loyal and faithful followers' (Xifra, 2008, p. 194). From a relationship management point of view, public relations is concerned with social and identity cohesion (Xifra, 2008) and the formation of allegiances through events, celebrity icons and drama.

CULTURE IN SPORT

There are a number of ways in which we can think about the relationship between culture and sport. Each different sport has its own culture arising from its history, values, practices and ideology. Thus rugby culture is very different to that of windsurfing. 'Lifestyle' or 'adventure' sport espouse in some cases an anti-competitive ideology, for example, skateboarding

(L'Etang, 2009). Furthermore, sport is played within very different national or ethnic cultures, for example, there are challenges that face women who wish to participate and compete at athletics in some Muslim cultures. And within some sport ethnic tensions and sectarianism may be played out through sub-cultures within a sport, as has been the case in parts of British football and in Mauritius where local football has developed along ethnic and religious lines (http://news.bbc.co.uk/sport1/hi/football/world_football/5278046.stm). Fan culture crosses cultures in support of major teams such as Manchester United (there are fan clubs for Man United, Liverpool and Chelsea in Mauritius chosen in preference to the local Super League). Or fan culture may enact nationalist aspirations as in the case of the Catalan football team, 'Barça' (Barcelona Football Club – BFC) where sport may be regarded as a form of 'civil religion' to which fans pay homage, make pilgrimages, experience community bonds and envisage through collective celebration the as yet unfulfilled national status (Xifra, 2008, p. 193).

These issues are not solely of academic interest but are taken seriously within the business community as part of brand value illustrated by the comments of the Editor of *Sport Business International* Kevin Roberts:

> *FC Barcelona...the sexiest brand of all...a club whose brand identity has been forged by history rather than being artificially inseminated in a boardroom specimen bottle...a rallying point for the people of Catalonia... A focal point for regional identity amid turbulent and often bloody periods in Spanish history and the most visible manifestation of Catalan pride...the club history provides many examples of the incidents that conspired to create the identity and its relationship with the community...It is a people's club – proud, independent, anti-authoritarian, stylish and successful...as the marketing men will tell you, these are very compelling attributes....*
> (Roberts, 2006, p. 22)

In conversation with Roberts, Esteve Calzada commented:

> *We kind of represent a nation here...[the fans] use the club to show who they are, how they feel...The brand is consistent around the world and when we play in China, Japan and elsewhere, you'll see Catalan signs and flags in the crowd. We work hard to leverage that uniqueness and to define ourselves as different...Our research suggests that the brand attributes are important to global growth and our research shows that they are attributes to which young people and women respond particularly well....*
> (Roberts, 2006, p. 22)

In a globalized world, however, there is also the issue of personal affiliations and choice regarding national identity, for example, there have been a number of cases of sportspeople changing their national allegiance for various reasons, due to emigration, some opportunistic, which may, from a sport business perspective, have brand implications.

> *The more tenuous the link, however, the more sceptical fans will be. And it can be particularly difficult for fans to swallow when the athlete has previously represented another country…New Zealand rugby player Shane Howard represented Wales on 19 occasions before rugby officials later discovered he was not qualified to play for the country as originally thought. It turned out he did not, in fact, have a Welsh grandparent. And he was not the only one….*
>
> (Smith, 2006a, 2006b, p. 70)

Some athletes have not only changed their nationality but also their name, for example, Bulgarian Angel Popov became Said Asaad and Kenyan Stephen Cherono became Saif Saaeed Shaheen (Poli and Gillan, 2006).

Sport is also a sub-cultural or micro-cultural element of both national, ethnic and organisational cultures. National leaders use sport to enhance national identity and to endeavour to unify national culture. Organisations, both public and private sector, also utilize sport as a form of public relations to enhance employee relations. And since sport reflects many of the dominant culture's features, current issues and debates will also be mirrored in sport, some of which may require public relations management, for example, issues of security and terrorism, gender issues, religion and race.

CROSS-CULTURAL COMMUNICATION

Cross-cultural communication is usually defined as a comparative approach to exploring communications in different cultures, for example:

> *Cross-cultural communication [is] the comparison of face-to-face communication across cultures…[and grew out of cultural anthropological studies of communication processes in different cultures].*
>
> (Gudykunst and Mody, 2002, p. ix)

Cross-cultural communication is therefore a specific form of anthropology that explores how specific cultural environments influence communication, for example, communication practices in different cultures at weddings or at sport events (the 'Mexican wave' emerged during the World Cup in 1986). Cross-cultural communication needs to be separated out from some other similar terms: intercultural communication, international communication and development communication, all of which are relevant to both public relations and sport. Cross-cultural communication is distinguished from *intercultural communication* (Gudykunst, 2002), which describes communication between one culture and another, a form of communication highly relevant to globalized industries such as sport. It has been described as generally involving: 'Face-to-face communication between people from different national cultures' (Gudykunst and Mody, 2002, p. ix).

A cross-cultural communications approach to sport public relations requires us to understand political, economic and social history and international relations which frame the emergence of sport in different cultural contexts. As Guilianotti and Armstrong (2004, pp. 1–27) pointed out:

> *Football cultures in any location tell us much about the societies that play and understand the game in the distinctive ways they do…Colonialism, neo-colonialism and neo-liberalism provide the circumstances within which African people's make and remake their cultural identities and practices…Sport…has been destroyed, reintroduced and refashioned through this interplay of historical, political, economic and cultural influences…fledgling European sport traditions were taught to young African males by Western missionaries, teachers, soldiers, administrators and businessmen…some indigenous traditions did survive, notably the pan-African games known in southern Africa as* mancula *and* moraba-raba.

International communication describes communications, which arise as part of international politics, state diplomacy and public diplomacy – a feature of the field of international relations (IR) (Bramam, 2002). This term also has a high degree of relevance to sport given not only its global scope, but also its large scale funding by political masters, and sport's role in the expression of national, racial and ethnic identities. International communication: 'Deals with power, politics and the process of influencing other nation–states…and grew from research into the two World Wars…" (Gudykunst and Mody, 2002, p. ix).

In other words, sport may be used for political ends, to bolster a nation's pride and confidence, to enhance national identity, to unify a country in a common cause, to distract a population from political or economic crises and to improve health statistics and medical epidemiology. Hosting major events such as the Olympics represents a major opportunity for public diplomacy. For example, 'Asia's use of sport as a nation-building tool is important…' (Fry, 2006, p. 44).

International communication is grand-scale analysis looking at nations 'world systems, groups and movements' (Gudykunst and Mody, 2002, p. ix). It also explores mass-mediated communication and thus highly relevant to international public relations and international sport public relations in particular. International communication includes the use of sport for *public diplomacy* (communication with domestic publics of other nations, often about issues which have international and domestic implications – known as intermestic publics). For example, Denmark launched a Year of Sport in 2009, designed to communicate and project 'Danish-ness', Lars Lundov, Director of Sport Event Denmark, the government body leading the initiative, explained that the goals of the Year of Sport are to show the world that Denmark is a friendly and attractive country, that Danish organisations are efficient and that the country is a good destination for international events.

> *We don't think that Denmark is very well-known abroad…We are not a well-known European country like France, the UK or Germany and many people around the world would not be able to point us out on a map! But we believe that, using sport, which is an international language, we can show guests and visitors the Danish qualities…efficiency with a smile… hygge [the relaxed atmosphere found whenever Danes are with family and friends]…our journey is some kind of sport politics…*
>
> (McCullagh, 2009, p. 24)

Discussion Question

How would you project your own culture through sport to those from other cultures?

International organisations or movements may also seek to communicate their messages through sport. One example of this has been the second Sport and Peace Conference held in December 2008 in Monaco, which was, according to Kevin Roberts, Editor of *Sport Business International*:

> *Life-affirming, gut-wrenchingly frustrating and hugely moving …once one managed to cut through a thick outer skin of political posturing and mutual appreciation to get to the core…[speakers told of] the role that sport has played and continues to play in helping reconcile peoples and create social progress in countries as diverse as Rwanda and Ireland. Here was a reminder that for every $1 million-a-month superstar there are millions of kids for whom sport represents a taste of something approaching normality in lives devastated by famine, war, gang culture and/or HIV.*
>
> (Roberts, 2009, p. 7)

However, the Sport and Peace Conference scheduled to take place in South Africa in 2009 had to be shelved because the South African Government would not permit the Dalai Lama to attend, which Tibet's government-in-exile claimed was due to the fact that China is South Africa's largest trading partner (http://abcnews.go.com/International/wireStory?id=7156674). Other similar initiatives have included more broadly focused international conferences exploring the role that sport can play in development and peace.

Corporations may use sport as a means of *corporate diplomacy*, as a way of enhancing relationships with external groups in areas of strategic business or marketing interest. Both public diplomacy and corporate diplomacy are terms which describe a strategic form of public relations – where public relations action is driven by management policy to prioritize reputation management and embark on 'hearts and minds' campaigns.

A more recent form of diplomacy and public relations has arisen around cities, particularly those that bid for major international events such as the Olympics, Asian Games, etc.

Cities have gained in importance in the study of global communications, culture and information: the notion of a "world city" appeared…in the 1980s…and approaches to study of the city now include those that look at urban centres as command and control sites for the intermeshing of global financial, production, and distribution systems…economic engines because they are dense in information resources…serving global functions because of their cultural creativity…as edges or links between nodes, rather than nodes in themselves…as symbolic sites.

(Comor, 2002, p. 404)

It is not too far fetched to describe this emergent form as *city diplomacy*, or 'city public relations' and it has reached its apogée in the development of Sport Cities, such as Dubai, Doha and Oman. Dubai Sport City is regarded as a benchmark, including:

A state-of-the art futuristic indoor and outdoor multi-purpose stadia, dedicated cricket and hockey stadia and world class sport facilities and training academies… sited in a 50 million square foot area within Dubai-land, a "biosphere" of leisure, tourism and entertainment.

(Glendinning, 2006, p. 50)

Such cities are designed to attract sport tourists (L'Etang et al., 2006) and they offer an extraordinary opportunity for 'the tourist gaze' (L'Etang, 2006a, Urry, 2003).

Another example is Oman's 'Blue City' development planned as a tourist destination with ports, venues and academies, which is supposed to create thousands of jobs, important as all Gulf States seek to diversify their carbon-based economies (Glendinning, 2006). Bahrain, which made its name when it hosted the Formula 1 Grand Prix in 2004 has 'Khalifa Sport City' and Doha (Qatar) not only hosted the 15th Asian Games (bigger than the Olympics in terms of the number of sport) but, 'Is also one of the best places in the world for sport sciences…[which means] it could partner with the Australian Institute of Sport (Glendinning, 2006, p. 50).

In public relations terms, these elite centres of population seek elite partners and strategic alliances to build brand and enhance their reputation.

The Gulf States have positioned themselves on the global map for elite sport to provide an alternative income stream. In 2006 a number of sport academies had relocated or established training centres there, for example Manchester United Soccer School, David Lloyd Academies (leisure, spa and tennis), International Global Cricket Academy and the Butch Harman School of Golf (linked with Troon, Scotland) (Glendinning, 2006).

These examples demonstrate: the complexity and interconnections between the international business of sport, national economies, tourism and the cult of the 'mega'. Public relations in such a context is potentially political, promotional, propagandistic and undeniably complicated in terms of stakeholder management and corporate social responsibility.

Discussion Question

What cultural issues arise that impact public relations and reputation for the newly emerging sport cities and why?

Development communication explores communication structures and practices in developing regions, not only in relation to the developed world, but also, more reflexively, in terms of how communication contributes to processes of change and development such as nutrition, health, literacy and sport.

Development communication is the study of social change brought about by the application of communication research, theory and technologies to bring about development – defined as a widely participatory process of social change in a society, intended to bring about both social and material advancement (Rogers and Hart, 2002, pp. 9–10).

An example of this can be cited in the work of the Mathare Youth Sport Association (MYSA) which, since 1987, has grown to become the largest youth organisation in Africa, focused on football as a way of strengthening self-esteem and belief and to alter distorted images of Africa (Hognestad and Tollison, 2004). It thus entails the ambition of an international media campaign, as well as utilizing sport as a form of communication that can bestow individual and community confidence. An optimistic view is that: 'Sportification of Africa can indeed be a positive rather than a negative component establishing peaceful and viable social relationships' (Giulianotti cited in Hognestad and Tollison, 2004, p. 224).

> **Discussion Question**
> Can sport solve social and economic problems, and, if so, how and why?

Thus, sport public relations ('relations with publics, including the general public') and communications can be utilized in many different ways and contexts, for national diplomacy or for local development.

Finally, I should highlight the fact that some authors, including those in public relations, incorrectly use the terms cross-cultural communication, intercultural communication and international communication interchangeably, which is why I have gone to some trouble to distinguish them here, not least because each has a particular implication for public relations work in sport.

GLOBALIZATION

Faster and more accessible travel and digital technologies have contributed to the phenomenon of globalization, which to some is a form of capitalist imperialism. McLuhan's 'global village' appears to have been realized in many respects, in multi-cultural societies, and in the availability of similar goods and services throughout (the richer) parts of the globe where: 'The same set of economic rules [apply] everywhere in an increasingly interdependent world' (Rogers and Hart, 2002, p. 12).

Trans-national advertising has been held partly responsible for this aspect of globalization, described as: 'The fire that lights the path towards capitalism and consumption...it...promotes particular worldviews and ideologies...what we must aspire to...That is, it has a social control function' (Viswanath and Zeng, 2002, pp. 359–361). Similarly, public relations involves discourse work and the construction and management of symbols in promotion (of sport events), likely to be connected to powerful elites who finance such events (political class, capital class).

Cross-cultural comparisons are evident where people are on the move either individually or in groups. Increased mobility and more open borders enhance nomadic possibilities because:

Global transformation compels us to stretch the limits of our usual ways of thinking. At the forefront of this reality are countless people who are on the move across cultural boundaries – millions of immigrants, refugees, and other long-term re-settlers who seek a better life. Others re-locate temporarily for a narrower set of purposes – artists, musicians, writers, business people, construction workers…diplomats and other government employees…missionaries and journalists.

(Kim, 2002, p. 259)

Athletes, coaches, amateur sport participants, spectators, officials, sport business practitioners and marketers contribute to the international sport diaspora. Major sport events facilitate cross-cultural comparisons when national teams are accommodated in temporary global sport villages.

Globalization contributes to homogenization of goods and services across the globe, and the dominance of those perceived as aspirational – and often dominant cultures. This can contribute to a decline in locally offered goods and services (sport is a service if defined as entertainment). For example:

The Asian Football Confederation has been…arguing that fans in some parts of Asia prefer to watch the FA Premier League on ESPN Star Sport than attend a local league match or play themselves…the Chinese Basketball Association is worried about the talent drain to the NBA while the Japanese Baseball's ruling body is reluctant to let the USA's major league Baseball take too much of a lead in global development of the sport…

(Fry, 2006, pp. 44–46)

Globalization demands cultural sensitivity, competences and training. Public relations practitioners specializing in sport need to be able to understand a variety of sporting cultures, organisational and corporate cultures and ethnic and national cultures.

THE BUSINESS OF SPORT AND CROSS-CULTURAL COMMUNICATION

Sport is a massive international business that sells sport events, products and services to sponsors, media (media rights) and advertisers. Public relations is often seen as part of marketing and integrated communications, but has an acknowledged role in the activation of sport sponsorships, in corporate hospitality and luxury PR, in celebrity/sport star media relations (although this role may in fact be carried out by sport agents), in event management, in corporate social responsibility and of course in media relations and promotional publicity (L'Etang, 2009). It is probably fair to say that sport PR has not yet reached its potential and is still limited in many cases to the tactical technical level. However, the growth of security as an issue and the concomitant risk management aspects of the sport business (which impact insurance) may begin to see greater PR presence in issues and crisis management. The sport business practitioners operate in a global environment, constantly assessing new markets, for example, in Asia and China for growth in terms of sport programming and rights. For example:

> *The vision of sport as an economic driving force…is being replicated right across the Asian land mass. In China, Japan, Korea, India, Malaysia, Singapore. Hong Kong, Qatar, Dubai and Bahrain, investment in sport has become one of the most visible symbols of the way economic power is shifting inexorably east.*
>
> (Fry, 2006, pp. 44–46)

Sport business people have to be sensitive to cultural difference, for example, Richard Worth, MD of TEAM marketing, responsible for handling commercial developments of the Champions league on behalf of Union of European Football Associations (UEFA) commented: 'The point is that there is a big difference in the way the competition and the brand is perceived from territory to territory. In the UK it would have one characteristic and in say, Finland or Japan it would have others' (Roberts, 2006, pp. 46–47).

Globalization of the sport business also requires sensitivity in terms of local markets and the requirement to 'think global, act local'. This has been particularly so in Asia of which it has been argued:

> *There are many obstacles to being commercially successful in the region…the number of financially active consumers is lower…growth is an urban phenomenon…150 million Chinese live on less than 1$ a day…political goodwill in Asia is hardcore. Formula 1 and the ATP tennis Tour spent 10 years* pressing the flesh *before they began to make real inroads into China.*
>
> (Fry, 2006, p. 44 – emphasis added)

This suggests that long-term strategic public relations has a considerable role to play in developing and enhancing business relationships well in advance of any propositions.

Yet despite the extent of globalization, there are still some key cross-cultural differences, for example:

In Europe and North America, there is a lively TV rights market. But in Asia it is extremely difficult to get a decent rights fee out of a broadcaster (with the partial exception of Japan)…some networks are strapped for cash (Philippines, Indonesia)…others form cartels to bid for rights…some have capricious legislation (India)…in others…. there is a local monopoly (China, Vietnam)…some pay-TV piracy massively undermines the commercial clout of local platforms when buying rights (Thailand).

(Fry, 2006, p. 44)

Business is also quick to pick up on sport which do cross cultures, such as baseball which attracted sponsorship from Anheuser-Busch, Gatorade, Mastercard Inc, MBNA, Benco Mercantil, Konami, Tourism of Puerto Rico, as Judy Hector, Director of Business Affairs and Licensing for the major league Baseball Players Association said: 'The World Baseball Classic is a tribute to the global popularity of baseball – a fact that has not gone unnoticed by the international corporate community' (Smith, 2006a, 2006b, p. 10).

To practice public relations in sport business requires a close knowledge of sport business and international business and not just of sport.

MEDIA AND CROSS-CULTURAL COMMUNICATION

A challenge for public relations practitioners operating internationally is that media structures, ownership, regulation and control, editorial freedom, gate-keeping practices and source-media relations and practices vary cross-cultur-ally. It is for this reason that effective intercultural communication draws on the combination of global resources and local knowledge ('glocalization'), which has led to the mantra of 'think global, act local'. For example, media outreach or saturation will be limited by depressed levels of literacy (Sriramesh and Vercic, 2003). Cross-cultural variance in media practices depends upon political systems, levels of economic development, the legal system, the extent of activism or single-issue public relations activity (Sriramesh and Vercic, 2003).

Digital TV, online coverage (including fantasy games) has widened opportunities to view and download coverage, at least for those in developed countries. For example, in the UK there is access to BBC News 24, Sky News, Sky Sports News and the ITV News Channel and these 24/7 news channels often feature sport press conferences (Boyle, 2006, p. 129). There have been increased links between media outlets such as Sky News affiliation with the UK national commercial radio station TalkSPORT, and in Sweden SPORT-*Expressen* TV channel was the consequence of collaboration between the

Expressen newspaper, a sport rights distribution company IEC and a technology company Hego (Boyle, 2006). These burgeoning opportunities suggest that there will be a consequent expansion of opportunities in sport media relations.

The US cable TV network, ESPN is dedicated to sport broadcasting but has largely focused on US football and baseball. In December 2008, however, they indicated that they might bid for British Premier League TV rights, as reported by Kelso (2008).

> *A major player in US sport rights, the Disney-owned company have been circling European football rights for some time, and in September Disney president Dick Iger indicated they would bid for live Premier League…Their recent involvement in Germany may be instructive. ESPN were thought to be contenders for live Bundesliga rights and their apparent interest pushed pay-TV channel Premiere to pay €1 billion. In fact ESPN had only bid for the less valuable Bundesliga 2 rights. If they have a similar impact in England there will be no complaints from club boardrooms.*
>
> (Kelso, 2008, *online*)

Sport media is therefore a big international business and is driven by commercial imperatives and profit. Thus programming is dominated by popular sport and, within that, male sport. While public relations practitioners and press agents may have to work very hard to keep footballers out of the papers and broadcast media, and spend large amounts of time managing club web pages and forums, those who work on behalf of minority sport will need all their creativity to achieve a modicum of coverage. It certainly seems, in sport media, that the sport public sphere is indeed dominated by sport elites.

By way of contrast, Transworld Sport takes a cross-cultural approach to its programming, in that it purports to give a round-up of sport action around the globe and includes a wide variety of culturally grounded sport such as a complicated and ancient stone throwing game in Bhutan lasting half a day, often played on religious festivals (20th anniversary edition of TWS 6/5/07 shown on Channel 4).

International media are also crucial in the portrayal of different nations with developing countries being presented less favourably. For example, Larson and Rivenburgh (1991) studied the TV coverage of the opening ceremony of the Seoul Olympics by the British Broadcasting Corporation (BBC), the United States' National Broadcasting Corporation (NBC) and Australia's TEN network and found that a large majority of developing countries received no mention whereas developed countries received positive and extended coverage (Sriramesh and Vercic, 2003). Likewise, De Moragas et al.'s international content analysis of TV coverage of the Barcelona Olympics around the world showed that for many cultures around the world, the Olympics creates more a sense of participating in the festival of 'others' than of participating in a universal event' (Libby, 1995; De Moragas et al., 2004).

In sport, international communication is instigated by international sport organisations (see Chapter 13, this volume) but is realized through the global sport media market. As Comor (2002, p. 321) pointed out:

> Global media corporates are important...[because] media corporations are pivotal agents in the production and distribution of information and images throughout the world...[and because] they contribute some of the most influential entities in the emerging history of the Internet and related digital technologies in terms of how these will be structured, who will have access to them, and how they will be used.

SUMMARY

From this survey of some of the cultural issues in sport, it can be seen that popular elite sport fuels major global economic activity that is tied in to other sectors, especially travel and tourism. Public relations is an activity which follows economic activity and economic policies, and is present at all levels, even though it may not be recognized as such, it should be clear that sport is both entertainment (promotion) and politics (diplomacy). Public relations necessarily supports sport international marketing, although it is not limited to this role, and it is required to engage and communicate with culturally different media, stakeholders, audiences and publics. The importance of intercultural training has been highlighted in the business world by Roland Chavillon, development officer for the FIFA Master course which focuses on sport management and marketing: 'Providing a truly international and multi-cultural dimension is key, as well as integrating the sport industry with the curriculum...countries with emerging sport industries are much in need of education and know-how' (Smith, 2006a, 2006b, p. 9).

As strategic communicators, sport public relations practitioners need to be attuned to cultural differences and sensitivities and to issues that arise from the globalization of dominant sport. They also need to be aware of history and politics, which shape, and arise from, culture and produce ideological tendencies which are reflected in sport and communicative practices. Sport public relations operates strategically and interculturally on behalf of states and sporting institutions and corporations; at the technical level, the nuances of communication are apparent in the study of rhetoric in official documentation and public communication. Thus intercultural sport public relations is a complex affair, challenging its practitioners.

KEY TERMS

Culture Shared patterns of behaviour, common values and assumptions about daily living within a particular community.

Promotional Culture Entails a particular discourse through which organisations and individuals seek to 'sell' themselves and their vision.

Cross-Cultural Communication Usually defined as a comparative approach to exploring communications in different cultures.

Intercultural Communication Describes communication between one culture and another.

International Communication Communications which arise as part of international politics, state diplomacy and public diplomacy.

Public Diplomacy Communication with domestic publics of other nations, often about issues which have international and domestic implications.

Corporate Diplomacy A way of enhancing relationships with external groups in areas of strategic business or marketing interest.

DISCUSSION QUESTIONS

1. Why is public relations in a sporting context a matter of intercultural communication?

2. What are the implications of culture for sport public relations?

3. How does culture influence sport practice?

4. How does culture inform and shape sport public relations?

GUIDED READING

Coakley, J., Dunning, E. (Eds.)., 2000. 'Sport and Society Research Around the Globe', Handbook of Sport Studies. Sage, London, pp. 521–522.

L'Etang, J., 2006. Public relations and sport in promotional culture. Public Relations Review 32 (4), 386–394.

L'Etang, J., 2009. Sport public relations: context, issues & critique. Sage, London.

Xifra, J., 2008. Soccer, civil religion, and public relations: devotional–promotional communication and Barcelona Football Club. Public Relations Review 34 (2), 192–198.

RECOMMENDED WEBSITES

Official Website of 16th Asian Games – <http://www.gz2010.cn/en>.

Official Website of 16th Asian Games – Spirit of the Games – <http://www.gz2010.cn/special/0078002J/sight.html>.

REFERENCES

Allison, L., 2000. Sport and nationalism. In: Coakley, J., Dunning, E. (Eds.), Handbook of Sport Studies. Sage, London, pp. 344–356.

Allison, L. (Ed.), 2005. The Global Politics of Sport: The Role of Global Institutions in Sport. Routledge, London.

Aw, A., Tan, S., Tan, R., 2002. Guanxi and public relations: an exploratory qualitative study of the public relations – Guanxi phenomenon in Singapore firms. Seoul, South Korea. Paper presented to the Public Relations Division of the International Communication Association, July 15–19.

Banks, S.P., 2000. Multicultural Public Relations: A Social-Interpretive Approach, second ed. Iowa State University Press, Ames, IA.

Barnett, Lee, 2002. Its use in intercultural communication research. In: Gudykunst, G., Mody, B. (Eds.), Handbook in International and Intercultural Communication, second ed. Sage, Thousand Oaks, California, pp. 275–290.

Boyle, R., 2006. Sport Journalism: Context and Issues. Sage, London.

Braman, S., 2002. A pandemonic age: the future of international communication theory and research. In: Gudykunst, W.B., Mody, B. (Eds.), Handbook of International and Intercultural Communication. Sage, Thousand Oaks, pp. 399–413.

Chen, N., 1996. Public relations in China: the introduction and development of an occupational field. In: Culbertson, H., Chen, N. (Eds.), International Public Relations: A Comparative Analysis. Lawrence Erlbaum Associates, Mahwah, NJ, pp. 121–154.

Coakley, J., Dunning, E. (Eds.), 2000. Sport and Society Research Around the Globe. Handbook of Sport Studies. Sage, London, pp. 521–522.

Comor, E., 2002. Media corporations in the age of globalization. In: Gudykunst, W.B., Mody, B. (Eds.), Handbook of International and Intercultural Communication. Sage, Thousand Oaks, pp. 309–324.

De Moragas Spa, M., Rivenburgh, N., Larson, J., 2004. Local visions of the global: some perspectives from around the world. In: Rowe, D. (Ed.), Critical Reading: Sport, Culture and the Media. Open University Press, Maidenhead, pp. 186–209.

Edwards, A., Skinner, J., 2006. Sport Empire. Meyer and Meyer Sport, Oxford.

Falkheimer, J., Heide, M., 2006. Multicultural crisis communication: towards a social constructionist perspective. 6–9 September 2006. In: Eighth Annual

EUPRERA Congress. Strategic Communication in a Multi-cultural Context. University of Central Lancashire, Carlisle, Lake District, England.

Foster, K., 2005. Alternative models of the regulation of global sport. In: Allison, L. (Ed.), The Global Politics of Sport: The Role of Global Institutions in Sport. Routledge, London, pp. 63–87.

Fry, A., 2006. Understanding the Eastern promise. Sport Business International 111 (March), 44–46.

Glendinning, M., 2006. Building a winning platform. Sport Business International 106 (December), 49–56.

Jarvie, G., 2000. Sport, racism and ethnicity. In: Coakley, J., Dunning, E. (Eds.), Handbook of Sport Studies. Sage, London, pp. 334–344.

Grainger, A., Newman, J., Andrews, D., 2006. Sport, the media and the construction of race. In: Raney, A., Bryant, J. (Eds.), Handbook of Sport and Media. Lawrence Erlbaum Associates, Mahwah, NJ, pp. 447–469.

Grunig, J., Grunig, L., 2008. Excellence theory in public relations: past, present and future. In: Zerfass, A., van Ruler, B., Sriramesh, K. (Eds.), Public Relations Research: European and International Perspectives and Innovations. Verlag fur Sozialwissenschaft, Wiesbaden, VS.

Gudykunst, W.B., 2002. Cross-cultural communication: introduction. In: Gudykunst, W.B., Mody, B. (Eds.), Handbook of International and Intercultural Communication. Sage, Thousand Oaks, pp. 19–24.

Gudykunst, W.B., Lee, C.L., 2002. Cross-cultural communication theories. In: Gudykunst, W.B., Mody, B. (Eds.), Handbook of International and Intercultural Communication. Sage, Thousand Oaks, pp. 25–51.

Gudykunst, W.B., Mody, B. (Eds.), 2002. Handbook of International and Intercultural Communication. Sage, Thousand Oaks.

Guilianotti, R., Armstrong, G., 2004. Drama, fields and Metaphors: an introduction to football in Africa. In: Armstrong, G., Guilionatti, R. (Eds.), Football in Africa: Conflict, Conciliation and Community. Palgrave Macmillan, Basingstoke, pp. 1–27.

Hargie, O, Tourish, D. (Eds.), 2000. Handbook of Communication Puppets for the Organisations. Routledge, Newyork.

Hargreaves, J., 2002. Globalisation theory, global sport, and nations and nationalism. In: Sugden, J., Tomlinson, A. (Eds.), Power Games: A Critical Sociology of Sport. Routledge, London, pp. 25–44.

Hofstede, 1984. Cultures Consequences, first ed. Sage.

Hofstede, 2001. Culutres Consequences, second ed. Sage.

Hognestad, H., Tollison, A., 2004. Playing against deprivation: football and development in Nairobi, Kenya. In: Armstrong, G., Guilianotti, R. (Eds.), Football in Africa: Conflict, Conciliation and Community. Palgrave, London, pp. 210–228.

Holtzhausen, D., 2000. Postmodern values in PR. Journal of Public Relations Research 12 (1), 93–114.

Holtzhausen, D., 2002. Towards a postmodern research agenda for PR. Public Relations Review 28 (3), 251–264.

Huang, Y.H., 2000. The personal influence model and *Gao Guanxi* in Taiwan Chinese public relations. Public Relations Review 26, 216–239.

Huang, Y.H., 2001. A cross-cultural, multiple-item scale for measuring organisation–public relationships. Journal of Public Relations Research 13 (1), 61–90.

Kelso, P., 2008. Premier League welcomes ESPN interest in TV rights. *Daily Telegraph*, Retrieved 16 December 2008 from: <http://www.telegraph.co.uk/sport/football/leagues/premierleague/3796008/Premier-League-welcome-ESPN-interest-in-TV-rights.html>.

Kim, Y.Y., 2002. Adapting to an unfamiliar culture: an interdisciplinary overview. In: Gudykunst, W.B., Mody, B. (Eds.), Handbook of International and Intercultural Communication. Sage, Thousand Oaks, pp. 259–275.

L'Etang, J., Pieczka, M. (Eds.), 1996. Critical Perspectives in Public Relations. Thomson Business Press, London.

L'Etang, J., Pieczka, M. (Eds.), 2006. Public Relations: Critical Debates and Contemporary Practice. Lawrence Erlbaum Associates, Mahwah, NJ.

L'Etang, J., 2006. Public relations in sport, health and tourism. In: L'Etang, J., Pieczka, M. (Eds.), Public Relations: Critical Debates and Contemporary Practice. Lawrence Erlbaum Associates, Mahwah, NJ.

L'Etang, J., 2006. Public relations and sport in promotional culture. Public Relations Review 32 (4), 386–394.

L'Etang, J., Falkheimer, J., Lugo, J., 2006. Public relations and tourism: critical reflections and a research agenda. Public Relations Review 33 (9), 68–76.

L'Etang, J., 2008. Public Relations: Issues, Practice and Critique. Sage, London.

L'Etang, J., 2009. Public relations and promotion of adventure sport. In: Wheaton, B.J., Ormrod, J. (Eds.), On the Edge: Leisure, Consumption and the Representation of Adventure Sport. Leisure Studies Association, pp. 43–70.

L'Etang, J., 2009. Sport Public Relations: context, issues & critique. Sage, London.

Larson, J., Rivenburgh, N., 1991. A Comparative Analysis of Australian, US and British telecasts of the Seoul Olympics opening ceremony. Journal of broadcast and electronic media 35 (1), 75–94.

Libby, J., 1995. Television in the Olympics. University of Luton Press, London.

Leitch, S., Neilson, D., 2001. Bringing publics into public relations: new theoretical frameworks for practice. In: Heath, R. (Ed.), Handbook of Public Relations. Sage, London, pp. 127–138.

McCullagh, K., 2009. The language of sport. Sport Business International (142), 24–25.

Maguire, J., 2000. Sport and globalization. In: Coakley, J., Dunning, E. (Eds.), Handbook of Sport Studies. Sage, London, pp. 356–370.

Maguire, J., 2006. Sport and globalization: key issues, phases and trends. In: Raney, A., Bryant, J. (Eds.), Handbook of Sport and Media. Lawrence Erlbaum Associates, Mahwah, NJ, pp. 435–447.

McKie, D., Munshi, D., 2007. Reconfiguring Public Relations: Ecology, Equity and Enterprise. Routledge, London.

Motion, J., Leitch, S., 1996. A discursive perspective from New Zealand: another world view. Public Relations Review 22, 297–309.

Palmer, C., 2000. Spin doctors and sport brokers: researching elites in contemporary sport – a research note on the Tour de France. International Review for the Sociology of Sport 35 (2), 364–377.

Philipsen, G., 2002. Cultural communication. In: Gudykunst, W., Mody, B. (Eds.), Handbook of International and Intercultural Communication. Sage, Thousand Oaks, pp. 51–68.

Poli, R., Gillan, P., 2006. Nationality in sport: issues and problems. CIES Conference 2006.

Public Relations Anthropology – a new concept. In: Sriramesh, K., Vercic, D., (Eds.), Culture and Public Relations.

Public Relations Anthropology – towards a research agenda. In: Hodges, C. Edwards, L. (Eds.), Society, Culuture and Public Relations.

Raney, A., Bryant, J. (Eds.), 2006. Handbook of Sport and Media. Lawrence Erlbaum Associates, Mahwah, NJ.

Riordan, J., Kruger, A. (Eds.), 1999. The International Politics of Sport in the 20th Century. E & FN Spon, London.

Roberts, K., 2006. Barça basking in brand play. Sport Business International 110 (February), 22–23.

Rogers, E.M., Hart, W.B., 2002. The histories of intercultural, international and development communication. In: Gudykunst, W.B., Mody, B. (Eds.), Handbook of International and Intercultural Communication. Sage, Thousand Oaks, pp. 1–18.

Rowe, D. (Ed.), 2004. Critical Reading: Sport, Culture and the Media. Open University Press, Maidenhead.

Smith, D., 2006a. Your country needs you. Sport Business International 106 (December/January), 70.

Smith, D., 2006b. Equipping yourself for a career in sport. Sport Business International 112 (April), 10.

Sriramesh, K., 2009. The relationship between culture and public relations. In: Sriramesh, K., Vercic, D. (Eds.), The Global Public Relations Handbook: Theory, Research and Practice. Routledge, London, pp. 47–61.

Sriramesh, K., Vercic, D. (Eds.)., 2003, 2009. The Global Public Relations Handbook: Theory, Research and Practice. Routledge, London.

Tan, S.L., 2000. Guanxi and Public Relations in Singapore: An Exploratory Study. Masters' Dissertation. Nanyang Technological University, Singapore.

Tilson, D., Alozie, E. (Eds.), 2004. Toward the Common Good: Perspectives in International Public Relations. Allyn & Bacon, Boston, Pearson.

Tilson, D.J., 2006. Devotional–promotional communications and Santiago: a thousand year public relations campaign for St James and Spain. In: L'Etang, J., Pieczka, M. (Eds.), Public Relations: Critical Debates and Contemporary Practice. Lawrence Erlbaum Associates, Mahwah, NJ.

Urry, J., 2003. The Tourist Gaze. Sage, London.

van Ruler, B., Vercic, D. (Eds.), 2004. Public Relations and Communications Management in Europe: A Nation-by-Nation Introduction to Public Relations Theory and Practice. Mouton de Gruyter, Berlin.

Viswanath, K., Zeng, L.B., 2002. Transnational advertising. In: Gudykunst, W.B., Mody, B. (Eds.), Handbook of International and Intercultural Communication. Sage, Thousand Oaks, pp. 359–380.

Wernick, A., 1991. Promotional Culture: Advertising, Ideology and Symbolic Expression. Sage, London.

Willner, B., 2006. Not a classic – yet? Sport Business International 112 (April), 10.

Xifra, J., 2008. Soccer, civil religion, and public relations: devotional–promotional communication and Barcelona Football Club. Public Relations Review 34 (2), 192–198.

CHAPTER 11

New Communications Media for Sport

Rob Lewis, Paul Kitchin

London Metropolitan Business School, University of Ulster

Learning Outcomes

Upon completion of this chapter the reader should be able to:

- Develop an understanding of the evolution of media
- Identify the main building blocks of current media
- Understand the shift from the broadcast paradigm to the interactive paradigm of sport communication
- Assess the opportunities for the Sport Public Relations and Communications (SPRC) function to utilise these effectively

CHAPTER OVERVIEW

This chapter sets out to describe the evolution of media in the context of Public Relations (PR) and Communications in sport over the last 20 years (roughly the life of the Internet from birth through to integral part of the way we live and organise ourselves in society). It will survey the impact of changing media (and underlying technology) on the practice of PR and Communication, in the context of the role and purpose of that function within the overall concept of sport management. The chapter will develop a framework of definitions, ideas and concepts for Sport Public Relations and

Communications (SPRC) to adapt and use *new media* to develop its capabilities and increase its effectiveness.

THE NEXUS BETWEEN MEDIA AND SPORT PR AND COMMUNICATIONS

The role of SPRC is being more and more recognised as a major element in the overall strategy of sport organisations (Hopwood, 2007a). For many years, SPRC has traditionally been seen as a function limited to ensuring that the organisation gets favourable coverage in the press and television media and is the main reactive function when any crisis occurs, which threatens the relationship between the sporting organisation and the wider public. As such it is functionally concerned with the production and distribution of press releases, the handling of media contacts, the day-to-day interface with sponsors and the management of programmes designed to build and maintain the organisation's relationship with the local community (Stoldt et al., 2006).

The primary media interfaces have always included local and national press, plus television (depending on the size and nature of the sporting activity). As such, the SPRC function has been established very much as the public face of the organisation, and a first port of call for the media. In return, the media have been cultivated and managed so that news about the organisation could be published, and the most favourable opinion created and maintained, thus playing a critical role in maintaining the symbiotic relationship between sport and the public media that has lasted for over a century of organised sport (Nicholson, 2007). Although a specifically sport-related PR definition has been slow in being formally defined, a distinctive definition of SPRC was being formulated which stressed the relationship building and maintenance over time, through appropriate communications, between the sporting organisation and its relevant stakeholders or publics. In this way the SPRC role made a significant contribution to the legitimacy of the sporting organisation within a wider social and commercial world (Hopwood, 2007b).

This chapter seeks less to define the SPRC activity itself, than to create a view of the necessary nexus between the functional activity and the media available for the operational implementation of that function. To approach this, the chapter will take as its starting point the impact of the Internet on sport marketing, with a specific reference to the SPRC role, and also bring into account the impact of new technologies that are transforming the way in which the media produces and allows consumption of communications between sporting organisations and their wider publics. The continuing growth of the Internet means that any statistic on number of users and growth rates is out of date the moment it is published. Rather than providing spurious accuracy of number of users by location, the reader is advised to look at sites such as http://www.internetworldstats.com/, which is one of many useful sources of up-to-date information. However, it is incontestable that the Internet is embedded in the way people consume and create information, and the transformation this has wrought means that old assumptions about relationships between message and medium need recalibrating.

THE INTERNET 1996–2005 – PROMISE UNFILLED?

Awareness of the potentially transformative power of the Internet and the *World Wide Web* (WWW) (the Internet is the underlying connectivity network, and the world wide web is the content available on that network – we shall use the terms almost interchangeably as opposed to pedantic distinctions) for the role of PR and for sport marketing in general came early in the 1990s. From the specialist PR view, the benefits of the Internet were the following:

- Extension of reach into target publics across national and cultural boundaries.
- Direct communication between the organisations without the gate keeping function of the mass media.
- Greater interactivity and feedback.
- Increased opportunities for integration between real world and virtual world in communication programmes.
- Lower cost of communication.
- Availability 24/7.
- Global reach.
- Speed of information provision and change.
- Support of multiple content types from text to video.
- Interactivity.
- Adaptability and customisability for different sectors of the market (White and Raman, 1999; Ihator, 2001; Ki and Hon, 2006).

From a sport marketing perspective, websites could be positioned to support:

- Product information and key messages
- Sport promotion

- Capturing customer information
- Database marketing
- Support of transactions and commerce such as ticket and merchandise sales
- Direct advertising
- Sponsor sales and relationships
- Market surveys
- Cost reduction of marketing activities and
- Customer service (Stoldt et al., 2006; Delpy and Bosetti, 1998; Duncan and Campbell, 1999).

The growth in sporting organisations' web presence meant that by the early years of the twenty-first century, analysis of how sporting organisations were using the web was becoming relatively commonplace. Outstanding examples of this work are Beech et al. (2000), Carlson et al. (2003a) and Brown (2003). However it became clear, and was unambiguously stated by Brown in his survey of US professional sport marketers, that the use of the web was really analogous to recreating online what had been available offline, but at reduced cost, and with added benefits of being able to tap into *e-commerce* to grow sales of merchandise and tickets (the latter also being a significant cost reduction over traditional methods). Turner (2007) in his analysis of the development of the Internet in sport marketing noted a growth in the use of the sporting website in the context of creating a Customer Relationship Management (CRM) capability in the organisation. Adamson et al. (2006) noted not only the opportunity available but also that sport organisations were often seduced into the attractions of database marketing without realising the resource requirements and investments needed to build successful programmes.

The promise of interactivity and in particular the use of fan community message boards (Auty, 2002) was largely underplayed, and the virtues of interactivity that has driven much of the vision of the Internet were not utilised. The success of Manchester United in building a global fan forum was a rare exception, as more resources were made available to have multilingual forums to capture the global appeal of the Manchester United brand (Flavian and Guinaliu, 2005). Research into the use of message boards in Major League Baseball (MLB) also shows that the message boards are important to fans as a means of attempting to engage with other fans and the organisation, even though there was little evidence that organisations actively responded (Woo and Cho, 2008).

In many sports the fan-based comment and input were seen as at best a necessary evil, or at worst a distraction and threat in the case of potentially libellous comment being attributed to the club by appearing on its website (Lewis, 2006). The growth of alternative websites for supporters of sporting clubs, or the sport itself, and the shift of traditional media such as broadcasters and newspapers into providing comment and message board areas on their websites was seen as a relief for the sporting organisations in that it diffused away much of the traffic and relieved them of participation and the need to monitor activity. The potential for message boards to generate abusive comment and rant was more accepted in North American sport, where greater resources were devoted to managing and moderating comments before they appeared on the website (Stoldt et al., 2006).

Overall, the early experience of the web had not led to greater interactivity as once foreseen, but had created increasingly sophisticated and content-rich static sites, which downplayed the communicative elements in favour of asymmetric communication of selected news and messages. SPRC managers were often given responsibility of the organisation's website, but the principal utilisation was one within a broadcasting paradigm, with little customisation or flexibility available to the viewer of the site (Arnott and Bridgewater, 2002). This was a result of the inflexibility of early website design tools which accentuated the ease of publishing content, and which were often proprietary software, and which required expertise in IT and programming. This was the era of the Webmaster (usually a technologist) who controlled the website from a technology-oriented standpoint.

One other important aspect of the web is the ability of stakeholders within a sport to create their own web presence and gain much more attention through a website than through traditional media (Wilson, 2007). In this sense the web and Internet have facilitated activist groups in disseminating their messages and gathering support through online petitions and simple registrations of supporters. In sport many of these sites can function as alternatives to the official site and in many instances can be as professionally produced as the 'official' site (Carlson et al., 2003b). As well as providing certain groups of stakeholders with a voice and presence, they may influence other media through their content and releases of information.

van der Merwe et al. (2005) suggest that there are four broad strategies for organisations facing Internet-based activism:

- *Removal* – through getting rid of the need for the site – either by embracing it or by subsuming it into one's own communications.
- *Reformative* – taking action to render the site redundant by solving the problems as they arise.

- *Resourceful* – create the site and colonise the space before anyone else does.
- *Redundancy* – ensure there is no need for the site in the first place.

We return to a case study used in Chapter 7 to illustrate the use of the Internet in creating wider awareness of a social issue affecting Australian Rules Football and the spill over into Rugby League. In the case, contrasting reactions of two sporting organisations are described and may be considered as an example of how traditional sport have failed to adapt to the influence of the Internet and indeed to use it positively to manage a PR crisis.

CASE STUDY 11.1: The Purple Armband Games

In the first few years of this century Australian Football ('Aussie Rules' as it is known) suffered a series of scandals based around alleged sexual misconduct by its star players. The response of the governing body was a consultation with specialists in sexual assault and law enforcement and the issuing of a policy that focused more on how women should behave to avoid being entangled in serious sexual assault as opposed to targeting the behaviour of the players. Public reaction led to many women boycotting games, and a feeling that the Australian Football League (AFL) was out of touch both with its female supporter groups, and the cultural norms of society. A few fans created a movement called 'Footy Fans Against Sexual Assault' (FFASA) that attempted to mediate between the fans, the clubs of the AFL and specialists in gender violence prevention. The dominant idea was not about blaming the clubs or the sport, but on educating them and their players to do something positive and provide leadership and role models. The key to the campaign was to get the fans on side as *fan advocacy* was seen as far more powerful than the advice of experts as solicited by the sport governing body. To symbolise their stand against sexual violence the clubs were asked to wear purple armbands at particular games to show solidarity with the cause. The AFL stepped in and banned the wearing of armbands without stating why and within a few months had actually fined a club for wearing armbands to support a different charity. The FFASA used this opportunity to revive their concerns and reopen the discussion. They also broadened their campaign to include the Australian Rugby League which was going through a similar set of crises and proved more open to discussion than the AFL.

The key to the success of FFASA was its ability to cultivate excellent relations between different stakeholders in the government (local and national) and non-governmental organisations in the same field. The key to this was the creation of a dedicated website which served both as a source and a repository of information to the media, and a well-managed database that supported regular e-mail communication with site registrants and thus was able to convert visitors into supporters very easily. The viral nature of the information was also promoted as all registered members of the site were given pre-prepared messages to post on their local club sites to promote the cause. In addition, the FFASA created a draft preferred policy document on their site and invited members to collaborate and comment in drafting the final version, which was substantially redrafted as a result of input from members of the website.

The success of this fans advocacy movement was the acceptance by both sports of the need for better player education and role modelling, plus acceptance of the purple armband being worn at designated games as a symbol of support for the aims of the group. The major success of the group was to encourage widespread adoption of the purple armband being worn at all levels of the sport, and the handing over to every club the materials and advice to manage their own implementation of the symbol, and the advice and guidance provided by FFASA. Thus the 'purple armband' became a widespread symbol of clubs at all levels striving to implement the positive messages of good behaviour and respect advocated by the group.

The key to the operation was the mobilisation of support and sustaining that support through the use of the website. Without having this as the hub of the movement it is highly unlikely that the group could have stayed united and succeeded in mobilising so much support over an extended period of time. The site also supported media relations, which maintained the prominence of the story in traditional media as well as online. As it developed positive feedback so the movement grew in stature, and its ability to hand over to clubs the materials and advice to run their own versions it gained respect as an authoritative voice but not a controlling presence. The contrasting reactions of the two sports – AFL which tried to ignore the situation and manage top–down within its own sport, and the Rugby league management which openly embraced the opportunity also shows how sport even recently has major problems with fan dialogue and acceptance of the views of key publics as a natural role in policy making. Without the Internet, it is difficult to see how this activist group could have succeeded in producing such a spectacular advocacy based on garnering and nurturing fan opinion (based on Dimitrov, 2008).

WEB 2.0 – THE CHANGING COMMUNICATIONS PARADIGM

Holtz (2002) claimed that PR professionals were less than comfortable with the web because although they were familiar with their own web publishing activities, and using the web for research, they did not participate in the burgeoning communities that were shaping the way the web would be used. At the same time, PR professionals were certainly very aware of both the power of the web in the minds of their clients, and how being positioned as 'web savvy' helped to win new business (Sallot et al., 2004).

However, the standard Internet model was being subtly undermined through a combination of new technologies that would enable a massive transformation in the way people interacted with the web and how this new interaction would affect the dominant paradigm of web presence, web content creation and publication (Christ, 2005). Christened with the term 'Web 2.0' (O'Reilly, 2004), the emerging web model was based upon a radical simplification of content creation and upload to the web, open standards between applications to enable new applications to be created through combinations of features, increased sophistication of search engines enabling far more precise targeting of information. When added to this was the vastly reduced costs of storage (which enabled large video files to be stored cheaply on servers attached to the Internet), the vastly increased speeds of access networks as digital lines replaced dial up access to the Internet, and cleverer, cheaper consumer technology for data capture, storage and upload (the netbook, the mobile camera phone, the portable video recorder, and the mp3/Ipod store and playback devices), this nexus of technological innovation and change created, and will continue to create, a major impact on tlhe way in which new media changes the way the world is seen and presented.

As the Internet and web have been transformed by these technology changes, so has the role and function also altered. The main characteristic of this transformation is the shift in the locus of control of content from a publishing/reader model aligned more with the press/television consumption paradigm, to one where the user generates content in the shape of text, video and audio and loads it onto the web. This phenomenon of 'user-generated content' is rapidly taking over the web (IDC Technologies, a technology forecasting company, forecasts 70% of all web content will be derived from users by 2010 (e-consultancy, 2007)), and as it does, so it changes the web from a top–down, centralised, linear, consumption-driven model into a more non-linear, networked model of creating and sharing of information between peers (Schipul, 2006).

The other major aspect of this change is that as users go about creating content, the Internet and web become more and more closely interwoven into their lives as the web becomes the point of contact between people and their friends, their sources of information and entertainment, learning and of course, shopping. The growing importance of Web 2.0 and its cognate terms 'Social Media' (which reflects the social interactivity that characterises much of users web activity) does and will lie in the way in which it affects traditional models of organisation to customer/citizen relationships (Weber, 2007).

The key phenomena of Web 2.0 are:

Blogs: Created as a noun and as a verb from the word 'weblog', the term took on currency in the Internet world in the late 1990s, and then became one of the most visible signs of the change in web usage in the early years of the century. Essentially a blog is a journal entry with the latest entry on top when displayed on the screen. Readers can type in comments on whatever is written, and the blog can develop into a conversation between bloggers and readers very easily. Each blog has archives of past entries and comments, and usually contain links to other sites on the web so the reader can see what interests the blogger, and where they may source their initial stimulus. It is estimated that there were over 100 million blogs available on the Internet in 2008 (Technorati, 2008), with many (estimates range from 1 to 5 million) blogs that have regular readership. Traditional media, and many journalists working in their spare time, have joined the 'blogosphere', and the most read blogs are now usually to be found on the websites of traditional media such as the *New York Times*, *Huffington Post*, *The Guardian* newspaper and *ESPN*. Many bloggers have emerged as opinion formers, and it may be that in the future traditional media and the blogosphere will merge and journalists will cite blogs as their source as easily as they do other media today (Weber, 2007).

One trend has been for companies to encourage their employees to create blogs that allow engagement between the company and its customers. Although this has not been universally adopted, in many companies even the CEO uses a blog as a means of communicating with stakeholders, and a means of simplifying and making immediate issues, and encouraging dialogue with customers and other stakeholders (Wyld, 2008). For this to work, the blog must retain the values of openness and spontaneity, and not be seen as being in 'corporate speak' or blatantly promotional or self-serving (Marken, 2006). Almost all traditional sport media, and specialised sport websites such as cricinfo.com, have blogs which are side comments on the news or stories in the press that allow for a freer style of comment than traditional researched journalism. The major North American sports (National Football League (NFL), MLB, NBA and the National Hockey League (NHL)) have adopted blogging on their core sites, as have the vast majority of the teams. Outside the USA, there are a fewer examples. At the moment of writing there did not seem to be any major attempts by professional sport clubs and bodies in Europe to follow this trend, which may be linked to their initial attitude towards the web as one of corporate information and content control, with far less emphasis on interaction with the fan and wider community via the web.

The following comment from Dan Gillmor of *Knight Ridder*, a traditional news media conglomerate, sums up the 2008 state of play:

From a journalistic perspective: Blogging and other conversational media are entering a new phase when it comes to community information needs — they're growing up. Traditional media are using these tools to do better journalism, and are beginning to engage their audiences in the journalism. Entrepreneurial journalists are finding profitable niches. Advertisers are starting to grasp the value of the conversations, and so on. The big issues remain, including the crucial one of trust. Here, too, we're seeing progress. The best blogs are as trustworthy as any traditional media, if not more. The worst, often offering fact-challenged commentary, are reprehensible and irresponsible. But audiences are learning, perhaps too slowly, that modern media require a more activist approach. We need to be sceptical of everything, but not equally sceptical of everything. We need to use judgement, to get more information — and to go outside our personal comfort zones.

(Technorati, 2008, *online*)

The most recent development in blogging is the launch of 'micro-blogging' (the most successful being the almost ubiquitous 'Twitter' service) based on SMS messages of less than 140 characters where people simply send messages, such as statements of what they are doing, where they are, what they are thinking, and questions to a directory of friends who receive them and may reply. This instant blogging has already been used by the US Professional Golfers' Association (PGA) to provide quick updates to followers of a golf tournament (Sport Marketing 2.0, 2008). Many sport personalities have Twitter accounts to communicate with fans, and this is the fastest growing instance of social media as we write in 2009.

Closely linked to the blog is the podcast, an audio or video digital-media file distributed over the Internet to portable media players (the word podcast is a portmanteau term linking the initially most popular personal media player, the Apple iPod, and the 'cast' from broadcast) and personal computers. Though the same content may also be made available by direct download or streaming, a podcast is distinguished from other digital-media formats by its ability to be *syndicated*, subscribed to and downloaded automatically when new content is added. Podcasts can be made up of spliced-together content such as interviews, commentary and can include music. Video can also be incorporated to enrich the mix. Many sport media sites such as the BBC, *The Times* and *The Guardian* newspapers have podcasts available, and increasingly sport clubs such as Manchester United, Arsenal and almost all U.S. professional sport teams now have podcasts available as a means of communication with fans.

The important word in the above definition is the use of syndication or updating of content sent out from the initial site to interested users. Really Simple Syndication or RSS allows users to in effect bookmark websites and then be automatically informed when new content is available. This has increased the personalisation of the web experience as now users are specifically tracking certain content and having it delivered as opposed to searching for it and clicking through the pages of corporate websites.

Syndication itself is being improved through the use of better search engines which allow users to target more precisely the content they want by the location within a website, thus avoiding the navigation through the front page. This means that owners of websites who expect the user to see messages on the front page will be outflanked, and thus render some static web strategies that are less useful (Scott, 2007). The revolution in search created by Google now means that there is a struggle between the sites that want to attract users and the users need to go directly to the source of the information they need. Search Engine Optimisation (or SEO) is a way in which websites can use certain keywords to ensure that their content comes out on top of users search, and thus ensure they control what is being found about them on the web. Another aspect of this shift in search is the need for organisations to create separate landing pages or micro-websites which are themselves searchable so that users arriving via search get an appropriate response from the website as opposed to being delivered at the front page and having to navigate (Scott, 2007).

Whereas it is possible to create video-based blogs, the real phenomenon of the Web 2.0 world has been the growth in homemade videos posted to web, a capability pioneered by YouTube (now acquired by Google). Current research estimates that over 150,000 short videos are posted to YouTube everyday in 2008 and the total content on the site would take over 400 years to view in a single sitting (Digital Ethnography, 2008). Videos vary from home movies, comedy clips, music clips, sport clips, personal diaries and commercial content (12% as brands create their own 'channels' on the site).

The power of YouTube is in the ability for the word of mouth to spread the popularity of a clip very rapidly via e-mail, blogs and personal profiles on social networking sites such as MySpace and Facebook. In 2008, a short clip of an NBA star player being outplayed in a one-on-one situation while visiting a local community in London as part of a promotional exercise reached 3.5 million views within days of appearing (Barkham, 2008). Overall sport videos make up about 7% of YouTube content, although this will increase as traditional media companies such as ESPN licence content to the site. One reason for this is the fear of sport media rights owners that 'free' content created by end users will both degrade the value of their commercial rights and result in legal infringement of content exclusivity contracts with broadcasters.

'*Wikis*' or collaborative definition, of which the most successful instance is *Wikipedia*, which allows contributors to create definitions in an encyclopaedic format thus building up knowledge through collaboration and sharing. This comes from the willingness of participants to agree to common rules and practice and vigilance against misapplication or abuse of the process. Web 2.0 may be machine enabled, but it is very human in the way it is produced, monitored and managed (Quiggin, 2006, Paramesswaran and Whinston, 2007). Up to now the authors have not found sport organisations using wikis as an interactive tool with sport fans and consumers. However, its potential to engage enthusiasts has been shown by the numerous sport-related entries on Wikipedia itself, and it is suggested that one area where sport organisations could use wiki tools is through allowing fans to create a history of the club or organisation and collaborate to sustain its culture and heritage.

Perhaps the most visible area of Web 2.0 has been the growth in social communities on the web. The two best-known social networking sites, Facebook and MySpace, have over 500 million members with active profiles, and it is claimed that for the current younger generation (under 25) the social network site is what television was to their parents. Many sport teams have created profiles on these sites and encouraged other members to sign up as 'friends of'. In some cases the social site is simply a static page, which links back to the main site, in others, the social network has been integrated into their marketing as a low cost way of creating messages and relationships with fans. Other brands such as Coca-Cola, Nutella, Dell and Intuit have created vibrant online communities which act as a new mode of interaction through the web with a community of users and consumers which supports increased brand loyalty and genuine user interest in the products and services (Sicilia and Palazon, 2008). These communities can also be used to support innovation through real-time customer research and ideas seeking (Rowley et al., 2007).

In the sporting domain, many smaller teams in the USA have adopted a social networking approach to marketing because it enables them to easily target their audience and share content and comment through links to video and blogs thereby communicating with the audience in a familiar way (Viera, 2008). Sport sites such as Takkle.com act to support school and amateur sporting communities as a platform for the creation of sporting communities. The authors would argue that at present there are few successful examples of these sites, and the whole area of participatory sport is comparatively underdeveloped to date apart from those dedicated to sport goods (e.g. Nike runs a website, Nike +, dedicated to amateur runners which has many features of a social network and allows runners to communicate, post messages, record training and performance times).

However, the most recent phenomenon in Web 2.0 social media is the rise of *Twitter* which utilises 'micro-blogging' (or 'tweets') based on SMS/ web-based messages of less than 140 characters where people simply send messages, such as statements of what they are doing, where they are, what they are thinking, and questions to a directory of friends who receive them and may reply. This is instant but *broadcast* blogging, i.e. followers of a person tweeting automatically get updates sent to their mobile or computer, creating instant community updates. Twitter is now incorporated in most social media applications and web presence. In sport an early, functional use of Twitter was by the US PGA to provide quick updates to followers of a golf tournament (Sport Marketing 2.0, 2008). The use of Twitter has grown so fast between its inception and mid-2009 (as this chapter is written) that it is now a staple factor of communication in sport PR. From team websites having a Twitter feed on latest events, through to individual sport stars having their private Twitter followings. Sites such as BBC sport carry Twitter updates from reporters at events, and the uncontrolled nature of the communication can result in PR lapses (as when the Australian cricket player Philip Hughes announced on his Twitter account that he had been dropped from the team before the official Australian cricket team announcement) (Briggs, 2009). In PR terms control of Twitter has become a major headache, with organisations attempting to limit usage by players (Maese, 2009), and even fans using the service to comment to each other during matches (Azpiri, 2009). The most prominent users of Twitter to date have been the NBA, led by the presence of Shaq O'Neal who uses Twitter to stay in close touch with fans, and even to invite them to dine with him, or receive free tickets to games! The NBA's official Twitter feed has roughly 1.25 million followers, as much as Major League Baseball, the NFL and the NHL combined (Robbins, 2009).

How one sporting team, The Indianapolis Colts, an NFL franchise, set out to create their own community site is the subject of the case study below, which illustrates some of the issues and challenges associated with creating sport-centric communities.

CASE STUDY 11.2: Mycolts – A Social Network Experiment

The Indianapolis Colts are one of the leading NFL franchises, ranking third in terms of most affiliated fans in the USA. As with all other NFL teams, the Colts have an official website as part of the NFL's umbrella web domain, and a team site. Whereas the NFL site is linked to NFL sponsors and advertisers, and focuses very much on news, merchandise and tickets, the team website has more information targeted at the immediate fans of the team, with links back to the NFL. In 2006, the marketing team at the Colts was excited by the idea of using Web 2.0 tools to create a site that was far more fan-centric and which would make full use of social media to create a new community. The trial site was launched in 2007, and growth to date has been impressive, reaching over 25,000 members by the middle of 2008. The site was relaunched into a more sophisticated version during early 2009.

What Is Mycolts.Net?
Firstly it is a site where the content is exclusively generated by the members. Based very much on the social networking paradigm of Facebook and MySpace, the community allows fans to create content from starting and contributing to blogs or forum-based discussions, uploading personal profiles detailing their likes and dislikes such as personal favourites in terms of books, films and television, including videos and photographs, to contributing content to different areas of the site. It contains links to the main websites (and these are reciprocated) and carries very little direct advertising apart from the team's main sponsorships. Fans (and the club) can even create and post their own surveys as a way of finding out what the community thinks.

Continued

'Colts Cred'

'Colts Cred' is an approval rating of contributors' contents on MyColts.Net. It takes into account of how often people's pages are looked at and how they rate the content loaded onto the site. Points are awarded based upon activity inside MyColts.Net, e.g. blog posts, comments, uploading photos and videos, as well as reporting inappropriate content accurately. This has both an incentive scheme (the more 'cred' points the more the chance to win prizes such as VIP days out with the team, social emulation (the top 'cred' points earners are displayed on the site) and a form of self-monitoring that restricts or at least points out inappropriate behaviour which might also include infiltration by opposing fans posting denigratory content.

One of the initial findings from analysing the 'cred' scores is that females who make up 33% of the site's membership actually score 55% of the points, i.e. are more dedicated to using the site proactively (no points are awarded simply for observing content). Early data also suggest that these female fans do not visit the fan forum on the main site but prefer the social network.

User-Generated Content

The approach on the site is to 'take what they give us' – as Pat Coyle, the Colts marketing manager puts it 'We've come to realise there's an opportunity to let fans do the talking, and still generate the valuable traffic we want. That's a big reason why we are building the Colts Fan Network – it allows us to expand the amount of user generated content on our site...and allows fans to create the content that, we hope, will attract even more fans to visit and soak it up.' This reaching out to the fans and facilitating their ability to create their own views of the club and share these is central to the site, and central to the idea of building the community united around the team. Again Coyle comments:

> On our social network site things get a bit more interesting. First of all, I found it curious that our loyal forum members wanted NOTHING to do with the social net when we launched it last year. I suppose this is human nature. Many of them were concerned that we would take away the board to

> which they'd grown accustomed. We decided not to do that when we witnessed a distinct audience using the social net. Further, the social net is quite different from the board. We see a lot of community building going on...folks meeting offline and forming friendships. They talk about a lot more non-football stuff on mycolts.net. They can upload photos and videos and decorate their pages ... much more room for self expression and self-actualisation'. So there seem to be two distinct, and perhaps two gender-skewed communities growing up around the team.

(Coyle, 2008)

Long Tail – of Fans

Chris Anderson's (2006) discovery of how the Internet enables the 'long tail' of content to reach a market (i.e. the low to non-existent costs of distribution of encoded data on the web means back catalogues of book and music can be stored, reproduced and sold to very small market segments otherwise impossible to serve effectively when holding infinite real-world inventory) has been tweaked by the Colts to look at their distribution of fans across the USA.

Overall 65,000 Colts fans attend the stadium on 10 Sundays each year and 8 million Colts fans visit the website, and 10 million Americans say the Colts are their favourite team. The big issue is how to connect the non-attendees into a focused community and then ensure that this can be used to reinforce the fan affiliation and feeling of attachment to the team.

As NFL franchise marketing has usually looked to the stadium and the fans locally as the prime market, the new wider market opens up new challenges and opportunities for building relationships and widening the sense of belonging to the team.

The Problem – What do you do with a Social Network?

As the Colts develop the infrastructure for a community of fans, the issue being raised is one of 'well now we think we can build it, how are we going to monetise it?' At the moment there is more worry about building and sustaining the community but the future will pose further challenges to integration of this community into the marketing strategy of the team. At one level it would seem that this might be an experiment that has no defined end point, and current concerns over monetisation – may be via sponsorship of the community – are premature. How far can the discussion shift to the public relations logic that might position such a community as the way in which the Colts build one form of relationship with its target audience, in terms of fan loyalty and commitment, i.e. a core cost of being in the spectator sport business?

The core question for this initiative, and the others that are being built around commitment to sport, will centre on whether the sporting organisation can utilise the dialogic and relationship building power of communities or whether it simply sees it as another form of segmenting and parcelling up audiences for sponsors and advertisers. The Colts are adamant that this community of avid fans represents an opportunity for affiliation with a sponsor, but in what sense does a heterogeneous crowd of people united only by the passionate support of a team represent a viable target audience for a single sponsor? These are first steps on a long journey.

Interestingly, the use of Twitter between fans has been slow to take off – mainly perhaps because the fan base demographic tends to be over 35 years and therefore not as used to social media conversations as using the website to exchange messages and gather information.

IF THIS IS THE SOCIAL MEDIA, WHY DOES IT MATTER?

The core argument in recent public relations theory has centred on the relationship between PR, as a distinct area of competence, and the marketing function, as increasingly companies and organisations speak about marketing or brand communications as a single area of competence (Batchelor and Formentin, 2008). Others have gone further and stated that the future of Web 2.0 means the imminent collapse of marketing, PR and even customer service into a single integrated relationship focused communication path with the customer (Scott, 2007; Solis, 2008). If the premise behind the growth of social media is that marketing can no longer be divided into functional areas of expertise, then the impact on SPRC management and practice will be profound. However, despite the perhaps lacklustre use of web-based PR tactics and strategy in the past, the arrival of a new web paradigm may be an opportunity for sport PR managers to utilise expertise and knowledge of how the media is evolving to take a leadership role in the development of relationship-based approaches to the stakeholder base for the sporting organisation. Commenting on the need for SPRC expertise, Hopwood (2007c, p. 2) has noted:

> Public relations is much more than simply media relations, publicity and event management, it is a fundamental component of today's integrated marketing communications mix…The important word for sport organizations…is 'relationships' as it relates to the relationship

management notion that any organization with effective public relations will attain positive public relationships.

Social media demands an understanding of how organisations will interact in a continuing dialogue between themselves and their stakeholders – from fans to community to sponsors to internal staff. Expertise in this area will be less concerned with immediate exchange-based objectives and more with long-term nurturing and development of both the relationship between the organisation and the stakeholders as much as it will be in enabling intra-stakeholder communication (Solis, 2008). One of the complicating factors of the new web is the increased ability for stakeholders to hold conversations between themselves outside the control of the organisation, and rather than consider this a drawback, organisations will need to understand how to facilitate and intervene and negotiate within such conversations, moving from an organisation-centric model to a relationship-centric mode of operation (van der Merwe et al., 2005)

In her book, *PR 2.0*, Deirdre Breakenridge summarises what customers believe they want from social media interactions with organisations:

- Receive direct unmediated communications.
- Have easy access to information about the products and services on offer.
- Be able to ask questions (and get answers) about products and services.
- Get a quick response for an enquiry.
- Hear a voice from the organisation on issues which affect that organisation's wider environment.
- Believe they can trust the people from the organisation.
- Drive and control their communications with the organisation.
- See how other people feel about the organisation and its products/services.
- Interact with people who have similar viewpoints.
- Easily share information with others through video, pictures blogs, podcasts, etc.
- Discuss their interests and viewpoints on a number of issues from soap operas to politics with people inside a community with shared values and interests.
- Create information and content within an open forum (Breakenridge, 2008).

These needs are not that dissimilar from the original hopes for the Internet in terms of organisation–customer relationships, but the rise of Web 2.0 capabilities offers greater facilitation and the promise of greater effectiveness.

One aspect of change in the sport marketplace is the rise of a youth market that has grown up without the experience of traditional television and press dependence for sport. The markets of Generation Y and Generation X, post-date the 'baby boomer' population of the post-war developed world, who were the early adopters and drivers of the Internet. The 13–24 generation spend over 50% of their Internet time on user-generated content sites, versus 35% for Generation X (25–41) and 27% for the baby boomer generation of 42–60-year-olds. This 2007 figure will undoubtedly continue to change in favour of user sites versus organisational sites, especially as traditional media morphs into a sea of blogs and community networks centred on user interests (Breakenridge, 2008). The younger demographic is also far less likely to use or trust traditional media versus the web (Pew Research Centre, 2006) and will continue to mediate its world via a web of social contacts in cyberspace. For sport this is both an opportunity and a threat. The sport that manages to master social media to build and sustain relationships with their target audiences (and also mediate their role in the world via the media preferred by their stakeholders) will be better placed to enjoy the trust built up with that community. They will also be at the forefront of interpreting user needs and requirements as they change over time.

In addition, developing communications with customers and stakeholders in the social media world has operational benefits over traditional media – it is both the preferred way for target consumers to interact with the sport, and it can be a far lower cost and wider reach medium than traditional promotional alternatives. This is especially true for sport organisations which do not enjoy major television coverage, or who are trying to reach out to the community at large to promote and/or develop sport participation. In these cases bloggers are often becoming the new journalists as media cut back coverage of all but the most popular sport.

Here is the marketing manager of DC United, a US-based soccer franchise commenting on the rise of new media and relationships with target audiences:

> We believe that traditional media (print, radio and TV) is both
> ineffective and cost prohibitive. The rise of social networks and
> soccer club websites represent a much more cost-effective way of
> reaching our audience. When you combine that with the 400 player
> appearances that our players make each year we are able to much
> more efficiently convert these player touches into fans….It is
> absolutely imperative that owners of sport franchises understand
> how to reach their audience with geographic and personalized

relevance with new media. Those who don't will fall hopelessly
behind.

(Trost, 2008, online)

The importance attached to the combination of old methods (personal appearances by players in the community) with reinforcing this through web-mediated communications using social media shows that the new SPRC role will be at the forefront of how new media reinforces and enhances relationship building with the target community.

There is still, however, a long way to go. It has been noted that in the past sport organisations have treated the web as mostly a notice board or repository of information which was then made available. Most sport managers are still focused on the short term and growing revenues and attendance as opposed to building relationships and exploiting new technology for the longer term (Favoriso, 2008). In many cases this is down to a mindset formed by the view of media relations being at the core of the SPRC function, and a failure to appreciate how channels of communication can be used to forge and support relationships with key stakeholders, and in particular with the fans. With the advent of social media there is a far more likely scenario of the consumer or stakeholder being in a position of controlling just what information they need from a sport, and to trust sources such as bloggers outside the sport organisations or established media (Scott, 2007; Weber, 2007).

An additional factor is that sponsor brands are far more advanced in the use of social media as they develop strategies for engaging competitively in the marketplace against other brands and seek to build up new and loyal brand adherents. As an example the 2008 Beijing Olympics saw many innovative uses of media by the core Olympic sponsors who had used the Olympic events as a backdrop to promote their products and services. McDonald's launched an 'alternate reality game' called '*The Lost Ring*', with an accompanying Wiki and a YouTube site, using a subtle tag line associating the brand with the sport 'McDonalds is proud to sponsor The Lost Ring and bring the spirit of the Olympic Games to people around the world'. Lenovo the PC manufacturer sponsored athletes' blogs, while Nike and others created YouTube channels to show off user-generated content on an Olympic theme.

In South Africa, the sponsor of a Pro20 cricket match series launched their sponsorship with a 'social media press release' detailing how the sponsor's site will encourage supporters to get involved and create content using social media channels like blogs, Facebook, Twitter, MXit and YouTube. Whereas it is no doubt comforting that the cricket authorities and players will get the value of the sponsors money, here it is the sponsor who is building the relationship as opposed to the sport, and one might have expected a better execution which led to a cricket event-based community linked to the sport as opposed to a sponsoring bank.

HOW SHOULD SPORT PR AND COMMUNICATIONS APPROACH SOCIAL MEDIA?

The new media available to sport organisations provides a challenge and opportunity to harness a new mode of communication through a more direct and participative approach to building relationships. This is not to say that the new media will replace the traditional formats, but that the ethos of social media will become integrated into how communications and interactions with stakeholders will take place in the future. We have observed that traditional media is increasingly devoting more effort and resource to web-based content that involved users interacting, and that virtual communities supporting brands such as Coca-Cola, Dell and Intuit are being incorporated into those from daily business processes, while sites such as YouTube are colonised and utilised by brands to encourage consumer interaction and creativity. For the sport organisation what are the likely benefits of beginning to adopt social media as a key part of their PR and communications planning and implementation?

- More direct interaction with fans and other stakeholders.
- Greater information on what are the key issues faced by their audience.
- Ability to gain greater knowledge of the stakeholder base and tailor messages to support stronger relationships.
- Ability to reach out to people over a wider area and bring them closer to the club through providing features and facilities that enable them to have a closer relationship through interactions with other like-minded people and the club's own people.
- Ability to develop greater fan loyalty through closer interaction with blogs and community forums to allow the organisation to have a closer relationship with its audience.
- Ability to link the organisation and its messages to other websites, communities and blogs to widen its scope and appeal.
- Ability to generate greater coverage and awareness through the facilitation of fan-based media coverage and content creation.

Whereas the established model of excellence in PR has always focused on the Grunig derived two-way symmetrical continuum (Grunig, 1992) the development of a more European-centric model by van Ruler and Vercic

(2005) attempts to position the role of PR within the commercial and societal relationships of the organisation. In effect they are splitting the focus of the organisation between managerial concerns of commercial profit and the legitimacy or reputation/longevity aspects of the organisation in its wider environment, and on the other hand, placing the role of communications as mediating between the organisation and its immediate target audience – from customers where there is a strong commercial relationship, through to wider societal constituents or weak stakeholders who are potential publics if an issue or crisis arises that has an impact beyond the immediate market or audience of the organisation. In the case above, the instances of sexual assault in Australian sport proved to engage not only the immediate public – the fans – but also engaged a wider constituency of people concerned with gender-specific violence in Australian society.

By simplifying the van Ruler/Vercic thesis the following broad model can be created (while admitting that within the management of any organisation setting communication goals will be a constant dialectical tension between different forces). In the top right quadrant, where the concern is over legitimacy of the organisation within the social sphere, crises can subvert reputation unless there is swift response – hence this is seen as dominated by crisis management, although at a lower level there will be a continuing stream of communications that discursively attempt to manage any debate about the organisation inside a context set and managed by the organisation's own rhetoric. This might be termed a negotiating stance. Other quadrants may be interpreted in terms of the commercial focus versus the public reputation, and the need to target what might be crudely termed the 'paying' audience, and society at large. This leads to the labels and modes as shown in Figs 11.1 and 11.2.

One of the advantages of the explosion in new media is that it allows the organisation to consider a more differentiated and more direct approach to each area of activity, without having to rely on the intermediation of mass media (while remembering that in many cases it may be the mass media that itself creates the content for the communication as this operates within a tangled web of interrelated networks of communication and stakeholders).

Figure 11.2 attempts to place the appropriate use of media in the appropriate quadrant while remembering that this is merely indicative as opposed to prescriptive analysis.

The purpose here is to show where different aspects of the Web 2.0 and social media may play a role within an overall communications strategy. It also shows a move away from 'one size fits all' for the website – and the need to consider the different purposes of commercially oriented sites and the need for communities and public facing vehicles of communication. Whereas it does not purposely show the traditional media, there will remain a role for

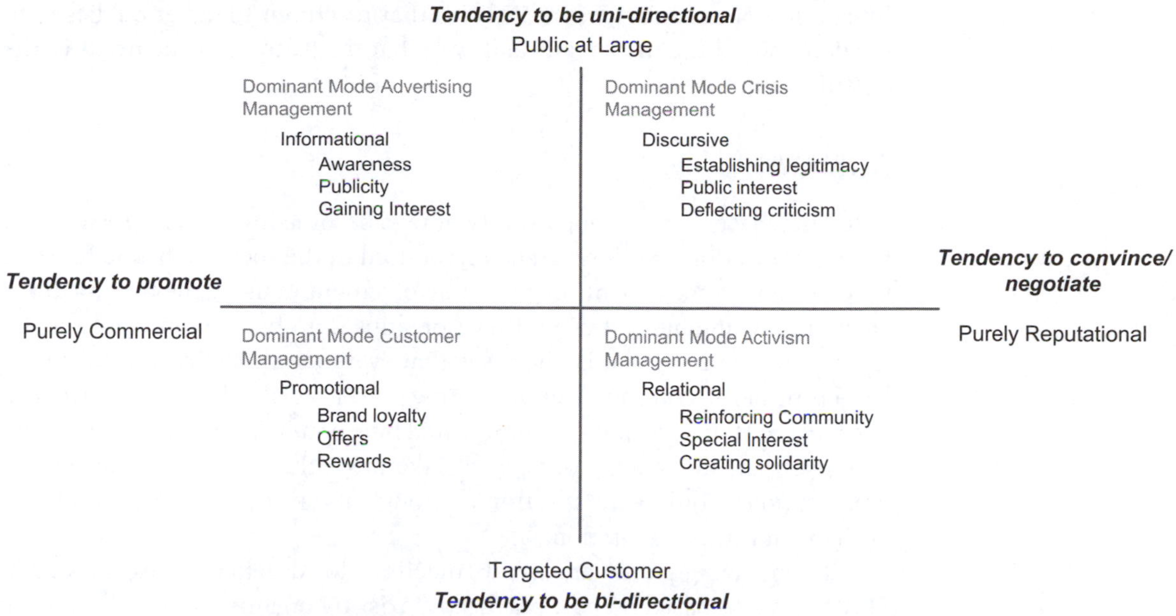

Tendency to be uni-directional
Public at Large

Dominant Mode Advertising Management	Dominant Mode Crisis Management
Informational	Discursive
Awareness	Establishing legitimacy
Publicity	Public interest
Gaining Interest	Deflecting criticism

Tendency to promote   *Tendency to convince/ negotiate*

Purely Commercial   Purely Reputational

Dominant Mode Customer Management	Dominant Mode Activism Management
Promotional	Relational
Brand loyalty	Reinforcing Community
Offers	Special Interest
Rewards	Creating solidarity

Targeted Customer
Tendency to be bi-directional

FIGURE 11.1 *A Model for Mapping Communication Flows in PR*

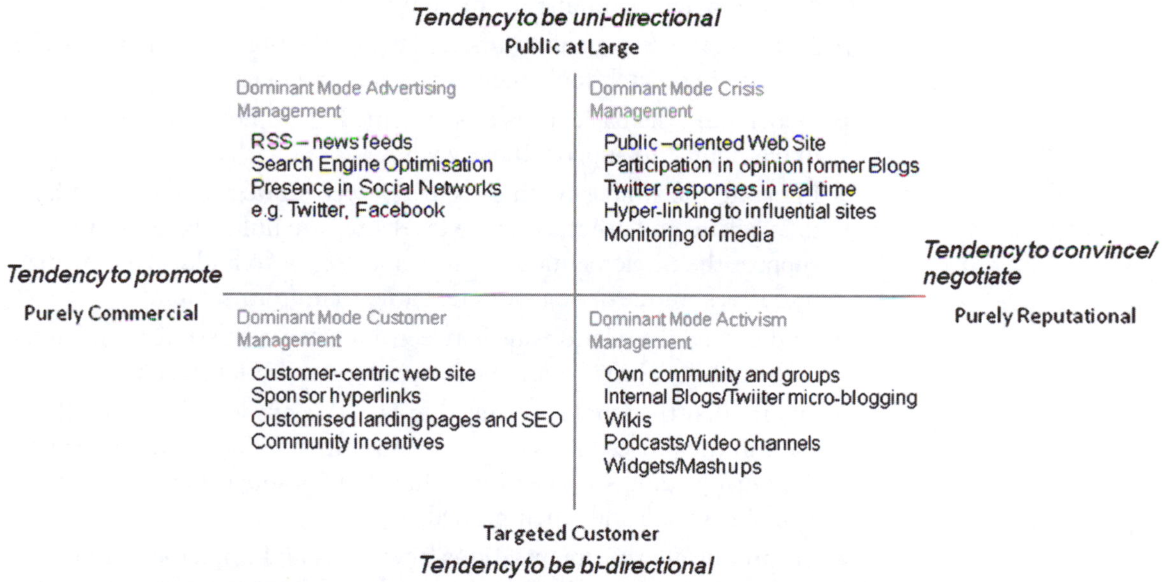

Tendency to be uni-directional
Public at Large

Dominant Mode Advertising Management	Dominant Mode Crisis Management
RSS – news feeds	Public –oriented Web Site
Search Engine Optimisation	Participation in opinion former Blogs
Presence in Social Networks	Twitter responses in real time
e.g. Twitter, Facebook	Hyper-linking to influential sites
	Monitoring of media

Tendency to promote   *Tendency to convince/ negotiate*

Purely Commercial   Purely Reputational

Dominant Mode Customer Management	Dominant Mode Activism Management
Customer-centric web site	Own community and groups
Sponsor hyperlinks	Internal Blogs/Twiiter micro-blogging
Customised landing pages and SEO	Wikis
Community incentives	Podcasts/Video channels
	Widgets/Mashups

Targeted Customer
Tendency to be bi-directional

FIGURE 11.2 *A Model for Mapping Communication Flows of new Media in PR*

integration of the activities on Web 2.0 that reach out to target publics with the demands of the media, and ability of that media to meet the needs of the organisation.

SUMMARY

SPRC managers have an opportunity now to become involved in the world of their organisation as it is seen and reproduced in the social web, and to begin to work though the benefits of greater involvement in using the new media to create more tangible and vibrant relationships than has been possible before the rise of Web 2.0. That is not to say that everyone should rush into simply launching blogs, communities or creating presences on all the social network sites just for the sake of it – an unupdated blog or a member-less community is worse than not having one at all. Like any other business strategy, the organisation should carefully think through its aims, goals and resources available for implementation.

The following points are broad guidelines for developing a social media SPRC strategy, based on best practice in existing organisations.

- Understand what its goals are and how building closer relationships with stakeholders will help.
- Communicate internally and where possible with key stakeholders to discover their requirements and issues.
- Audit what is being communicated about the organisation across the web – using search tools including searching blogs.
- Understand the basic ideas of social media and how this could be implemented to support those goals.
- Integrate the strategy with the current web strategy and ensure that the website and other associated websites are linked together to support the implementation – it is a lot easier to build social media initiatives from existing website traffic than from scratch.
- Understand the relationship between a social media strategy and links with traditional media and how to reinforce and leverage these.
- Ensure that the whole organisation is aware of the roll out and their roles in the process – issues in a community will affect all aspects of the organisation, so it is critical that there is support and resource available where and when needed.
- Communicate the organisations new plans and implementation using existing channels and new modes of communication – internally and externally.

- Implement the plan and monitor performance – ensuring that there is full commitment to implementation – nothing is worse than an attempt at dialogue that simply tails off into silence.
- Create a goal in the short and medium term which acts as a definition of success.
- Define the key metrics which support this.
- Review the implementation based on feedback and listening to the reaction from key stakeholders.
- Look for ways to improve the flow of dialogue and use it to discover new ideas and possibilities.
- Do not try to manage, censor or control or direct the flow of the dialogue unless absolutely necessary.
- Find out who your community of stakeholders think is most influential – it may be easier to build a relationship with such a person's blog than create one that competes.
- Make sure all members in the target community can exchange views with each other – this is a network not a broadcast.
- Always respond where appropriate in a timely fashion – whoever is in charge of responses must have the trust of the internal management as well as earn that of the community.

The most important factor is to have a passion for what you are implementing and to communicate this internally and externally. The new media is a challenge and an opportunity to refashion relationships within the nexus of communication between the sport organisation and its public – it can offer a whole new way of thinking about marketing the organisation and building relationships which are more intensive not only in terms of time and effort but also more effective and efficient than traditional media, or indeed, traditional media flatly translated into a static, one-sided web presence, never mind how impressive the graphics and content.

KEY TERMS

New Media   A collection of digital communications techniques that are synonymous with the growth of the Internet revolution.

World Wide Web   The collection of information that is accessed through the Internet. In this chapter these terms are used interchangeably.

e-Commerce   A term used for a collection of commercial techniques that are facilitated through or operate on electronic platforms and systems.

Web 2.0   A paradigm of web presence, web content creation and publication. Furthermore a web model which is based upon simplification of content creation and uploads to the web, open standards between applications, increased sophistication of search engines enabling far more precise targeting of information.

Blogs (Weblogs)   Essentially a blog is a journal entry with the latest entry on top when displayed on the screen.

Syndicated   A form of content licensing that allows updates to be transmitted to users through digital tools such as web browsers.

Wikis   Also termed collaborative definition, which allows multiple contributors to create definitions in an encyclopaedic format thus building up knowledge of a given topic through collaboration and sharing.

Twitter   A social media application that allows individuals or organisations to utilise 'micro-blogging' (or 'tweets') based on messages of less than 140 characters. These messages can send statements of what they are doing, where they are, what they are thinking, and questions to a directory of friends who receive them and may reply.

Social Media   A term which reflects the social interactivity that characterises much of users web activity.

DISCUSSION QUESTIONS

1. Visit a few sporting websites from different sports. How do different sports use electronic media to build relationships with their supporters? What examples of Web 2.0 behaviour can you find? Are there differences in approach between different sports and why might this be the case?

2. There is considerable debate within sports over the use of fan-generated images and video of sporting events. What are the pros and cons of allowing fans to capture and communicate their experiences of a sporting event on the web?

3. Many sports stars have created blogs and micro-blogs such as Twitter. If you were managing the SPRC for a sporting organisation, how would you position blogs and micro-blogs in your overall plan?

4. How does the rise of social media affect the SPRC model and the relationship with traditional media?

GUIDED READING

The reference list contains many useful sources of information relevant to the topic, however, the authors recommend three sources in particular:

Scott's *The New Rules of Marketing and PR* touch on many of the issues discussed in this chapter and considers how new media sources and technology are changing long-standing ideas on marketing and PR and replacing them with a new paradigm.

Favoriso's *Sport Publicity: A Practical Approach* examines PR from within the sport industry from a more practical and less academic angle. Students can use these insights to then develop areas where social media may look to pick upon opportunities that old media could not.

Finally Rein, Kotler and Shields examined the existence of *The Elusive Fan* (2006-McGraw Hill) and in doing so provided a call to reconnect with old and new fans alike in order to continue the development of sport, which is under increasing pressure from other entertainment options.

RECOMMENDED WEBSITES

Using and Population Statistics – <http://www.internetworldstats.com>.
Cricinfo – <http://www.cricinfo.com>.
High School & College Sport Recruiting – <http://www.Takkle.com>.

REFERENCES

Adamson, G., Jones, W., Tapp, A., 2006. From CRM to FRM: applying CRM in the football industry. Database Marketing and Customer Strategy Management 13, 156–172.

Arnott, D., Bridgewater, S., 2002. Internet interaction and implications for marketing. Market Intelligence and Planning 20, 86–95.

Auty, C., 2002. Football fan power and the Internet: net gains? Aslib Proceedings 54, 273–279.

Azpiri, J., 2009. Social media banned at college stadiums: SEC bans Twitter et al. NowPublic. Retrieved 30 August 2009 from: <http://www.nowpublic.com/sports/social-media-banned-college-stadiums-sec-bans-twitter-et-al>.

Barkham, P., 2008. Slam dunk 'English chap' beats US basketball star at his own game. Retrieved 24 April 2009 from: <http://www.guardian.co.uk/sport/2008/oct/17/gbbasketball-ussport>.

Batchelor, B., Formentin, M., 2008. Re-branding the NHL: building the league through the "My NHL". Public Relations Review 34, 156–160.

Beech, J., Chadwick, S., Tapp, A., 2000. Surfing in the premier league: key issues for football club marketers using the Internet. Managing Leisure 5, 51–64.

Breakenridge, D., 2008. PR 2.0: New Media, New Tools, New Audiences. Financial Times, Prentice Hall, London.

Briggs, D., 2009. The Ashes: Phillip Hughes' manager takes the blame for Twitter gaff. The Daily Telegraph. Retrieved 30 August 2009 from: <http://www.telegraph.co.uk/sport/cricket/international/theashes/5940738/The-Ashes-Phillip-Hughes-manager-takes-the-blame-for-Twitter-gaffe.html>.

Brown, M.T., 2003. An analysis of online marketing in the sport industry: user activity, communication objectives, and perceived benefit. Sport Marketing Quarterly 12, 48–55.

Carlson, J., Rosenberger, P., Muthaly, S., 2003a. Nothing but net!: a study of the information content in Australian professional basketball websites. Sport Marketing Quarterly 12, 184–189.

Carlson, J., Rosenberger, P., Muthaly, S., 2003b. Super 12s rugby union: comparing the information content and infotainment usage in Australian, New Zealand and South African super 12s websites. In: Rugimbana, R., Nwankano, S. (Eds.), Cross-Cultural Marketing. Thompson Learning, London, pp. 354–361.

Christ, P., 2005. Internet technologies and trends transforming public relations. Journal of Website Promotion 1, 3–14.

Coyle, P., 2008. Are female NFL fans more socially active online? Retrieved 24 April 2009 from: <http://sportsmarketing20.com/profiles/blogs/are-female-nfl-fans-more>.

Delpy, L., Bosetti, H., 1998. Sport management and marketing via the world wide web. Sport Marketing Quarterly 7, 21–27.

Digital Ethnography, 2008. YouTube statistics. Retrieved 24 April 2009 from: <http://mediatedcultures.net/ksudigg/?p=163>.

Dimitrov, R., 2008. Gender violence, fan activism and public relations in sport: the case of 'Footy Fans Against Sexual Assault'. Public Relations Review 34, 90–98.

Duncan, M., Campbell, R., 1999. Internet users: how to reach them and how to integrate the Internet into the marketing strategy of sport businesses. Sport Marketing Quarterly 8, 35–41.

e-consultancy, 2007. Will the growth in user generated content swamp our ability to monitor it? Retrieved 24 April 2009 from: <http://www.e-consultancy.com/forum/106086-will-the-growth-in-user-generated-content-swamp-our-ability-to-monitor-it.html>.

Favoriso, J., 2008. Sport Publicity: A Practical Approach. Butterworth-Heinemann, Oxford.

Flavian, C., Guinaliu, M., 2005. The influence of virtual communities on distribution strategies in the Internet. International Journal of Retail and Distribution Management 33, 405–425.

Grunig, J. (Ed.), 1992. Excellence in Public Relations and Communications Management. Lawrence Erlbaum Associates, Hillsdale, NJ.

Holtz, S., 2002. Public Relations on the Net, second ed. AMACOM, New York, NY.

Hopwood, M., 2007a. The sport integrated marketing communications mix. In: Beech, J., Chadwick, S. (Eds.), The Marketing of Sport. Pearson Education Limited, London, pp. 213–238.

Hopwood, M., 2007b. Sport public relations. In: Beech, J., Chadwick, S. (Eds.), The Marketing of Sport. Pearson Education Limited, London, pp. 292–331.

Hopwood, M., 2007c. It's football but not as you know it: using public relations to promote the world game in Australia. Retrieved 10 June 2009 from: <http://epublications.bond.edu.au/cgi/viewcontent.cgi?article=1175&context=hss_pubs>.

Ihator, A., 2001. Corporate communication: challenges and opportunities in a digital world. Public Relations Quarterly Winter, 15–18.

Jo, S., Kim, Y., 2003. The effect of web characteristics on relationship building. Journal of Public Relations Research 15, 199–223.

Ki, E.-J., Hon, L., 2006. Relationship maintenance strategies on Fortune 500 company websites. Journal of Communication Management 10, 27–43.

Lewis, R., 2006. Understanding Internet-Based Marketing in English Rugby Union and Cricket. Unpublished MA Dissertation. London Metropolitan University, London.

Maese, R., 2009. With Twitter, NFL loses control of image game. NBC Sport Website. Retrieved 30 August 2009 from: <http://nbcsports.msnbc.com/id/32254402/ns/sports-washington_post/>.

Marken, G.A., 2006. Blogosphere or blog with fear. Public Relations Quarterly Retrieved 10 June 2009 from: <http://findarticles.com/p/articles/mi_qa5515/is_200612/ai_n21407203/>.

Nicholson, M., 2007. Sport and the Media: Managing the Nexus. Elsevier, Oxford.

O'Reilly, T., 2004. What is web 2.0: design patterns and business models for the next generation of software. Retrieved 17 June 2009 from: <http://oreilly.com/web2/archive/what-is-web-20.html>.

Paramesswaran, M., Whinston, A., 2007. Research into social computing. Journal of the Association for Information Systems 8, 336–350.

Pew Research Centre, 2006. Audience segments in a changing news environment: key news audiences now blend online and traditional sources. Retrieved 17 June 2009 from: <http://people-press.org/reports/pdf/444.pdf>.

Quiggin, J., 2006. Blogs wikis and creative innovation. International Journal of Cultural Studies 9, 481–496.

Rein, I., Kotler, P., Shields, B., 2006. The Elusive Fan: Reinventing Sport in a Crowded Marketplace. McGraw Hill, New York, NY.

Robbins, J., 2009. Super social: Twitter is all the buzz in NBA, Orlando Sentinel. Retrieved 30 August 2009 from: <http://www.orlandosentinel.com/sports/orlando-magic/orl-sportsnba-twitter-29082909aug29,0, 3874758.story>.

Rowley, J., Kupiec-Teahan, B., Leeming, E., 2007. Customer community and co-creation: a case study. Market Intelligence and Planning 25, 136–146.

Sallot, L., Porter, L., Alzuru, C., 2004. Practitioners web use and perceptions of their own roles and power: a qualitative study. Public Relations Review 30, 269–278.

Schipul, E., March 2006. The Web's Next Generation: Web 2.0. Tactics, p. 23.

Scott, D., 2007. The New Rules of Marketing and PR. John Wiley, Hoboken, NJ.

Sicilia, M., Palazon, M., 2008. Brand communities on the Internet. Corporate Communications 13, 255–270.

Stoldt, G., Dittmore, S., Branvold, S., 2006. Sport Public Relations. Human Kinetics, Champaign, IL.

Solis, B., 2008. The state of social media. Retrieved 24 April 2009 from: <http://www.briansolis.com/2008/09/state-of-social-media-2008.html>.

Sport Marketing 2.0., 2008. Retrieved 24 April 2009 from: <http://www.sportsmarketing20.com/group/sportssocialnetworks/forum/topics/1736840:Topic:15676>.

Technorati, 2008. The state of the blogosphere. Retrieved 24 April 2009 from: <http://www.technorati.com/blogging/state-of-the-blogosphere>.

Trost, E., 2008. An interview with D.C. United's Will Chang. Retrieved 24 April 2009 from: <http://socialmediatoday.com/SMC/44496>.

Turner, P., 2007. Direct, database and on-line marketing in sport. In: Beech, J., Chadwick, S. (Eds.), The Marketing of Sport. Pearson Education Limited, London, pp. 239–266.

van der Merwe, R., Leyland, P., Abratt, R., 2005. Stakeholder strength: survival in the Internet age. Public Relations Quarterly, 39–46. Spring.

van Ruler, B., Vercic, D., 2005. Reflective communication management: future ways for public relations research. In: Kalbfleish, P. (Ed.), Communications Yearbook. Taylor and Francis, e-library, Philadelphia, PA, pp. 239–273.

Viera, M., 2008. Befriending generation Facebook. Washington Post Retrieved 24 April 2009 from: <http://www.washingtonpost.com/wp-dyn/content/article/2008/07/14/AR2008071402144.html>.

Weber, L., 2007. Marketing to the Social Web. John Wiley, Hoboken, NJ.

White, C., Raman, N., 1999. The world wide web as a public relations medium: the use of research, planning and evaluation in website development. Public Relations Review 28, 408–419.

Wilson, B., 2007. New media, social movements, and global sport studies: a revolutionary moment in the sociology of sport. Sociology of Sport Journal 24, 457–477.

Woo, C., Cho, S., 2008. Sport PR in message boards on Major League Baseball websites. Public Relations Review 34, 169–175.

Wyld, D., 2008. Management 2.0: a primer on blogging for executives. Management Research News 31, 448–483.

CHAPTER 12

Public Relations for Players

James Skinner
Griffith University

Learning Outcomes

Upon completion of this chapter the reader should be able to:

- Define the concept of Public Relations (PR)
- Describe the public relations role of players/athletes
- Describe the public relations role of fans
- Detail public relations consequences for players/athletes of their on- and off-field behaviour and attitude

---

CHAPTER OVERVIEW

Bruce and Tini (2008) indicate that with sport it is the media rather than sales and advertising strategies that are the key to conveying sport unique imagery and meaning. They suggest that the impact of high-profile scandals, however, can turn what is mainly positive media coverage into unbalanced and misinformed press that has the potential to cause long-term damage. As this media coverage is harder to control than advertising or sales promotion there are positive and negative implications that need to be managed by the sport public relations professional. If a player or a sport organisation receives positive press, Bruce and Tini suggest that it will assist in forming a stronger connection with fans and create and further channel the need and desire for more sport content. Unsavoury or bad press about players and sport organisations has the potential to call into question a player's reputation and lead to poor public perception of the sport organisation or sport. This can then filter through to future participation problems and a reduction in a range of revenue streams including sponsorships and player endorsements. As will be highlighted in this chapter, this is particularly the case in professional sport given the extensive media scrutiny afforded to it. How sport public relations professionals deal with potential player(s) crisis and the wider implications for the sport organisation and sport requires a detailed understanding and ability to implement crisis communication strategies. As such, there is little doubt that public relations has a key role to play in professional sport. With particular emphasis on the work of Summers and Morgan (2008), this chapter explores the role of public relations in professional sport with particular emphasis on how public relations and communication strategies can be used when dealing with potentially damaging situations for players, the sport organisation and the sport itself.

THE PUBLIC RELATIONS ROLE OF PLAYERS/ATHLETES

Professional sport requires large investment and to do this it draws on a range of revenue sources. These sources add a layer of complexity to how a sport organisation and its employees (players) are managed. Sponsors, the media, the corporate sector and the broader community may all have conflicting agendas regarding what they wish to achieve through their engagement with professional sport. According to Summers and Morgan (2008, p. 176), 'this has forged an important symbiotic relationship between the media, global public relations activity, professional sport and the players and spectators of sport. Each needs the other to sustain an existence far beyond simply providing televised coverage of a sport'. The more professional sport promotes its hyper-real emphasis on excitement, speed and power the more the public embraces it as a medium of entertainment. Players have been rewarded with higher salaries as a consequence of greater revenue streams. These revenue streams have resulted from the growing pool of potential high-profile sponsors such as globalised corporate giants like NBC, Coca Cola, McDonalds and Reebok investing in professional sport, and the emergence of global markets through telecommunication technologies expanding the sport audience beyond the wildest dreams of sport administrators. 'This constant demand and supply of information, competition and excitement breeds heroes, villains, celebrities and superstars. Indeed, intrinsic to this commercialisation of sport is the creation of the 'sport celebrity' as a product in their own right' (L'Etang, 2006, cited in Summers and Morgan, 2008, p. 176).

This growing public obsession associated with professional sport has changed the way it is reported and how it is presented in the media. 'Fan interest' is the essential element that drives demand for professional sport. Fans have an identification or association with a particular team, typically founded on a geographic or an emotional connection. Fans are consumers, they are the demand-side of the market for professional sporting competitions. They are the market for team merchandise, souvenirs and the other products of team sponsors. They buy the newspapers that report on the matches and the subscription TV channels that provide exclusive live coverage. They are also the consumers who buy the tickets and fill the stadiums – and therefore become part of the product itself, as part of the spectacle of the live event that is sold to other consumers (Borland and Macdonald, 2003). The obsession of fans with professional sport can lead to 'unfettered hero worship and idolisation of sporting stars by their fans who expect their sporting heroes to display exemplary sporting behaviour, courage, loyalty and bravery' (Summers and Morgan, 2008, p. 177). Moreover, Summers and Morgan (2008, p. 177) suggest that 'certainly this is part of the reason the media and sport commentators are so quick to criticise and vilify sport stars when their behaviour does not live up to our social ideals'. An example of this is highlighted in the following case study.

CASE STUDY 12.1: Michael Phelps – From Hero to Hophead – and Back to Hero Again

When the 2008 Beijing Olympic Games had ended, the world had a new swimming hero. Michael Phelps had surpassed Mark Spitz' 1972 record of seven gold medals in one Olympic Games, by winning eight. In the process he set seven world records, and his total Olympic medal tally stood at 16, with 14 of them being gold. His future looked bright with estimates of his potential earnings from product endorsements and spokesperson roles estimated to reach $100 million in his lifetime (Crouse, 2009). Among the companies quick to sign on the swimming superstar were Visa, AT&T, Kelloggs, Mazda and Subway.

This bright financial future was threatened on 1 February 2009 when the British Tabloid 'News of the World' published a photograph of Michael Phelps supposedly smoking marijuana from a bong. Reaction to the story was swift. Through his marketing agency, Octagon, Phelps issued the following statement:

I engaged in behavior which was regrettable and demonstrated bad judgment, Phelps said. I'm 23 years old and despite the successes I've had in the pool, I acted in a youthful and inappropriate way, not in a manner people have come to expect from me. For this, I am sorry. I promise my fans and the public it will not happen again.

(Crouse, 2009, p. D8)

Continued

The United States Olympic Committee was also quick to comment, saying that it was 'disappointed in the behavior recently exhibited by Michael Phelps', describing him as a role model who was 'well aware of the responsibilities and accountability that come with setting a positive example for others, particularly young people' (Crouse, 2009, p. D8).

Worse was to come for Phelps, with USA Swimming suspending him for 3 months, and one of his major sponsors, Kelloggs, declining to renew their contract with him. Another major sponsor, Mazda, insisted on a video apology by Phelps, which was apparently sufficient to ensure that the reported US $1 million deal for Phelps to promote Mazda cars in China would continue. In a statement issued by Mazda they stated that Phelps' 'expression of remorse and his determination to make amends, and especially his video apology and expression of thanks to the Chinese people, give us confidence that Phelps can make a healthy return to the pool and have even more brilliant achievements' (Zinser, 2009, p. D2).

The media as well had mixed opinions of the scandal and the likely impact on Phelps and his career. While he was condemned for setting a bad example to young people, he also received sympathy in some quarters. George Vecsey wrote in the New York Times that:

> Like it or not, by winning eight gold medals in Beijing, Phelps automatically became a role model by virtue of being sent out there as a highly paid spokesman for multinational corporations. We like our sporting heroes to be perfect, but it's hard to be perfect in the 24-hour electronic buzz where everybody is a blogger and has a cellphone camera within reach.
>
> (Vecney, 2009, p. D1)

When the dust finally settled over the 'bong photo' scandal, the consequences to Michael Phelps could be seen to be relatively minimal. He lost the contract with Kelloggs, but Mazda, Speedo, Omega and Subway were among the major sponsors to stand by Phelps. As Dan Neil (2009) from the LA Times commented: 'To the extent that endorsement opportunities are a rough metric of how well someone in public life is liked, admired, respected, the bong-heard-around-the-world scandal might as well never have happened. With the benefit of hindsight, Kellogg execs might well be kicking themselves.'

Giulianotti (1999) notes that star players have become an intrinsic part of contemporary popular culture. To sell newspapers and further bond the relationship between sport consumers and players the instinctive and unpredictable behaviours of star players are frequently featured in the media. The general public has been inadvertently drawn to media reports of the behaviour of sport stars they may not necessarily associate with in a sporting sense but are drawn to by their high media profile. Carefully selected player imagery, information and the public interest are the apparatus the media use in their public relations activities to create an image of sport stars that many believe to be a reality (Summers and Morgan, 2008). This identity is based on the fusion of the cultural and commercial dimensions of sport. Rituals, myths, escapism, display, tribalism and community have all been conflated into a complex interdependent cultural and commercial system dominated by the hyper-real and mediated media experience (Skinner et al., 2003).

Star players make lucrative livings in professional sport and it is clear that there are financial advantages that a high off-field media profile can provide.

These financial advantages are gained by employing marketing strategies such as players doing television commercials, having individual sponsorships with a variety of global brands and participating in strategically planned public appearances. Carefully crafted media profiles of this nature require sport stars to use public relations experts and organisations. Summers and Morgan (2008) suggest that it is not unusual for athletes with a high public profile to contact media and public relations organisations to manage and shape their image and profile. They suggest that when it comes to professional sport 'winning and losing' needs to be balanced against how a player looks, the public perception of that player and if they can generate media attention. They point to the example of David Beckham who although now in the twilight of his football career is earning more from his product endorsements and his image than from his craft of football. Similarly, former Russian professional tennis player Anna Kournikova, who was once ranked eighth in the world, has achieved most of her fame and fortune from the publicity surrounding her personal life, as well as numerous modelling shoots. Kournikova made her debut at the US Open in 1996 as a 15-year-old. Her natural beauty attracted the attention of the world's media and it did not take long for pictures of her to start appearing in numerous magazines with global distributions. Kournikova was able to attract with relative ease numerous sponsorships and product endorsements. As a 19-year-old she became the new face for Berlei's shock absorber sport bras, and successfully featured in the billboard campaign 'only the ball should bounce'. She quickly became a hit in various men's magazines, including the 2004 *Sport Illustrated Swimsuit Issue*, *FHM* and *Maxim*. Kournikova made into the list of *People's* 50 Most Beautiful People on numerous occasions and was voted 'hottest female athlete' on ESPN.com. In 2002, she was also placed first in *FHM's 100 Sexiest Women in the World* in US and UK editions. By contrast, when comparing media hype to sporting accomplishments as a singles player, ESPN ranked Kournikova 18th in its '25 Biggest Sport Flops of the Past 25 Years'. Similarly, in the ESPN Classic series 'Who's number 1?' Kournikova was also ranked number 1 when the series featured sport's most overrated athletes. Despite this she had a highly lucrative and successful sporting career based on her media image (Wikipedia.org, 2009).

A sport star who complains about media attention does so at their own peril. Not only do they fail to recognise the importance of proactive and detailed public relations strategies designed to create an engaging public image but they also open themselves up to potential bad press and the construction of a media image contrary to that desired. A carefully designed public image is even more important if we acknowledge that sporting stars take on the mantle of role models to the young and impressionable, and are seen as vehicles for installing national pride and are hero-worshipped by their fans (Summers and Morgan, 2008). Just as sponsorship, merchandising and stadium naming rights provide sporting organisations with a revenue base so too does the sporting star. Sporting organisations and their governing bodies cannot service the increasing spiralling costs of player wages, provide development programs across the globe and armchair-viewing access via global communications technologies without the additional revenue they leverage from the sporting stars (Giulianotti, 1999; Summers and Morgan, 2008). As such, the global shift from hard news to soft news has led to the development of a sport star industry. In this industry 'personality, image and behaviour are valuable both as news, and as products to be managed responsibly by the public relations industry' (Carroll, 2002; Turner et al., 2000, cited in Summers and Morgan, 2008, p. 181).

PLAYERS AND SPORT: HOW AN IMAGE IS CONSTRUCTED?

Bruce and Tini (2008) point to North American studies that have highlighted the interdependence between sport journalists and sport public relations professionals and how in some ways this does provide some form of control over what is reported in the media despite the intense media scrutiny of professional sport and its players. Although the media plays a key role in marketing professional sport, exaggerating player performance, suppressing player criticism or supporting players under pressure, Bruce and Tini suggest that communications technologies such as team and personal player websites have also provided sport organisations and players with a more direct way to communicate with fans and the media. This relationship between sport, the media and commercial organisations has resulted in sport organisations using the Internet to create a sense of community among users through interactivity, partnerships and entertainment activities focused on the loyalties of the sporting fans. Members can obtain exclusive access to various sections of a website that provides information not yet available to the wider public through other media sources (Edwards and Skinner, 2006). Furthermore, the interactive possibilities that attract the sport Internet consumer are 'intrinsically' well-suited to the formation of what are termed 'online communities' (Evans and Smith, 2004). For example, the Washington Capitals are using the Internet to build up a strong sense of community among fans and see the use of the Internet as a vehicle to build cyber-communities for sport fans (Morrow and Hamil, 2003; Shilbury et al., 1998).

Hopwood (2007) suggests that there is evidence that sport cyber-communities are not immune from some of the more negative aspects of human behaviour. She cites the example of the Newcastle Falcons Rugby Club supporters' chat community facility on the Club's website which had to be closely monitored as some 'fans' were using it as a forum to undermine the players by publicly criticising them and encouraging what could be described as 'virtual subversion' among the cyber fan community. Thus, 'the Internet and digital media has allowed fans to actually publish their own 'news' to a global audience and they have become as much a part of the production cycle as the consumption' (Summers and Morgan, 2008, p. 177).

Dimitrov (2008, p. 91) suggests that 'the transformation of players into 'stars' has blurred the boundaries between their play and their life. Every detail of the sport stars' life – on-field and off-field – is potential news'. Wilson et al. (2008, p. 102) suggest that negative player transgressions are excessively represented in the media and has resulted in the reporting of incidents that in the past would not have been considered newsworthy, leading some to refer to the media as an 'insatiable beast'. Summers and Morgan (2008, p. 177) support this view and suggest media stories of sporting stars in 'trouble are high-interest stories'. This has led to media coverage 'that has evolved into a global medium far beyond the archaic notion of the nightly half-an-hour broadcast, news managers struggle to balance the need to fill time with the journalistic rules and fact checking of the past' (Hall, 2004, cited in Summers and Morgan, 2008, p. 177).

THE PUBLIC RELATIONS ROLE OF FANS

Contemporary sport fans have become a complex and sophisticated consumer and many professional sports are seen as a commodified product. This commodification of the fan has an ambiguous effect on professional sport and its capacity to communicate with fans. The growth of professional staff in marketing, sponsorship, advertising, brand management, licensing and public relations has also become evident (Dimitrov, 2008). The commodification of professional sport and its fans can be seen in the commodification of its cultural heritage. While some fans may feel alienated by the increasing commercialisation of their club, there is no escaping from their own part in this commodification process. Even searching for a link with the pre-hyper-commercialisation of their club by purchasing, for example, a 'classic' football shirt or viewing classic matches on video or DVD, the fan is still contributing to the current commercialised status of their favourite team. As Giulianotti (1999) asserts, professional sport economic relationships are extremely complex, and fans are contributing either directly or indirectly to this commodification process. Summers and Morgan (2008, p. 177) suggest that there is still, however, an expectation from fans in relation to player behaviour, yet the impact of bad behaviour or bad press is largely dependent on 'the general profile of the athlete and whether or not the event was sport related'.

The utilisation of sport stars in advertising, promotional activities and sponsorship deals is not a phenomenon unique to the latter part of the twentieth century. In the nineteenth century, for example, the uniquely recognisable visage of English Cricket captain W.G. Grace endorsed a range of domestic products (Skinner, 2009). It is the difference in the scale of commercial involvement that uniquely defines the contemporary professional sport. As a consequence, sport starts of today live a charmed life that would be considered surreal to the general public. This rising media profile of sport stars 'removes any obligation to treat sport stars with the same degree of privacy that we would impart to our fellow workmates or colleagues and definitely brings with it high expectations of on- and off-field behaviour and image… and has led sport stars themselves attempting to bridge this gap through the provision of information, gossip, photos and statistics in order to keep sport fans interested and emotionally and financially connected to the sport' (Summers and Morgan, 2008, pp. 177–179).

Public relations experts use their expertise to construct a sport star's public image and in turn it raises the public expectations of how sport stars should act. Expectations of sport stars being involved in charities, undertaking volunteer work in community sport settings and fulfilling the role as the model parent and citizen are raised. At the same time there is a public desire for sport stars to be likeable, at times perhaps controversial and larger than life, but display traits that suggest a deep social conscience is always evident (Summers and Morgan, 2008). These 'role model' expectations are often questioned by the sport stars themselves. Chalip (1996) points to the example of Charles Barkely who stated: 'I am not a role model. I am paid to wreak havoc on the basketball court. Parents should be role models. Just because I dunk basketballs doesn't mean I should raise your kids' (Smith and Press, 1993, cited in Chalip, 1996, p. 52).

Although Dietz-Uhler and Lanter (2008) point out that sport fans are loyal to their team, to its players and to the sport, Summers and Morgan (2008) suggest that they demonstrate a multifaceted and generally impractical set of expectations. For example, Chalip (1996, p. 43) notes the importance of sport stars to demonstrate humility and not be self-centred as this is an expectation of fans. Similarly, portraying 'rebelliousness and anti-establishment images are to be avoided. Yet athletes like Muhammad Ali have been both rebellious and anti-establishment', but Ali is idolised and applauded for these traits by many sport fans.

It seems that sport fans have complex and high expectations of sport stars but lack patience and are quick to criticise performance. Sport stars who fail to perform on the field of play can be assigned labels such as 'past their use by date', 'getting old' or 'enjoying too much of the good life', consistent poor performances can lead to sport stars receiving advice that can be at best described as direct and to the point (Summers and Morgan, 2008). Because many professional sports by their nature involve a degree of on-field physical intimidation – shouting, swearing and public humiliation are commonly used to express dissatisfaction. Public expectations of sport stars to behave in socially responsible ways are promoted in the media, yet such actions are not being consistently modelled by sport consumers. The media is complicit in creating these expectations as it portrays sport stars 'as 'god like', exciting and glamorous stars [which] confirms and encourages sport fans high expectations and idealised views' (p. 180).

THE CONSEQUENCES OF BAD BEHAVIOUR BY PLAYERS

Although we expect sport stars to excel in their chosen field of endeavour, the general public also expect them to demonstrate consistently high standards of behaviour and moral conduct. Unsavoury off-field behaviour of players can lead to a negative public perception that creates problems for sport public relations mangers. Just as the media can create a positive image of a sport star they can change this image and if they desire recreate the positive image again (Crawford, 2004). 'This rollercoaster treatment by the media can be seen in numerous sporting careers, such as those of David Beckham, Dennis Rodman and Diego Maradona' (Andrews and Jackson, 2001, cited in Crawford, 2004, p. 133). Similarly, the media may compare the behaviour of one player with another in order to create contrasting images. Crawford points to how the good conduct of ex-English soccer captain Gary Lineker was compared to the media 'hard man' image construction of Vinnie Jones, 'or the outlandishness of Denis Rodman was opposed to the wholeness of Michael Jordan' (p. 133). In more recent times the Australian media sought to compare the conduct of cricketers Shane Warne and Adam Gilchrist. In this light we can see that the media construction of a sport star can 'often lack depth of character'…and can be 'frequently painted as one-dimensional' (p. 133).

Fink et al. (2009) suggest that at any given time of the year the questionable and sometimes deceitful behaviour of players can surface. They point to examples of professional baseball players being accused and subsequently admitting to steroid use and a professional football team having nine players arrested in 9 months. Summers and Morgan (2008) suggest that this is the core of the debate about the expectations of the public and their opinions of sport stars and their behaviour. They suggest that 'if sport fans acknowledge that high-profile sports are based on aggressive competition, where physical contact, foul language and trickery are an expected part of the performance, why then are sport fans surprised and even outraged when those who play sport at the elite level are caught behaving in similar ways off the field' (Joyner and Mummery, 2005, cited in Summers and Morgan, 2008, p. 179).

When the bad behaviour of players can have negative consequences for sport organisations and/or sport how does the sport public relations manager deal with negative media coverage? For example, the greater the popularity and profile of the sport star the quicker the media is to highlight socially unacceptable behaviour ranging from 'drunken exploits, domestic abuse, infidelity, drug abuse and violence' (Lines, 2001, cited in Summers and Morgan, 2008, p. 179). Fink et al. (2009) suggest that when a player engages in untoward behaviour the sport fan will attempt to reconcile the positive feelings they have for the team against the bad behaviour of the player. This could lead fans to react in one of two ways, 'either by exhibiting an in-group bias effect, or by exhibiting the black sheep effect' (p. 144). The 'in-group bias' effect suggests that members of the group will maintain loyalty to the group even when information may suggest that a group member has broken the expectations of the group. They suggest groups do this as they draw on copying mechanisms to help them reconcile the behaviour of a player within the expectations of the group. This may be achieved by questioning the reliability of the information and suggesting the media is using unreliable witnesses and is conducting a 'witch hunt'. Similarly, sport fans may suggest that there were mitigating circumstances and the player was simply in the wrong place at the wrong time. Such strategies are often used by sport public relations managers. The key feature of this strategy is the sustained support for the player. Summers and Morgan (2008) suggest that the ethical problem with this approach is that it can also lead to situations where there is an expectation that the bad behaviours of players may be different. This raises the possibility that players could consider themselves above the social norms and laws of the community and 'as a consequence we experience recalcitrant, unlawful and unethical behaviour' (p. 179).

When embracing the 'black sheep effect' the sport public relations manger may chose to label the player as 'different'. They may choose to present a case that supports this view as it may have a less detrimental public relations impact on the sport organisation. Such an approach allows sport fans to maintain positive feelings about the team despite negative press, as they do not consider the behaviour of the 'black sheep' to be representative of the team. From a public relations point of view there is a tendency for the sport organisation and sport fan to distance themselves from the player in question. Summers and Morgan (2008), however, argue that in most cases sport fans are capable of separating the on-and off-field behaviours of players and are prepared to make a distinction and subsequently moderate their expectations. As indicated by Fink et al. (2009), unacceptable off-field behaviours are often played down by sport public relations managers as a result of 'mitigating circumstances'. For example, sport fans should not be too harsh in judging the behaviour of a young, immature and vulnerable sport star who may have been displaying the behaviours of any other young male, as long as the on-field performance of the player remains high.

It seems that the public is almost resigned to sport stars behaving badly or inappropriately (Summers and Morgan, 2008). Wilson et al. (2008) highlight several examples in Australia. The severity of these incidents is communicated in headlines such as 'TAC set to dump Tigers, Magpies'', in relation to a major sponsor's reaction to drunk-driving offences by Australian Football League (AFL) players and "Footy Clubs Plagued by Sex Scandals", regarding sexual assault allegations against players in both the AFL and the National Rugby League (NRL)' (p. 99). While Wilson et al. provide examples of inappropriate off-field behaviour that has occurred in the Australian sporting context, they suggest that the phenomenon is widespread and is not isolated to the code of football. For example, the gambling controversy that has confronted international professional cricket could have led to potentially devastating impacts for the sport. However, despite the involvement of high-profile professional cricketers international cricket has survived the controversy and some would suggest it has expanded its market reach. This following case study provides insight into the public relations that was used to mange this controversy.

CASE STUDY 12.2: International Cricket and the Spectre of Illegal Gambling

Cricket is an international sport whose reputation has been seriously tarnished in recent times. A game that was not known for gambling in any form now attracts large sums of money in a variety of bets. Successful betting, however, depended not so much on skill and good fortune as on the corruption of players involved in the game.

Match fixing in cricket can be traced as far back as the 1970s when county and club games in domestic tournaments in England and other countries were allegedly fixed to secure points and league positions. From the late 1970s onwards more insidious and corrosive forms of fixing took hold, involving players under performing so that the result

Continued

of the match was determined in advance. This allowed bets to be placed with a certainty or high probability of winning. Betting on cricket grew in the 1980s and 1990s as a result of the interaction of a number of issues. In particular the two major issues were: (1) live television matches and the growth in the number of one-day internationals, and (2) betting on cricket grew even more with the widespread availability of mobile phones.

Corruption in cricket has many manifestations as every single aspect of a match can be bet upon. For example, betting can be made on the outcome of the toss, the end from which the fielding Captain will elect to bowl, the number of wides and no balls occurring in a designated over, players being placed in unfamiliar fielding positions, batsmen being out at a specific time in their innings, total runs in which the batting captain will declare and the time of a declaration (Rae, 2001). The level of involvement of a player in match fixing of any of the above scenarios can be so minimal as to be almost undetectable, yet the financial windfalls of successful betting can be huge.

There are a number of reasons why corruption in cricket is so widespread. These include the argument that international cricket players are paid less than other professional athletes and are therefore more vulnerable to corruption, professional cricketers have relatively short and uncertain careers so some seek to supplement their official earnings, some administrators turn a blind eye or are themselves involved in malpractice, cricketers play a high number of one-day internationals and nothing is really at stake in terms of national pride or selection, some professional cricketers take money from potential corruptors in turn for innocuous information and yet refuse to fix matches and it is too easy (Rae, 2001).

The Public Relations Response of the International Cricket Council to Ongoing Corruption Scandals

There have been numerous recorded cases of players being involved in match fixing allegations. No country appears to be exempt from these claims. For example, during a tour of Sri Lanka in 1994, Mark Waugh and Shane Warne accepted money from an Indian bookmaker in exchange for information about weather and pitch conditions. When these dealings were revealed in 1998, Warne was fined $AUS8000 and Waugh $AUS10,000. The most public instance of corruption in cricket was when the late South African cricket captain Hansie Cronjé accepted money from a bookmaker in exchange for information, pitch reports and match fixing. He was subsequently banned from all forms of the game (Rae, 2001).

The scandal involving South African Cricket Captain Hansie Cronjé was sufficiently serious to spur the International Cricket Council (ICC) to take decisive action. In April 2000, when investigating an unrelated matter, New Delhi Police while monitoring the telephone calls of an Indian national, overheard a telephone conversation in which Hansie Cronjé discussed match fixing. An investigation was launched by the New Delhi Police and focused on the association between Cronjé and other South African players, a London-based businessman and two Indian bookmakers. New Delhi Police subsequently charged Cronjé and three other South African players in May 2000 with cheating, fraud and criminal conspiracy. Cronjé, as well as the captains of India and Pakistan, Mohammed Azharuddin and Salim Malik were all subsequently banned for life (International Cricket Council: Anti Corruption Unit, 2001).

In order to effectively deal with the issue of match fixing and illegal betting and the impact this was having on the public image of International Cricket, the ICC established the Anti-Corruption and Security Unit (ACSU). It was set up as the investigative arm of the ICC. The ACSU was to work independently of the ICC but was funded by the sport governing body. It had no powers, no criminal proceedings could follow as a direct consequence of their findings, and they could not recommend punishment. The outcomes from its investigations were provided to the Chairman of the ICC's Code of Conduct Commission. The Commission then had the right to ban a player from the game from 5 years up to life (BBC Sport, 2000).

To further gain credibility with the public, the ICC appointed Sir Paul Condon a former Metropolitan Police Commissioner to lead the unit. Condon used his contacts within the police force to staff his six-man office in central

London. They then in turn used a powerful database developed by a Cambridge-based company which was used by police forces across England and around the world. The use of this database was publicly portrayed as a method to revolutionise the way match fixers and crooked bookmakers were tracked down.

The ICC suggests that because the Anti-Corruption Unit operates under public scrutiny, opportunities for match fixing have been drastically reduced. However, Paul Condon suggests that there is still a lot that has to be done and it would be naive to think that match fixing is not happening. As recently as August 2009, news reports surfaced of approaches having been made to an Australian player by a person suspected of having links to illegal bookmaking, following the Second Ashes Test at Lords in July. To maintain public confidence and protect the image of the game the ICC issued a statement confirming that the incident had taken place and also acknowledged that such incidents continued to occur and that it 'would be naive to assume otherwise; if they did not then there would be no need for the continuing existence of the ACSU… However, the ICC is confident that all approaches are being reported, it is proud that its systems and education processes in place have created a widespread culture of integrity among the world's top players and it is pleased those players have confidence in the ACSU to report such matters' (Cricket365.com, 2009). The ICC statement continued: 'Incidents such as the one reported in the media illustrate the need for constant and ongoing vigilance on the part of players, officials and administrators and there is no scope for complacency… However thanks to the ACSU, cricket is regarded by other sports as a world leader in the area of anti-corruption and the ICC wants it to stay that way' (Cricket365.com, 2009).

In cases like the above cricket case study it is necessary that sport public relations practitioners consider how they can effectively handle such a crisis. There is no doubt that some governing bodies and sport organisations have attempted to institute processes to prevent players engaging in behaviours that are not considered acceptable to the public or reflect community standards (Wilson et al., 2008). For example, Wilson et al. note 'that some teams promote that they have introduced a players' code of conduct to explicitly highlight appropriate behaviour, while others have considered formal education sessions to discuss how players can avoid potential compromising situations' (p. 104). They suggest that the key to the success of such strategies from a commercial point of view is the necessity to create a culture that encourages publicly acceptable on- and off-field behaviour. The presence of such a program assists the sport public relations managers in managing and alleviating any potential public fall out.

SUMMARY

It is paramount that modern professional sporting organisations and professional players recognise the enormous impact they can and do have on their communities due to the strong emotional element of the sport product and the high levels of attachment and loyalty of their fans (Hopwood, 2007). This chapter has highlighted how negative player behaviour can impact on the image of the individual and the public perception and reputation of a sport. It has highlighted that sport has become a commodity in which players lend their images to a wide variety of products, and are often paid far more for endorsements than they are paid to play their sport. The 'market value' of a player's image and the reputation of the sport hinges on public perception, which is the domain of the public relations professional. Sport public relations professionals nurture and defend a player's image and a sport's reputation. At its best public relations should be proactive in its efforts to create a positive player image and reputation, however, it is often forced to react to negative situations by using strategies to repair a tarnished player image or reputation in order to defuse a public perception crisis. Sport public relations professionals need to focus on protecting and enhancing a positive player image and reputation by building and maintaining mutually beneficial relationships with key publics, in particular their fans (Hopwood, 2007).

KEY TERMS

Public Relations Public relations is the deliberate, planned and sustained effort to establish and maintain mutual understanding between an organisation (or individual) and its (or their) publics.

Crisis Management To identify, respond to and mitigate negative actions or activities with the goal of repairing a public image or returning a public image to its pre-crisis level.

Fans Followers, devotees and enthusiasts.

Commodification When economic value is assigned to something not previously considered in economic terms; for example, an idea, identity or gender. It describes a modification of relationships, formerly untainted by commerce, into commercial relationships – such as a relationship between a professional sport team and its fans.

Black Sheep Effect When a player's bad behaviour is considered not to be the norm of the group.

Code of Conduct Usually a statement and description of required behaviours, responsibilities, and actions expected of employees of an organisation or of members of a professional body, including athletes. A code of conduct usually focuses on ethical and socially responsible issues and applies to individuals, providing guidance on how to act in cases of doubt or confusion.

DISCUSSION QUESTIONS

1. Identify a high-profile sport identity. Look at recent media coverage of that sport identity. Weigh up the balance of 'sport reporting' against 'celebrity reporting'. How much is fact and how much is unverifiable?

2. What is meant by the 'Black Sheep Effect'? Provide an example of how a sporting organisation has used this strategy to protect their public image and reputation.

3. Research a major sporting organisation such as the ICC, FIFA, or the IOC. Does the organisation contain athlete charters or espouse values and conduct commensurate with society's expectation of the conduct of their players and athletes?

4. Do such organisations enforce player/athlete conduct codes?

5. Should mainstream society be permitted to regulate player and athlete conduct? What role do fans have in determining any negative outcomes as a consequence of the behaviour of sport stars?

GUIDED READING

Fortunato, J.A., 2008. Restoring a reputation: the Duke University Lacrosse Scandal. Public Relations Review 34, 116–123. This paper is relevant to the content of this chapter as it examines the crisis situation that confronted Duke University when three players of its lacrosse team were charged with rape and sexual assault. The reputation of the university was called into question and thus the need for appropriate public relations communications strategies was required. Through these strategies the university attempted to restore its reputation and public image.

RECOMMENDED WEBSITES

Institute for Public Relations – <http://www.instituteforpr.org/>.

REFERENCES

BBC Sport, 2000. How to be corrupt in cricket. Retrieved on 28 August 2009 from: BBC Online <http://news.bbc.co.uk/1/hi/sport/cricket/710418.stm>.

Borland, J., Macdonald, R., 2003. Demand for sport. Oxford Review of Economic Policy 19 (4), 478–502.

Bruce, T., Tini, T., 2008. Unique crisis response strategies in sport public relations: Rugby League and the case for diversion. Public Relations Review 34, 108–115.

Cricket365.com, 2009. Betting scandal shouldn't impact Ashes. Retrieved on 28 August 2009 from: Cricinfo.com. http://www.cricket365.com/story/0,18305,6575_5500235,00.html.

Crouse, K., 1 February 2009. Phelps apologizes for marijuana pipe photo. Retrieved on 28 August 2009 from: New York Times <http://www.nytimes.com/2009/02/02/sports/othersports/02phelps.html>.

Chalip, L., 1996. Celebrity or hero? Towards a conceptual framework for athlete promotion. In: Shilbury, D., Chalip, L. (Eds.), Advancing Management of Australian and New Zealand Sport. Conference Proceedings Second Annual Sport Management Association of Australian and New Zealand (INC.) Conference. Learning Resources Services, Deakin University, Victoria, pp. 42–56.

Crawford, G., 2004. Consuming Sport: Fans, Sport and Culture. Routledge, London.

Dietz-Uhler, B., Lanter, J., 2008. The consequences of sport fan identification. In: Hugenberg, L.W., Haridakis, P.M., Earnheardt, A.C. (Eds.), Sport Mania: Essays on Fandom and the Media in the 21st Century. McFarland & Company Inc., London, pp. 103–113.

Dimitrov, R., 2008. Gender violence, fan activism and public relations in sport: the case of footy fans against sexual assault. Public Relations Review 34, 90–98.

Edwards, A., Skinner, J., 2006. Sport Empire. Meyer & Meyer Sport, Aachen, Germany.

Evans, D.M., Smith, A.C.T., 2004. The Internet and competitive advantage: a study of Australia's four premier professional sporting leagues. Sport Management Review 7 (1), 27–56.

Fink, J.S., Parker, H.M., Brett, M., Higgins, J., 2009. Off-field behaviour of athletes and team identification: using social identity theory and balance theory to explain fan reactions. Journal of Sport Management 23, 142–155.

Giulianotti, R., 1999. Football: A Sociology of the Global Game. Polity Press, Cambridge.

Hopwood, M.K., 2007. The sport integrated communications mix: sport public relations. In: Beech, J., Chadwick, S. (Eds.), The Marketing of Sport. Prentice Hall, Harlow, England, pp. 292–317.

International Cricket Council: Anti Corruption Unit, 2001. Report on Corruption in International Cricket. International Cricket Council, London.

Morrow, S., Hamil, S., 2003. Corporate Community Involvement by Football Clubs: Business Strategy or Social Obligation. University of Stirling, United Kingdom.

Neil, D., 2009. Michael Phelps ads prove a new cultural tolerance of marijuana. Retrieved on 28 August 2009 from: LA Times <http://www.latimes.com/business/la-fi-neil7-2009jul07,0, 2840859.column>.

Rae, P., 2001. Bribery and Corruption in the Game of Rugby Union. Referee Level 3 Course Participant. Australian Rugby Union.

Shilbury, D., Quick, S., Westerbeek, H., 1998. Strategic Sport Marketing. Allen & Unwin, Sydney.

Skinner, J., 2009. Sport sponsorship and marketing. In: Chadwick, S., Hamil, S. (Eds.), Managing Football: An International Perspective. Butterworth-Heinemann/Elsevier, Oxford, pp. 105–118.

Skinner, J., Stewart, B., Edwards, A., 2003. The postmodernisation of Rugby Union in Australia. Journal of Football Studies 6 (1), 51–69.

Summers, J., Morgan, M.J., 2008. More than just the media: considering the role of public relations in the creation of sporting celebrity and the management of fan expectations. Public Relations Review 34, 176–182.

Vecney, G., 6 February 2009. Phelps needs less idle time, not more. Retrieved on 28 August 2009 from: New York Times <http://www.nytimes.com/2009/02/07/sports/othersports/07vecsey.html>.

Wikipedia.org 2009. Anna Kournikova. Retrieved on 24 August 2009 from: <http://en.wikipedia.org/wiki/Anna_kournikova>.

Wilson, B., Stavros, C., Westberg, K., 2008. Player transgressions and the management of the sport sponsor relationship. Public Relations Review 34, 99–107.

Zinser, L., 13 February 2009. Mazda asks, and Phelps apologizes to Chinese. Retrieved on 28 August 2009 from: New York Times <http://www.nytimes.com/2009/02/14/sports/olympics/14phelps.html>.

CHAPTER 13

International Sport Public Relations

James Skinner, Kristine Toohey
Griffith University

Learning Outcomes

Upon completion of this chapter the reader should be able to:

- Explain the reasons for the growth of international public relations
- Discuss the importance of culture in international public relations and the wider implications inherent in a cultural perspective
- Identify the critical role of public relations for sport and international sport organisations
- Appreciate the value of public relations when international sport organisations are confronted with a crisis

---

CHAPTER OVERVIEW

As the importance and financial rewards of global sport have increased so too the practice of public relations on an international basis has continued to expand and more public relations practitioners represent organisations that transcend national boundaries (Dickerson, 2005). As practicing international public relations tales place across national boundaries 'public relations becomes a cultural artefact, bound by cultural beliefs, perceptions and notions' (Curtin and Gaither, 2007, p. 20) which presents many unique challenges. This chapter identifies that culture should be at the centre of understanding the role of international public relations. Sport, however, is often overlooked in international public relations despite the fact that sport can cross national boundaries and focus the attention of the international community. It has the capacity to 'shape relationships at numerous levels: diplomatic, cultural, economic and organisational' and thus implies 'a role for public relations' (L'Etang, 2006, p. 386). By using the Olympic Games and the International Olympic Committee (IOC) as examples this chapter highlights the role that public relations has and can play in promoting and protecting the place that sport occupies in the international community.

INTERNATIONAL PUBLIC RELATIONS

The practice of public relations is now very much an international phenomenon. There are considered to be three key reasons for the increased interaction among organisations and publics across the globe, which, in turn, has necessitated the need for international public relations. According to Seitel (2004, p. 378), these reasons are:

■ The expansion of communications technology has increased the dissemination of information about products, services and lifestyles around the world, creating global demand.

■ The realignment of economic power, caused by the formation of multinational trading blocks, such as the North American Free Trade Agreement (NAFTA), Asia Pacific Economic Conference (APEC), Organisation of African Unity (OAU) and the European Economic Community (EEC). Such alliances have brought global producers and consumers closer.

■ People around the world are uniting in the pursuit of common goals, such as reducing population growth, protecting the environment, waging the war against terrorism and fighting disease.

In exploring the link between public relations and international public relations it is clear that culture plays an important role. Culbertson (1996, p. 2) suggests, 'international public relations tend to focus on the practice of public relations in an international or cross-cultural context'. This distinction is important because it highlights that 'public relations takes place across realms, not only geographically and organisationally, but more important culturally, this is why public relations in one country is propaganda or persuasion in another' (Curtin and Gaither, 2007, p. 20). For example, Curtin and Gaither point to the example of, when numerous media reports suggested that Islamists were ahead in the propaganda war on terror, the US government hiring a Washington DC-based public relations firm. The public relations organisation organised 'an anti-Saddam propaganda effort and included two clandestine radio stations, videos, skits and comic books which were critical of the former Iraqi leader' (Pentagon Hires, 2001, cited in Curtin and Gaither, 2007, p. 21). The term international public relations, according to Curtin and Gaither, suggests that public relations is not just a Western practice and its definitions, roles and challenges are influenced by cultural factors.

One of the challenges international public relations has had to confront has resulted from the growth of multinational organisations. A large percentage of cross-border business ventures fails largely because organisations routinely sacrifice cultural sensitivity and communication for an uninformed commitment to organisational strategy and profit (Morosini, 2002, cited in Curtin and Gaither, 2007). Huntington (1996) predicts that the source of future international conflicts lies in the differences in cultural, rather than the political and ideological traditions and beliefs. Those engaged in international public relations work in an environment in which the actions of individuals and organisations in one part of the world can be felt instantly and irrevocably by people around the globe. As a consequence, multinational corporations must be sensitive to how their actions might affect people of different cultures in different geographies. What happens in Japan can affect business thousands of kilometres away, a phenomenon known as 'cross-national conflict shifting'. The term refers to the idea that public relations challenges in one part of the world affect the operations of an international corporation elsewhere in the world. Essentially, this means that the new global economy makes it impossible for a multinational corporation to neutralise public relations challenges in one country without some effect on its global operations (Curtin and Gaither, 2007).

INTERNATIONAL SPORT AND PUBLIC RELATIONS

Sport is often overlooked in international public relations. This is despite the fact that international sport can be used as a vehicle to generate national unity, promote social change and celebrate national values and identity (Curtin and Gaither, 2007). One well-known example is the 1936 Berlin Olympic Games in which the organisers attempted to convince a sceptical audience that Germany was not a threat to international peace (L'Etang, 2006). Berlin was awarded the 1936 Olympics in 1931, 2 years before the Nazi party came to power. Adolf Hitler immediately seized on the games as an opportunity to showcase the efficiency and might of his regime. In the

USA, a move to boycott the Olympics was led by Judge Jeremiah T. Murphy, President of the Amateur Athletic Union (AAU). Murphy and his supporters were concerned chiefly about Nazi anti-Semitism, since Jewish sport clubs throughout Germany had been shut down. However, in 1935 the AAU voted by a narrow margin to sanction participation and Murphy resigned. He was replaced by Avery Brundage, who went to Germany on an inspection tour and reported that everything looked acceptable. Despite Germany's attempts to portray itself as benign many athletes and members of the press were alarmed by the nationalistic and militaristic atmosphere in Berlin. The ever-present swastika and icon-like portraits of Hitler and the martial music that blared endlessly through loudspeakers were deeply disturbing to many. Nor did it help that many journalists, suspected of anti-Nazi sentiments, discovered that their rooms had been searched by the secret police (Toohey and Veal, 2007).

Similarly, international sport can become a focus of political protest and activism, providing an international stage and guaranteed media attention for a cause. The 1972 Munich Olympic Games are an example of this. On the evening of September 5, in an attempt to raise international public awareness of the plight of the Palestinian people eight Palestinian terrorists broke into the Israeli team's headquarters in the Olympic Village. Two Israelis were killed immediately and nine others were held hostage. The terrorists demanded access to the world press, transportation out of Germany and freedom for some 200 prisoners in Israel. After lengthy negotiations with German authorities, the terrorists, along with their hostages, flew by helicopter to the airport, where a failed rescue attempt resulted in the killing of all nine captives and several of the terrorists (Toohey and Veal, 2007).

The Montreal 1976 Olympic Games were also used to raise awareness of an issue and subsequently became the victim of the first large Olympic boycott. It was spurred by Tanzanian leader Julius Nyerere, who rallied more than 20 African nations to boycott the Games. It was based on the premise that New Zealand should be excluded because its famous 'All Blacks' rugby team had toured South Africa, at the time a country banned from competition by the IOC because of its government's racist policies, known as apartheid. The IOC denied the African countries' request because rugby was not a sport under the Olympic umbrella, and despite negotiations the African states made good on their threat (Toohey and Veal, 2007).

The Moscow Olympics in 1980 was also subject to a large-scale boycott. The first Games to be held in a communist country, they were disrupted by an even larger boycott than that which occurred at the Montreal games. This boycott, led by US President Jimmy Carter, was part of an initiative to protest the December 1979 Soviet invasion of Afghanistan. After Carter's deadline for the withdrawal of Soviet troops from Afghanistan passed on 20 February 1980, Carter declared that neither he, nor the American people would support sending American athletes to Moscow, and his administration put enormous pressure on the US Olympic Committee to support his boycott. Carter also used his powers to block business involvement in the Moscow Games – including NBC's television plans, the US Postal Service's sale of commemorative stamps and postcards as well as the export of 'any goods or technology' related to the Games. Some governments, like Great Britain and Australia, supported the boycott but allowed athletes to decide for themselves whether to go to Moscow. No such freedom was given to American athletes. Carter not only threatened to take away future funding, but also the funding of any American athlete who tried to travel to Moscow (Young, 1988; Wiegand, 2006). The following Games in Los Angeles in 1984 were also boycotted, this time by Eastern Bloc countries. Since this time, boycotts have not interrupted the Olympic Games to the same extent as other political actions have affected the games (Toohey and Veal, 2007). One of the most recent examples of using the Olympic games as a forum for political protest and activism was the international Torch Relay that preceded the Beijing Olympic games in 2008. This is highlighted in the following case study.

CASE STUDY 13.1: Olympic Torch Relay

The Olympic Torch and the Olympic Flame are major ceremonial features of the Olympic Games. While flames were lit at the 1928 Amsterdam Games and the 1932 Los Angeles Games, the ceremony as practised today was introduced in the 1936 Berlin Games, at the instigation of Carl Diem, Chairman of the Organising Committee for the Berlin Games (Durantez, 1988). Diem instigated the practice of the torch being lit by the sun's rays at Olympia, in a ceremony conducted by classically attired 'priestesses', then being carried in relay procession to the host country. While there is no exact parallel in the Ancient Olympic Games, Durantez points out that torch relay races took place in classical Athens and ceremonies involving lighted torches took place at the Olympic Games, related to the lighting of sacrificial fires in religious ceremonies.

For the last few Games the lighted torch is carried by a relay throughout Greece (organised by the Hellenic Olympic Committee and then following this on an extensive international tour prior to the Games, including a nationwide, highly publicised tour in the host country, organised by the relevant Organising Committee of the Olympic Games (OCOG)). The torch's journey culminates in its entry into the Olympic Stadium and lighting of the Olympic Cauldron during the opening ceremony (Cahill, 1999). In the four most recent Summer Games, the Olympic Cauldron has been ignited by a national sporting hero.

Following the example of Los Angeles, the Torch Relay has now become a money-making aspect of the Games, with a major sponsor usually involved. Ceremonies and local festivals are held in designated host communities along the route. The relay therefore serves a key function in symbolically 'bringing the Games' to citizens throughout the host country. The international leg of the relay serves the same purpose on a larger level, as well as being a publicity vehicle to generate international interest in the upcoming Games. Unfortunately, much of the public's

Continued

interest in the Beijing 2008 Torch Relay was not positive and this turned into a public relations nightmare for the Olympic Movement. There were ongoing and at times violent demonstrations during the relay protesting the Chinese government's policy in Tibet, especially as it related to recent quelling of Tibetan dissent in many cities on the international route of the torch relay. At times these protestors attempted to extinguish the torch. According to Richard Pound, a current IOC member, former Vice President of the IOC and of the World Anti-Doping Agency (WADA):

> The nature of an international torch relay is an example of how the IOC should be assessing risk profiles in certain of its activities before the event and not in response to a crisis… What benefit is derived from a half-day event several months prior to the Games in a single city? Someone should have

> been paying greater and sooner attention to the likelihood of disruption of the relay, given the long-standing protests relating to China's domestic and foreign policies. While, in the end, the protestors damaged their own cause, there was initial and conflicting attention focused on the IOC and even the sustainability of the Games themselves. The situation got to the point that it was described by the IOC President as a 'crisis'.

> (Pound, 2008, pp. 2–3)

Once an organisation has such a crisis, good public relations can do much to repair the damage. However, it is costly in terms of time, stress and finances for the organisation involved. The better option is preventing such a situation occurring in the first place.

INTERNATIONAL NON-GOVERNMENTAL ORGANISATIONS, SPORT AND PUBIC RELATIONS

The power and influence of International Non-Government Organisations (INGOs) have also increased with the compression of time and space in a globalised world. Thousands of INGOs operate across most countries and are largely privately funded without assistance from governments and appear independent. Although the mandates and missions of INGOs vary their strength lies in their capacity to link diverse people to a common cause (Edwards and Skinner, 2006). Some INGOs that do this include Greenpeace, OxFam and the Red Cross. As international trade impacts societies INGOs have become increasingly influential in global affairs. In some cases they are consulted by governments as well as by international organisations, such as the United Nations, which have created associative status for them (Seitel, 2004).

The IOC by definition is an INGO as it has the 'capacity to bring together groups, associations, organisations and individuals from different countries who are non-state actors on the world stage with their interactions giving rise to transnational relations' (Chamerois, 2002, p. 14). In order to strengthen its global reach the IOC has developed a strong relationship with the United Nations. This relationship did not really begin to flourish until early in 1976 when Lord Killanin, the IOC President addressed Ministers and Bureaucrats who were in charge of Physical Education and Sport programs from around the world. Throughout the 1976 United Nations Congress there was a Charter drawn up which when completed constituted the 'International Charter of Physical Education and Sport'. This was followed by the formation of a 'Physical Education and Sport Committee' that was to oversee issues of physical activity and sport in all areas of the United Nations. This recognition of the positive values of sport and physical education has continued to be a central plank of United Nations policy and was highlighted in November 2003 with the proclamation that 2005 would be the *International Year of Sport and Physical Education* (IYSPE). This initiative invited governments, the United Nations system and international sporting organisations, such as the IOC, Fédération Internationale de Football Association (FIFA) and the Fédération Internationale de Volleyball (FIVB), to use sport and physical education as a tool in global development (Edwards and Skinner, 2006).

After Juan Antonio Samaranch's election to IOC President in 1980 he realised the need to establish working relationships with governments and the United Nations to provide political support and therefore shelter the IOC from world politics and future boycotts. Early attempts to achieve protection for the Olympics were largely unsuccessful. However, following an invitation to the United Nations Educational, Scientific and Cultural Organisation (UNESCO) to address the 1981 Olympic Congress cooperation agreements were signed by the IOC with UNESCO and the World Health Organisation (Edwards and Skinner, 2006).

Throughout his career Samaranch actively embarked on a public relations exercise that sought recognition of the IOC in terms of promoting humanitarianism. One of the initiatives Samaranch was successful in introducing and promoting was the Olympic Truce. This came about after the United Nations Security Council resolution in 1992 locked the former state of Yugoslavia out of the Olympic Games by placing sport on its restricted sanctions list. Following the support of the United Nations General Assembly a resolution on the observance of the Olympic Truce was unanimously adopted in 1993. This symbolism of the growing relationship between the United Nations and the IOC was highlighted at the 1998 Nagano Winter Olympics. At the Nagano Games the United Nations flag was flown at the Olympic Village and the Olympic stadium and this symbolism has been evident at all Olympic Games that have followed (Edwards and Skinner, 2006).

In July 2002, a United Nations Task Force evaluated how sport could be more intimately allied to the United Nations structure. The aim of the task force was to develop more efficient and logical use of sport in peace initiatives. The task force was empowered to: 'establish an inventory of existing sport for development programs, identify instructive examples, and encourage the United Nations system to incorporate sport into their activities and work toward achieving the Millennium Development Goals (MDGs)' (Sport as a Tool for Development and Peace: Towards Achieving the United Nations Millennium Development Goals, 2003, p. 1). Specific sport projects aimed at this included:

- In Somalia, UNICEF and UNESCO are working towards promoting peace through sport with programs that train youth in conflict resolution skills while doing sport training as well as providing resources and encouragement and support for inter-district and regional sport-peace tournaments. The aim is to build the capacity of sport while creating a protective environment to help rehabilitate and reintegrate young people living in a post-conflict situation.

- The International Labour Organisation (ILO) partners with FIFA and the African Confederation of Football to promote the 'Red Card to Child Labour' campaign.

- In Refugee camps, the United Nations High Commissioner for Refugees (UNHCR) uses sport as a means to lower tensions and to promote integration. Sport can cross cultures and sport programs can bridge social and ethnic divides. As a result, sport can be a powerful tool to promote peace, both symbolically on the global level and very practically within communities.

- 'Kicking AIDS Out' is a regional network of organisations in Southern Africa that uses sport to strengthen communities. It creates sustainable sport activities that increase awareness about HIV/AIDS, provide leadership training to at-risk youth and offer safe and healthy alternative activities.

- United Nations Environment Program (UNEP) is working with major sport organisations, including the Olympic Movement and the World Federation of the Sporting Goods Industry, to ensure that major sport events and sport goods are 'green' (Sport as a Tool for Development and Peace: Towards Achieving the United Nations Millennium Development Goals, 2003, pp. 1–19).

Although INGOs are not directly affiliated with any national government they often can have a significant impact on the social, economic and political activities of the country or region involved. INGOs do, however, face situation-specific public relations challenges. These include areas such as conflict of interest, local indifference and cultural misunderstanding (Curtin and Gaither, 2007). These challenges make effective public relations fundamental to any INGO, as highlighted below in the following case study.

CASE STUDY 13.2: The International Olympic Committee

The IOC was founded at the 1894 International Athletic Congress convened by Baron Pierre de Coubertin and held at the Sorbonne in Paris. Since that time, the Olympic Games have become unique in sport by having a declared philosophy, known as Olympism and being recognised as a 'movement' (Toohey and Veal, 2007). Olympism was conceived by de Coubertin and is defined in the *Olympic Charter* as:

> *a philosophy of life, exalting and combining in a balanced whole the qualities of body, will and mind. Blending sport with culture and education, Olympism seeks to create a way of life based on the joy found in effort, the educational value of good example and respect for universal fundamental ethical principles.... The goal of Olympism is to place everywhere sport at the service of the harmonious development of man, with a view to encouraging the establishment of a peaceful society concerned with the preservation of human dignity. To this effect, the Olympic Movement engages, alone or in cooperation with other organizations and within the limits of its means, in actions to promote peace.*
>
> (IOC, 2004, p. 9)

The Olympic Movement encompasses organisations, athletes and other persons who agree to be guided by the *Olympic Charter*. Currently, membership of the Olympic Movement is composed of:

- The IOC – a self-perpetuating body of about 115 members;
- International Sport Federations (IFs) – each representing up to 200 national sport governing bodies;
- National Olympic Committees (NOCs) about 200;
- The Organising Committees of the Olympic Games (OCOGs);
- National associations, clubs and persons belonging to the IFs and NOCs;
- Athletes;
- Other organisations and institutions as recognised by the IOC (IOC, 2004, p. 10; Toohey and Veal, 2007).

Importantly, in terms of its operations and, specifically, its public relations the IOC positions itself as an organisation which transcends sport because it has a philosophy (Olympism) and promotes itself as tool for peace and human rights (a role not generally associated with a sport organisation). Thus, in terms of its credibility and positive pubic relations throughout the world, it is important that it be seen as a scrupulously honest organisation, operating by its core values, transparent and above reproach in its business dealings. This has not always been the case. It is also difficult to achieve consistently around the world as cultural differences regarding what is acceptable or not vary greatly. An acceptable business practice in one country may be illegal in another. The following case study will illustrate that when the IOC fails to live up to its rhetoric, a public relations crisis can occur, be flamed by the international media and must be solved in a timely manner that does not conflict with its core values.

While the press has been influential in condemning certain actions of the IOC, arguably its most trenchant contemporary critic is Andrew Jennings. In *Lords of the Rings* (with Vyv Simson), *The New Lords of the Rings* and *The Great Olympic Swindle* (with Clare Sambrook), he has documented many alleged improprieties related to the Olympic Movement, especially the IOC. For a number of years Jennings was criticised because it appeared that there was little concrete evidence to substantiate his claims. However, the 1998/1999 Salt Lake City allegations concerning IOC members seeking bribes to vote for the city to host the 2002 Winter Olympic Games silenced many of Jennings' detractors. Always a man to 'take on a cause', he has recently turned his journalistic attention to FIFA for alleged improprieties in the book *Foul*, probably to the relief of the IOC as the Jennings' spotlight is focussing elsewhere.

The Salt Lake City Public Relations Crisis

One of the IOC's most divisive scandals and subsequently one of its greatest public relations disasters erupted in November 1998, when a Salt Lake City television station alleged that the Salt Lake City's 2002 Bid Committee had paid for an IOC member's daughter to attend an American University in Washington DC (Evans, 1999).

Continued

Following this, in December 1998, a Swiss IOC member, Marc Hodler, was quoted as saying that he believed that there was 'massive corruption' in the IOC, and that there were up to 25 corrupt IOC members whose votes for cities to host an Olympic Games could be bought. This corroborated the earlier claims of Simson and Jennings (1992) and Jennings (1996) that every Games for the last 10 years had been tainted by such bribery (IOC, 1999; Toohey and Veal, 2007).

Initially Hodler's claims were dismissed by the IOC and he was branded as a 'whistle blower', with an axe to grind, and to begin with he received little backing for his claims from other IOC members. Hodler was, however, 'a very senior member of the IOC, the author … of the so-called 'Hodler Rules' designed to limit the expenses incurred by candidate cities, as well as the President of the International Skiing Federation (FIS) for almost 50 years' (IOC, 1999, p. 4). His allegations could not easily be ignored, especially when the media and later the US Congress, especially Senator John McCain (who later stood as the unsuccessful Republican candidate for the 2008 presidential elections) also became involved. There was a range of allegations of impropriety in local, national and international levels involving a number of IOC members, their families and the Salt Lake Bid Committee (SLBC). These claims included:

- Payments to support members' children while at university or working in USA;
- Payments of tens of thousands of dollars for travel and hotel costs of members and their families to holiday in Utah and for 'side-trips', such as skiing or to the 1995 'Super Bowl' in Florida;
- Payment of medical costs for members while they were on trips to Salt Lake City;
- Direct cash payments, later claimed to have been passed on to NOCs or other sporting organisations in the IOC members' home countries;
- Cash payments for 'consultancy services';
- Provision of gifts valued at well above the IOC limit of US$250;

- Requests for favours for relatives and/or colleagues, such as guaranteeing them places in universities at no cost (Toohey and Veal, 2007).

The IOC scandal was news across the world. It headlined the front pages of newspapers, not just the sport sections. By itself the IOC was ill equipped to respond to the media with its deluge of requests for information and statements (Jennings, 2000). The IOC's position to deal with the escalating global media condemnation changed when a growing number of member organisations of the Olympic Movement put pressure on the IOC to improve its handling of the burgeoning public relations nightmare better. If they did not accede to their wishes there was the risk that the IOC would lose their support, as they did not want their own reputations to be tarnished through their association with the beleaguered organisation (Jennings, 2000). Sponsors seek a 'halo effect' in their association with the sponsored organisation, instead of which the opposite was occurring. As an example, the timing of the bribery revelations hampered the efforts of both the 2000 and 2002 Games organisers in seeking new sponsors. Additionally, existing sponsors were upset and expressed strong concern about the scandal, how it was being handled and some threatened that their sponsorship arrangements might be reconsidered if the IOC failed to address growing public relations nightmare in a timely manner. For example, the public relations manager of General Motors Holden, one of the Sydney 2000 Olympic sponsors, acknowledged that, 'It is difficult for a sponsor in the current environment to maximise its association with the Games as long as these revelations keep coming to the surface' (Evans, 1999).

McDonald's (Germany) Head of Marketing cautioned that 'if the corruption suspicions are confirmed, McDonald's will ask itself if sponsorship of the games still has a place in the group's image' (Hans Munichhausen, cited in Korporaal and Evans, 1999, p. 3). An American Olympic sponsor, the insurance company, John Hancock, withdrew its multi-million dollar Olympic theme advertising campaign on NBC (the US Olympic broadcaster), sending yet another strong message to the IOC that it needed help. Later, five sponsors called for Juan Antonio Samaranch to step down as IOC President (Toohey and Veal, 2007).

Thus, the IOC was being pressured by its important stakeholders to remedy the deteriorating situation or lose support. As a way forward out of the morass, it was suggested that an American firm, Hill & Knowlton be hired to handle the crisis, which was not going away, however, much the IOC wished it to. Hill & Knowlton, Inc. is an international communications consultancy, which according to its website (http://www.hillandknowlton.com/about) has its headquarters in New York, in 2008 it had 73 offices in 41 countries. It is part of WPP, one of the world's largest communications services groups.

The firm has a long history, dating back to 1927. In terms of public relations crisis management, its website notes that:

> Businesses spend years and invest millions in building credible and trustworthy reputations, capturing market share and achieving long-term growth. Yet a badly managed crisis can quickly undo all that effort, leaving investor, customer and employee confidence in tatters. Even for the most reputed companies, not being ready is simply not an option.

> Effective communication is crucial when defending an organization under attack. It needs to be carried out swiftly, with substance and with relevance to each audience. And it must be managed across geographies, business groups and media.

> Our global team of issues and crisis management consultants helps to build the defences needed to withstand attacks, manages crises when they happen and advises on strategies to rehabilitate reputations. We have more than 80 years experience across a range of sectors and issues, routinely preparing senior executives on how to effectively communicate key messages during a crisis and helping them to achieve the best possible outcome.

> (Hill & Knowlton, 2009)

The IOC was certainly in the unenviable position of needing such help. However, the use of Hill & Knowlton did not silence all of the IOC's critics. In fact it escalated some misgivings. For example, Jennings disapproved of Hill & Knowlton staff's strategy in dealing with past public relations nightmares for its client base. He noted that the company used 'personal connections with well-respected, authoritative and purportedly independent news organisations to plant positive stories …, secure warning of negative stories and get them rebalanced, or suppressed' (Jennings, 2000, p. 87). While this is an accepted public relations strategy, the IOC's philosophical position as an exemplar of honesty meant that its critics believed that using a company with such practices demonstrated that the IOC was more interested in saving face that addresses the root causes of its problems.

As it turned out, for the IOC, Hill & Knowlton implemented a more multifaceted, although similar strategy than that mentioned above. First, it advised the IOC to barrage the media with positive faxes and ensure that its other stakeholders had constant updates on how the IOC was moving forward to solve the crisis. Second, the number of IOC spokespeople talking to the media was to be curtailed. Those who were selected as spokespeople were to receive media training as were other IOC staff and members. The IOC President, Juan Antonio Samaranch's contact with the media was to be limited, as international public reaction to his initial handling of the crisis was negative. Thus his external credibility in this matter had been compromised, even though he had the support of the majority of IOC members. Third, Hill & Knowlton were to become closely involved with the IOC's more general public relations (rather than just the crisis management aspects). This turned out to be an ongoing and lucrative arrangement. Fourth, Hill & Knowlton conducted public opinion polls to gauge the public's viewpoint to the IOC. Finally, it advised the IOC to better promote its positive activities. This would also serve to deflect attention from the negative press it was receiving. These were only considered to be short-term solutions.

For the longer term, Hill & Knowlton advised that the IOC conducts ongoing market research to determine the public perception of the IOC throughout the world and to 'work synergistically with ongoing sponsor programming and utilise the full range of communications options: advertising,

Continued

web, direct marketing, public relations' (Jennings, 2000, p. 90). The object was for the IOC to be more transparent to the general public and sponsors and to operate by the values it espoused. As Jennings' comment suggests, this strategy would be achieved primarily via expeditious use of various media channels in order to reach a greater number and range of people. One of the chief strategies to achieve this was to use internationally well-respected individuals to endorse the IOC, in effect giving it the halo effect.

While Hill & Knowlton were leading the public relations clean up, the IOC did not sit idly by and not address the problem that had initially created the fiasco. The IOC and other members of the Olympic Movement finally began to investigate the growing number of claims of impropriety regarding its members. Some members obviously embraced this action more than others. The IOC established an ad hoc Commission of Inquiry, chaired by one of its Vice Presidents, the Canadian, Dick Pound (who later headed up the WADA). This IOC Commission was initially concerned only with Salt Lake City allegations, but later extended its brief to investigate all bids for Olympic Games since 1996. The Salt Lake Organising Committee (SLOC) itself established a Board of Ethics to investigate the bribery claims, reporting in February 1999 (Board of Ethics, 1999). The United States Olympic Committee (USOC) also established an inquiry, which reported in early March 1999 (Special Bid Oversight Commission, 1999). The United States Federal Bureau of Investigation (FBI) began enquiries to determine whether criminal acts had taken place, and the US Senate held hearings on the matter (Riley, 1999). The latter two investigations resulted in prosecutions.

The IOC Commission produced two reports, in January and March 1999 (IOC, 1999). The Commission adjudicated on 19 IOC members, recommending that 7 be 'excluded from the IOC', 10 be warned about their behaviour (ranging from 'warning' to 'serious warning' to 'most serious warning') and 2 be exonerated. Ultimately, there were 4 resignations, 6 expulsions and 10 official warnings that were a direct result of the Salt Lake City scandal.

At the same time, the Commission was critical of a number of the practices of the Salt Lake City Bid Committee and of the USOC. The Commission's report therefore fully vindicated Hodler and the external IOC critics, such as Andrew Jennings. In addition to adjudications on individual members, it made three recommendations to the IOC regarding its future practices in relation to its bidding processes. First, that changes be made to the bidding process, beginning with the 2006 Winter Games. Second, that limitations be placed on members' travel to bid cities and third, that an *Ethics Commission* be established (Toohey and Veal, 2007).

The first and third of these recommendations were acted on immediately: the Ethics Commission was established in April 1999 and bidding procedures were reviewed by the newly established 80-member *IOC 2000 Commission*. Additionally, since then a number of other reforms designed to make the IOC more transparent have been introduced, including the IOC Session being opened to the media for the first time. Thus the public relations crisis was solved by engaging an external public relations firm with a long history of dealing with such catastrophes on an international basis and by the organisation reforming itself. Although its credibility was tarnished, the Olympic Games have continued to grow and sponsorship and media rights are at record levels. It seems that the public has a short memory regarding IOC misdeeds, especially if the celebration of the Games are successful. The Sydney 2000 Games were judged to be 'the best ever'. The subsequent Athens Games took the Olympics back to the country where the Ancient Games were held. Indeed the short events were held in the ancient stadium at Olympia. Unfortunately, even this event was tarnished by drugs. Since then the Beijing 2008 Olympics have created both public relations problems (centring on highly organised and disruptive protests regarding China's human rights record during the international leg of the torch relay) and positive relations due to the successful staging of the Games themselves and the hospitality of the citizens of Beijing. Thus public relations forms an important part of the management of the Olympic Games at many levels.

The above case study clearly highlights that the Olympics may be the most prominent international sporting event promoting international relations, and competition to secure the Olympics is high. Russia's 2014 Winter Games organising committee hired the internationally respected public relations company Burson-Marsteller, with an estimated US$1 million budget to help them secure the international attention that comes with a successful bid (Curtin and Gaither, 2007). Although international sport provides a tool for diplomacy and improved relations, securing a mega sport event is increasingly expensive with estimates suggesting that 'US$12 million is required for a credible effort' (Zinser, 2005, cited in Curtin and Gaither, 2007, p. 30). This expense further widens the gap between the capacity of developed and developing nations to be successful in their bid and can lead to unsavoury business practices from the bidding cities and the bid decision-makers. A successful bid, however, can provide tremendous public relations opportunities. This point was highlighted by the Guardian newspaper the day London won the right to host the 2012 Olympic Games. The paper reported: 'the bonanza will have transformed the media, marketing, advertising and public relations industries reflecting the centrality of public relations to sport and vice-versa' (Brook and Tryhorn, 2005, cited in Curtin and Gaither, 2007, p. 29).

SUMMARY

This chapter has highlighted that in the twenty-first century public relations has become an international phenomenon. Major political shifts towards democracy throughout the world, coupled with the exponential growth of global communications and the move to form trading alliances of regional nations, have focused new attention on public relations. The collapse of communism, the coming together of European economies and the spread of democracy across the globe have further highlighted the importance of public relations in the international sphere (Seitel, 2004). The key, however, to opening the global gateways of public relations is to consider culture and the wider implications inherent in a cultural perspective. These are the adhesives that affect how governments operate, multinational corporations and INGOs function and sport flourish. How these entities present themselves internationally becomes a matter of international public relations (Curtin and Gaither, 2007).

Through a focus on the Olympics and the IOC this chapter has highlighted how public relations is a key element to future success and has the potential to minimise potential negative corporate and public perceptions.

Despite the possibility of the Olympic Games being used as a vehicle to raise public awareness of a cause that may have negative consequences for the host nation and city, and a corruption scandal that highlighted the unethical business practices that existed within the IOC, the commercial viability and public support for the Olympic Games continue to flourish. There is no doubt that this success is primarily because of the ability of sport to unify nations and influence national psyche, in turn, making it a powerful cultural agent (Curtin and Gaither, 2007). If history is to guide us, however, there is no doubt in the future that mega sporting events, such as the Olympics, and international sporting organisations, such as the IOC, will confront another crisis. Key to preventing this and reducing its possible impacts is following ethical business practices and applying sound international public relations strategies.

KEY TERMS

International Public Relations   The practice of public relations in an international or cross-cultural context (Culbertson, 1996).

Cross-National Conflict Shifting   The idea that public relations challenges in one part of the world affect the operations of an international corporation elsewhere in the world.

Global Economy   The expansion of economies beyond national borders, in particular, the expansion of production by transnational corporations to many countries around the world. The global economy includes the globalisation of production, markets, finance, communications and the labour force.

Activism   A policy of taking direct and often militant action to achieve an end.

United Nations   The United Nations officially came into existence on 24 October 1945. The purposes of the United Nations, as set forth in the Charter, are to maintain international peace and security; to develop friendly relations among nations; to cooperate in solving international economic, social, cultural and humanitarian problems and in promoting respect for human rights and fundamental freedom and to be a centre for harmonising the actions of nations in attaining these ends.

International Non-Governmental Organisations (INGOs)   Privately funded organisations that do not receive assistance from governments and appear independent. Their mandates and missions vary. INGOs have numerous strengths with one being their capacity to link diverse people to a common cause.

International Olympic Committee (IOC) An INGO, a non-profit organisation and the creator of the Olympic Movement. It exists to serve as an umbrella organisation of the Olympic Movement. It owns all rights to the Olympic symbols, flag, motto, anthem and Olympic Games. Its primary responsibility is to supervise the organisation of the summer and winter Olympic Games.

Olympism Seeks to create a way of life based on the joy found in effort, the educational value of good example and respect for universal fundamental ethical principles.

DISCUSSION QUESTIONS

1. What industries and areas are relevant to international public relations? Why?

2. How has the expansions of communications technologies necessitated the need for increased international sport public relations?

3. Provide an example of an international sporting incident that has threatened to undermine the credibility of the sport. As an international public relations expert discuss the strategies you would employ to reduce the negative consequences this incident may have on the sport.

4. When expanding a sport internationally what kinds of public relations practices should be observed by sporting organisations attempting to establish their sport in new markets? For example, if Australian Rules football attempted to expand into a new market with different cultural values what role would public relations play in this process?

GUIDED READINGS

L'Etang, J.L., Falkheimer, J., Lugo, J., 2007. Public relations and tourism: critical reflections and a research agenda. Public Relations Review 33, 68–76. Although this paper focuses on tourism it raises many issues that are relevant to sport, and in particular understanding the role of public relations in contemporary culture. Of key interest are the sections that address: the role of government and international relations; sport tourism, events and public relations and mega events, politics and diplomacy.

L'Etang, J.L., 2006. Public relations and sport in promotional culture. Public Relations Review 32, 386–394. This paper explores the links between sport and public relations. It is particularly relevant to international sport public relations as it argues that as sport is both international and part of everyday life it shapes relationships at every level including: diplomatically, culturally, economically and politically. As such, it suggests that sport is a key component of the cultural and business activity in contemporary society and the globalised world.

RECOMMENDED WEBSITES

International Olympic Committee – <http://www.olympic.org/uk/index_uk.asp>

REFERENCES

Cahill, J., 1999. Running Towards Sydney 2000: The Olympic Flame and Torch. Walla Walla Press, Sydney.

Chamerois, N., 2002. The Globalisation of the Olympic Games: From Seoul (1988) to Sydney (2000). Unpublished Doctoral Dissertation. University of Franche-Comte, France.

Culbertson, H.M., 1996. Introduction. In: Culbertson, H.M., Chen, N. (Eds.), International Public Relations: A Comparative Analysis. Lawrence Erlbaum, New Jersey, pp. 1–13.

Curtin, P.A., Gaither, T.K., 2007. International Public Relations: Negotiating Culture, Identity and Power. Sage, London.

Dickerson, M.A., 2005. One example of a successful international public relations program. Public Relations Quarterly 50 (3), 18–22.

Durantez, C., 1988. The Olympic Flame: The Great Olympic Symbol. International Olympic Committee, Lausanne.

Edwards, A., Skinner, J., 2006. Sport Empire. Meyer and Meyer Publishers, Germany.

Evans, L., 29 January 1999. Tainted IOC must draw the line to save itself. Sydney Morning Herald, 28.

Hill & Knowlton, 2009. <http://www.hillandknowlton.com/services/issuesandcrisis> (accessed 01.09.2008).

Huntington, S.P., 1996. The Clash of Civilizations and the Remaking of the World Order. Simon & Schuster, New York.

International Olympic Committee (IOC), 2004. The Olympic Charter. IOC, Lausanne.

International Olympic Committee (IOC), 1999. Report of the IOC ad hoc Commission to Investigate the Conduct of Certain IOC Members and to Consider Possible Changes in the Procedures for the Allocation of the Games of the Olympiad and the Olympic Winter Games. Presented to the Executive Board, January 24. IOC, Lausanne.

Jennings, A., 2000. The Great Olympic Swindle: When the World Wanted its Games Back. Simon & Schuster, London.

Jennings, A., 1996. The New Lords of the Rings: Olympic Corruption and How to Buy Gold Medals. Simon & Schuster, London.

Korporaal, G., Evans, M., 11 February 1999. Games people play. Sydney Morning Herald 2.

L'Etang, J.L., 2006. Public Relations and Sport in Promotional Culture. Public Relations Review 32, 386–394.

Pound, R., 2008. Future of the Olympic Movement: Promised Land or Train Wreck. Olympika: The International Journal of Olympic Studies 17, 199–203.

Riley, M., 11 May 1999. Atlanta bid files to be scrutinised. Sydney Morning Herald, 5.

Salt Lake Organizing Committee for the Olympic Winter Games of 2002, 1999. Board of Ethics Report to the Board of Trustees. SLOC, Salt Lake City, Utah.

Seitel, F.A., 2004. The Practice of Public Relations. Prentice Hall, New Jersey.

Simson, V., Jennings, A., 1992. The Lord of the Rings: Power, Money and Drugs in the Modern Olympics. Simon & Schuster, London.

Sport as a Tool for Development and Peace: Towards Achieving the United Nations Millennium Development Goals, 2003. Report from the United Nations Inter-Agency Task Force on Sport for Development and Peace. United Nations, Geneva.

Toohey, K., Veal, A.J., 2007. The Olympic Games: Social Science Perspective. CABI, Oxfordshire.

United States Olympic Committee, Special Bid Oversight Commission, 1999. Report. USOC. Available at: <http://www.teamusa.org/>.

Wiegand, T., 2006. The boycott of the 1980 Summer Olympics in Moscow: a research project outline. Journal of Olympic History 14 (3), 102–103.

Young, M., 1988. The Melbourne Press and the 1980 Moscow Olympic boycott controversy. Sporting Traditions 4 (2), 184–200.

Guideline Answers to Discussion Questions

CHAPTER 2: PUBLIC RELATIONS AND COMMUNICATION IN SPORT

1. The function of the Public Relations Transfer Process Model is to demonstrate how negative attitudes can be changed into positive ones through the use of public relations. Identify any recent examples of sporting events, incidents, entities or organisation where this model could be applied.

Students should highlight the value of the Public Relations Transfer Process Model to sport in general and then pick a specific example to which they should apply it. Such examples need not necessarily be from professional sport but they must clearly demonstrate an issue where negative attitudes have been changed into positive ones specifically through the use of sport public relations. Such issues might include the transformed reputation and/or behaviour of a sport organisation or individual; the acceptance of a 'new order' at a club or organisation; disgruntled supporters becoming happy supporters and so on.

2. For any sport organisation with which you are familiar, critically analyse its use of sport public relations and communication putting yourself in the position of a public.

Students are free to choose any sport organisation they like – professional or amateur – and they should imagine that they are a public. It is important that students identify which public they consider themselves to be – a supporter (external public) or a participant (internal public) because this will affect the way they approach their answer. Students should clearly apply the principles of sport public relations and communication discussed in the chapter in order to demonstrate that they can identify such practices within their chosen organisation – or not as the case may be.

3. A new girls' football team has been admitted to your local junior Sunday league and they have asked you to advise them on how they can raise awareness and build relationships in the local community. Develop a strategy on how they can use public relations and communication to achieve their objectives.

This answer lends itself very well to a group discussion and response. Students should apply the principles of sport public relations and communication discussed in the chapter and produce some ideas on how the girls' football team can use these principles and techniques in order to engage with the local community, for example, fundraising activities, visits to local schools, newsletters, volunteering and open days. Answers should not be marketing focussed, as students should be learning to differentiate between marketing and public relations.

4. How do you see the role of public relations in sport developing in the future?

This question is open to interpretation and answers will vary. Again, it could be a good group exercise in which students brainstorm their ideas and share them with the rest of the class. It would be an interesting way of finding the similarities and differences in ideas.

CHAPTER 3: SPORT RELATIONSHIP MANAGEMENT

1. Provide an example of an issue or situation which might require two-way symmetrical communications by a sport organisation to ensure that relationships are not compromised. Discuss.

Issues might include changes to organisational constitutions, league rules, branding, development of new facilities/stadiums, spending of funds and other issues related to organisational decisions or environmental changes that cause conflict between the organisation and its publics. Students should highlight the importance of conducting research into public attitudes and negotiating with the public in order to reach a compromise which best suits both the organisation and the public.

2. Develop a stakeholder map for your favourite sporting club. Discuss issues that could potentially arise between the club and one of those stakeholders and how the organisation might set about managing such issues.

Students should list individuals or groups of individuals who can affect, or be affected by, the behaviour and decisions of their favourite sporting club. Examples might include sponsors, investors, community groups, supporters, members, governing bodies, employees, suppliers, trainers, coaches, etc.

3. What factors are important to consider when sport organisations want to establish and manage relationships with volunteers that result in their long-term support?

   Recognising and thanking volunteers are the most important elements. Students should also discuss the importance of ensuring that volunteers are provided with an opportunity to contribute and have their opinions and experiences heard where possible, as well as ensuring that they feel a part of a team with other volunteers. Students might propose team building exercises that might be included (such as social functions or activities) that assist with this feeling of inclusion within the volunteer group.

4. How could stewardship be used by a sport organisation to manage relationships with an important sponsor?

   Students should discuss the four elements of stewardship: reciprocity, responsibility, reporting and relationship nurturing in regards to interactions with sponsors. They may choose to provide an example or outline these concepts generically within the context of a typical sport–sponsor relationship.

CHAPTER 4: SPORT MARKETING PUBLIC RELATIONS

1. For any sport organisation of your choice, identify how that organisation implements SMPR using The Rugby Ball Model as your theoretical basis.

   Students should refer to the chapter in order to illustrate how The Rugby Ball Model concept has been arrived at. They should then apply the different sections to the communication practices of their chosen organisation, focussing specifically on those strategies and techniques which fall into the SMPR category. Answers should demonstrate an understanding that SMPR strategies and techniques are those which are used to support the achievement of the marketing objectives of the sport organisation, e.g., early bird season ticket offers; discounted/first option to buy merchandise as a result of being a season ticket holder; using techniques other than advertising to promote the organisation; creating news stories around the organisation during the off season to keep supporters interested and so on. Examples given in the chapter will spark creative ideas.

2. Critically evaluate the differences between SMPR and Sport Marketing and give some examples of different Sport Communication incidences in which each could be implemented to good effect.

This question lends itself very well to group discussion. Students could brainstorm ideas and list the differences under separate column headings. The objective of doing this is not only for students to be able to distinguish between the two disciplines but also for them to be able to see some of the similarities. They should then consider a variety of Sport Communication situations – not just promotion and publicity, for example – and consider how each might be used based on the information given in the chapter and their roles as sport publics. For example, situations could include: aiming to increase season ticket purchases for the coming season by 5% on the previous season; engaging with local/junior clubs; attracting non-traditional publics to a club; attracting a new sponsor and so on.

3. Conduct some further research into Marketing Public Relations (MPR) and Corporate Public Relations (CPR) and consider how both types of Public Relations can be further applied within the sport context.

    Both MPR and CPR can be applied within the sport context because sport organisations are also sport corporates. Students should use the recommended reading sources to gain a deeper understanding of both concepts and then apply those to the sport context using specific examples. For example, MPR is used widely in attempts to achieve commercial objectives such as fans buying merchandise, tickets, etc. while CPR is used for non-commercial benefits such as attracting sponsorship, attracting investors, business partnership building and attracting new players.

CHAPTER 5: SPORT SOCIAL RESPONSIBILITY

1. Identify some potential benefits that a sporting organisation or franchise can offer to the wider community by following the principles of Sport Social Responsibility.

    Students should identify an international sport organisation or major national sporting franchise and look at community activities they provide that show the principles – in particular ethical or discretionary – of Sport Social Responsibility. For example, FIFA's support of the United Nations 1GOAL campaign, part of a major global education initiative, as well as sponsoring football and other sport programs across the Pacific and Africa.

2. Research a major sporting organisation such as the IOC or FIFA. Does the organisation espouse values and conduct commensurate with the

concept of Sport Social Responsibility? Does the sporting organisation have a published code of conduct or operation, and does this code go far enough in the current climate of community expectations of major sporting organisations?

Students can start by visiting the official website of a major international sporting organisation such as the IOC or FIFA, or a major national sporting franchise such as the NBL or NHL. Identify whether the organisation has a published code of conduct, responsibility or operation; whether there are examples of this code in action; does the organisation identify specific areas of community concern (i.e., environmental, racism) and how are they putting processes in place to address these issues.

CHAPTER 6: COMMUNITY RELATIONS AND ENGAGEMENT

1. Why would Barclays Bank be interested in working with a small charity like Cricket for Change?

Before attempting to answer this question instructors could ask their students to consider the Spaces for Sport scheme that was operated by Barclays Bank in the UK. There is some information about this scheme on the Barclays website (http://group.barclays.com/ Sustainability/Responsible-global-citizenship/Community-investment).

Students could consider the SPRC benefits of a large organisation such as Barclays gets from working with a small charity. Rodwell used the analogy for his organisation as an 'ideas factory'. It is possible that the small stature of the charity allowed it to respond to opportunities quicker than some other larger sporting organisations. Another reason could be that the bank had itself picked up on the SPRC activities of C4C and thought them well suited to the task.

2. Why is sport particularly well suited to Cause-RM initiatives?

At its best sport evokes a range of positive emotions (though this is not always guaranteed) and has the ability to reach large and disparate groups for their interest and enjoyment. As a key leisure activity many people who enjoy sport may connect these positive emotions with the partners that support sporting events. With the rise in ethical consumption discussed in the chapter sport could see some extra interest in events that take these needs into consideration.

3. How would you refocus the SPRC activity for the Cadbury's Get Active campaign to reduce negative associations?

This task is up to the students and/or the instructor however some pointers could be seen as follows:

- Launch SPRC to inform the public about how much chocolate is eaten each day in British schools.

- Reclassify the amount of chocolate required for a piece of sporting equipment. No longer should wrappers equal one piece of kit but bulk amounts of wrappers should obtain a series of sporting kit.

- In hindsight some recommendations are easy to suggest however the use of the sporting ambassadors should not have been reactive, they should have led the programme and possibly spread the message about current consumption and the sporting equipment this would have already generated.

- Additionally Cadbury's could have worked at the business-to-business level and worked with suppliers and wholesalers who deal with school canteens to offer the sporting equipment based on bulk orders of chocolate.

However the list of suggestions could go on.

CHAPTER 7: SPORT VOLUNTEERISM

1. Identify the potential benefits that your sport organisation or event can offer to potential volunteers. Use 2–3 key benefits to develop a core message that can be used to recruit volunteers for your organisation or event. Design a public relations campaign based on your core message.

The answer to this question depends on the particular sport organisation that the student chooses. For example, a swimming club might offer benefits such as helping one's family (if they are members of the club), opportunities to socialise with other (possibly influential members of the community), or learning how to teach swimming or to run a swimming competition. These might then be developed into a core message about being an active participant in the local community. The resulting public relations campaign would build images (e.g., photos) and stories about those aspects. For example, one set of stories targeted at local media might highlight families that participate jointly in the club, with some family members competing, and others providing vital administrative support. Related stories would show volunteers socialising at club social and competition events, including pictures of them interacting with high-profile members of the community when they are in attendance, such as a mayor or a city counsellor or a well-known local business person. Both sets of stories would then be complemented by others that provide colour and background by showing how the volunteers are developing new and useful (to them and to the community) skills while supporting their family and/or that enable them to do the things that cause them to socialise with others. Much the same tactic would be used for a sport event. Socialising, new skills, or possibly being on the inside of the event would be among the benefits that might be highlighted. Possible core messages could stress the community angle, or might stress the sense of becoming an insider, or might cleverly combine both. Stories and photos would then be organised to highlight those aspects.

2. Use a social networking site to search for sport volunteer groups. Analyse the effectiveness of the site for attracting and retaining volunteers. Analyse its effectiveness in creating or maintaining a positive image for the sport organisation or event. What elements can be created or enhanced by the organisation? Which are dependent on volunteers themselves? What recommendations would you make to the sport organisation to take advantage of the site? Why?

    The answer to this question will vary depending upon the social networking sites and the sport organisations that the students use. The key challenge for the students will be to think creatively about the ways that the sites they find can be built into an overall campaign. Here students should be encouraged to think in terms of an integrated communications campaign. The trick is not to think about the site in and of itself, but rather consider how to integrate it with other public relations tools, as discussed in this chapter.

3. Develop a story idea based on some aspect of the volunteer program (an interesting volunteer, a milestone in the program, the need for volunteers, etc.). To whom will you pitch the story? Why would the reporter be interested? How will you tailor your pitch to the specific reporter/publication/media?

    This question can be usefully linked to the preceding two questions. It is fine for students to come up with general ideas, such as those sketched out above with reference to Question 1. However, the core public relations challenge is to come up with story (and photo) ideas that could really find their way into print or broadcast. Students should be encouraged to think from the viewpoint of a reporter or an editor. What are the angles that might appeal to readers, viewers or listeners? In particular, they should be able to come up with realistic human-interest stories (i.e., features) that might be of interest. There should be something appealing about the people they can highlight, and the pictures should tie into that. Similarly, if they are suggesting stories around an event, the volunteers and their activities should provide useful colour pieces or backgrounders. Thus, students should be thinking how to link their stories into an overall framework of stories such that the volunteer stories support and are supported by other stories having to do with the organisation or event.

4. Outline a volunteer training program that will prepare volunteers to assist with the public relations efforts of a sport organisation.

In this case, students should be encouraged to take a systematic approach to what they develop. This will provide them with useful practice at reasoning logically through a training development task. First, they should identify those things they want volunteers to do that would support the overall public relations effort. This chapter provides more than ample suggestions. Second, students should then go through each of the potential means of support they have identified, and determine what specific knowledge and what particular skills would be required for each task. There will normally be multiple skills for each task. Only after these first two steps have been completed should they then endeavour to develop a specific curriculum. In this last step, they should formulate specific teaching methods that they feel will engage the potential volunteer, and that will help them to learn, reinforce and practice the skills and knowledge that they want the volunteers to have. Students should be encouraged to develop active learning methods, rather than simple lectures. The challenge is not merely to present the knowledge and skills, but rather to engage the volunteer and to help the volunteer to become both confident and proficient.

CHAPTER 8: CRISIS COMMUNICATION AND SPORT PUBLIC RELATIONS

1. Discuss the strengths and weaknesses of the Gonzalez-Herrero and Pratt's crisis management model as it applies to crises in sport.

Students should unpack and discuss Gonzalez-Herrero and Pratt's crisis management model and give attention as to how such a model addresses the broader context of sport management and the necessary skills and techniques required to identify, assess, understand and cope with a serious situation, especially from the moment it first occurs to the point that recovery procedures start. Students should view the model as a way of developing the necessary operational skills to deal with any major unpredictable event that threatens to harm the sport organisation, its stakeholders or the general public.

2. Discuss the view that the success of diversion as a crisis strategy bolsters the argument that public relations should focus on building quality relationships rather than on technical communication practices.

   Students should understand how to effectively achieve and build successful public relations through correctly managing the flow of information between an organisation and its publics. In order for successful public relationships to be developed, students need to identify with critical crisis strategies which nurture and protect positive public perceptions and promote quality interactions rather than developing technical communication practices.

3. Discuss the key elements of the crisis communication process that should be included in a sport crisis management plan.

   In order for students to understand this concept, they are required to comprehend the processes necessary for responding to a crisis. Students should develop an understanding as to how specific crisis communication processes are designed to protect and defend an individual, company or organisation facing a public challenge to its reputation. From this chapter, students will discuss crisis management plans which are aimed to assist organisations to achieve continuity of critical processes and information flows under crisis or event driven circumstances.

CHAPTER 9: THE PUBLIC RELATIONS ROLE OF FANS AND SUPPORTERS' GROUPS

1. As a sport fan or member of a supporters' group, evaluate what you consider to be *your* sport public relations role and how you might carry it out.

   This answer will vary from student to student but the important issue to draw from this exercise is how well students understand what public relations is. It will be helpful for students to reread Chapter 2 in order to answer this question though the examples given in this chapter will give them inspiration.

2. Visit the websites of the Barmy Army, the Fanatics and the Beige Brigade, all listed in the recommended websites section, and analyse

each in terms of their sport public relations and communication value. Decide which one you most prefer and give your reasons for your decision.

Again, answers will vary but students should be encouraged to visit each of these websites in order to form an opinion. The websites clearly illustrate how both public relations and SMPR are used and each of them varies in their degree of professionalism and quality. When giving their reasons, students should ensure that they focus on those which are sport public relations and communication related.

3. Visit the social networking sites for your chosen sport organisation, if they have them, or visit those of Chelsea Football Club given in the recommended websites. What do you think of these as a sport public relations mechanism?

Answers will vary but the key issue is that students are able to give analytical answers in terms of the sport public relations value of such media. Students may well find that they are able to bring in information gleaned from other chapters in this text into their answers but they are encouraged to focus specifically on the public relations benefits rather than potential marketing or promotional benefits.

4. Critically evaluate how any sport organisation of your choice carries out sport public relations and communication with its fans and supporters.

This question allows students to synthesise information from other chapters in the text into their answer. Both strategies and techniques should be included and, as an extension, recommendations for improvement could be made. Answering this question will allow students to be critical of their chosen organisation and they should be encouraged to highlight what they consider to be both good and bad practices.

CHAPTER 11: NEW COMMUNICATIONS MEDIA FOR SPORT

1. Visit a few sporting websites from different sports. How do different sports use electronic media to build relationships with their supporters? What examples of Web 2.0 behaviour can you find? Are there differences in approach between different sports, and why might this be the case?

This task is student led but could serve as a useful start to a lecture on this topic. Instructors could assign students this task the week preceding the class and then begin the lesson by examining the range of web behaviour and how it differs through sport.

2. There is considerable debate within sport over the use of fan-generated images and video of sporting events. What are the pros and cons of allowing fans to capture and communicate their experiences of a sporting event on the web?

   This is an interesting issue that is currently ongoing – not just with the use of fan-related images but also with images used for news organisations. In 2009 the Australian government weighed into the debate on the ban on news agencies gaining access to sporting venues in Australia. At the heart of this are sport organisations that feel that the images, sights and sounds produced at their sporting event are their intellectual property. To provide others with access that then permits the taking of non-authorised footage of the event is seen to breach this. However the debate can be constructed around the weighing up of the advantages and the disadvantages for the sport organisation in allowing their customers and fans to generate their own content. Some advantages are that it allows customers/fans to highlight their experiences with the sport or the brand leading to increased satisfaction and greater feelings of involvement than before. Disadvantages however can be represented by loss of potential earnings to sport organisations, issues over control of sport-related content and of course legal issues around hosting unedited content that is linked to the sport. Instructors could attempt to manage a class debate on this question.

3. Many sport stars have created blogs and microblogs such as Twitter. If you were managing the SPRC for a sporting organisation, how would you position blogs and micro blogs in your overall plan?

   This task is once again up to the students but could be used to place some of the concepts from this chapter the students understanding of developing a social media strategy. Each method has positives and negatives but from the chapter content there is clear growth in these areas.

4. How does the rise of social media affect the SPRC model and the relationship with traditional media?

   This is best addressed in two parts. First, the impact that social media will have on the SPRC model can be seen to create pressure on the sport to organise a more proactive public relations function. Second, the effect social media could have on the SPRC relationship with the traditional media could, once again, be seen best in positives and negatives. It is of no doubt, however, that social media is having and will continue to have a significant impact on the way that sport organisations deal with their many stakeholders.

CHAPTER 12: PUBLIC RELATIONS FOR PLAYERS

1. Identify a high-profile sport identity. Look at recent media coverage of that sport identity. Weigh up the balance of 'sport reporting' against 'celebrity reporting'. How much is fact and how much is unverifiable?

   Students should define what is meant by a celebrity. They should then examine the expectations of sporting celebrities and how the media reports on them. Students need to ask themselves the following questions: Are sporting celebrities treated differently to other celebrities, and if so why? Why is it in the interests of the media to report on 'sporting celebrities in this way?

2. What is meant by the 'Black Sheep Effect'? Provide an example of how a sporting organisation has used this strategy to protect its public image and reputation.

   Students need to review the social psychology literature about this effect. They should then search for examples in the media of how this effect may have been used or could be used in situations where the negative behaviour of a player could have long-term implications for the sport organisation or sport.

3. Research a major sporting organisation such as the ICC, FIFA or the IOC. Does the organisation contain athlete charters or espouse values and conduct commensurate with society's expectation of the conduct of its players and athletes?

   Students should begin by defining what a 'code of conduct' is and how it is developed. Students should ask themselves what are the core principles expressed within these codes and discuss how these codes are used by public relations experts to create a positive image of the organisation.

4. Do such organisations enforce player/athlete conduct codes?

   Students should be looking specifically at a player/athlete code of conduct. They should identify specific incidences where a player/ athlete from that sport has broken the code of conduct and document how the governing body of the sport or the club dealt with or failed to deal with the player. Was the action or non-action taken by the governing body or club reasonable given the 'code of conduct'?

5. Should mainstream society be permitted to regulate player and athlete conduct? What role do fans have in determining any negative outcomes as a consequence of the behaviour of sport stars?

Students should discuss the advantages and disadvantages of the general public and then fans acting as the moral regulator of what could be deemed as acceptable on-field and off-field behaviour. Students should then discuss if the commodification of the 'sport fan' provides a reasonable justification for 'sport fans' to have a greater say in how inappropriate player behaviour is managed.

CHAPTER 13: INTERNATIONAL SPORT PUBLIC RELATIONS

1. What industries and areas are relevant to international public relations? Why?

Students could discuss the growth of multinational corporations, the growth of travel and tourism and international sporting events. When students are doing this they should explore the implications of this growth.

2. How has the expansion of communications technologies necessitated the need for increased international sport public relations?

The expansion of communications technology has increased the dissemination of information about sport. How this information is managed and disseminated is vital to create positive perceptions about the sport organisation. Students could further explore this issue by examining if it is possible for international sport public relations experts to control this information flow, if so, provide examples of how?

3. Provide an example of an international sporting incident that has threatened to undermine the credibility of the sport. As an international public relations expert discuss the strategies you would employ to reduce the negative consequences this incident may have on the sport.

Students should identify an international sport. They should detail the particular incident that created the controversy and then discuss the strategies they would employ to reduce negative public perceptions of the sport. For example, international cricket has been plagued by allegations of corruption linked to gambling and match fixing. Students could discuss this and then detail what strategies they would employ to combat these allegations. Would different strategies be used in different countries? Why/Why not?

4. When expanding a sport internationally what kinds of public relations practices should be observed by sporting organisations attempting to establish their sport in new markets? For example, if Australian Rules football attempted to expand into a new market with different cultural values what role would public relations play in this process?

Students should identify that culture is at the centre of international sport public relations and therefore any international expansion of a sport needs to take into account the cultural values of the country. In order for that sport to be successful in a new country an international sport public relations expert needs to communicate that the practice of that sport conforms to and supports the cultural values of that society. Students should investigate the cultural values that underpin an Asian society and develop public relations strategies that would link Australian Rules football to those values.

Index

265